More Praise for

POSITIVE DISCIPLINE

"I do a lot of counseling with parents and often recommend your book as a fabulous tool for parents of strong-willed children. My own redheaded rebel, who is a delightful adult now, tried every bit of patience I had. When I attended one of your sessions at an AMS conference several years ago, I discovered your book! I buy them to keep on hand for parents who need help!"

—LINDA BERNSTORF, Nashville, TN

"As someone who has presented literally hundreds of classes and workshops based on *Positive Discipline,* I can attest to its power to change lives. And as our world grows in complexity with the attendant increases in stress on our families, we need *Positive Discipline* now more than ever."

—MIKE BROCK, licensed professional counselor, author, educator, and seminar leader, Farmer's Branch, TX

"As a family physician, I am constantly recommending *Positive Discipline* to parents to help them understand their children and themselves. I have seen countless numbers of parents and children blossom through the deep knowledge that they gain by reading and applying the principles of this book. As a parent, I had read many parenting books but none have spoken as clearly and honestly about the struggles we invite as parents. It has been invaluable to me and my family."

—DANIEL GOODMAN, M.D., Everett, WA

"What Jane Nelsen talks about in theory really works in practice."

—Robert L. Ater, Superintendent,
The International School of Brussels

"Easy to read. Easy to apply. *Positive Discipline* gives parents tools to guide their children positively and effectively."

—Marjorie Shulman, parent, Trumball, CT

"When parents and teachers use the ideas, processes, and techniques described herein, the results are remarkable. Students don't want to run away from school—they want to run to school."

—J. W. Rollings, Ed.D, parent/educator

"Your book has changed my life in the classroom—and my whole attitude toward teaching. It has helped by teaching my students to take on social and academic responsibility. During class meetings, students learn language skills through self-government, and classroom management skills that improve the total academic atmosphere of the classroom."

—Gene Ford, eighth grade teacher, Sacramento, CA

"Jane has been a keynote speaker at P.E.N. (Parent Education Network) conferences, and we use *Positive Discipline* for parent education classes. Participant evaluations have shown excellent ratings in all three areas."

—Muriel Kelleher, Executive Director, P.E.N.

"I have been using [this] book in workshops with teachers—they love it! It is exciting to see the improvements that have been made over the years with these marvelous ideas. You have made a valuable contribution."

—BOB BRADBURY, M. DIV., Pastor,
Admiral Congregational U.C.C.

"No one is perfect, but Jane Nelsen describes in an understandable way how we can have an almost perfect relationship with our children."

—ANGELIKE JAGER, parent, Bod Soden, Germany

"Walnut Grove Elementary School in Pleasanton, CA, adopted *Positive Discipline* and teachers enthusiastically used class meetings and experienced dramatic results. As principal, I facilitated several parent study groups. The net result was a school full of happy teachers, students, and parents working together in an atmosphere of cooperation to solve problems and improve social and academic skills. I cannot speak highly enough of this program and its benefits."

—ROBERT W. WAKELING, Superintendent,
Sunol Glenn School District, CA

POSITIVE DISCIPLINE

POSITIVE
DISCIPLINE

Jane Nelsen, Ed.D.

Ballantine Books   New York

Published in the United States by Ballantine Books, an imprint of The Random House Publishing Group, a division of Random House, Inc., New York.

BALLANTINE and colophon are registered trademarks of Random House, Inc.

Originally published by Sunrise Press, Fair Oaks, California, in 1981. Revised editions of this work were published by Ballantine Books, a division of Random House, Inc., in 1987 and 1996.

The chapter "Personality: How Yours Affects Theirs" is adapted from a chapter that first appeared in *Positive Discipline for Preschoolers* by Jane Nelsen, Cheryl Erwin, and Roslyn Duffy. Copyright © 1998 by Jane Nelsen, Cheryl Erwin, and Roslyn Duffy. (Three Rivers Press, an imprint of the Crown Publishing Group, a division of Random House, Inc. New York, 1998).

LIBRARY OF CONGRESS CATALOGING-IN-PUBLICATION DATA
Nelsen, Jane.
Positive discipline / Jane Nelsen.—Rev. ed.
p.   cm.
"Originally published in a different form by Sunrise Press, Fair Oaks, California, in 1981. First revised edition published by Ballantine Books, a division of Random House, Inc., in 1987"—T.p. verso.
Includes bibliographical references and index.
ISBN 0-345-48767-2
1. Discipline of children. I. Title.
HQ770.4.N43 2006
649'.64—dc22   2005057047

Printed in the United States of America

www.ballantinebooks.com

13 15 17 19 18 16 14

To Barry

I became pregnant with my sixth child while working on my master's degree. The university I attended was fifty miles from home. Because I deliver babies so quickly, and often early, during the last month Barry drove me to school (with our emergency birth kit in the back seat) and sat in an empty classroom while I attended classes. Mark was born during Christmas vacation. I love to nurse, so when school reconvened, Barry continued driving me and our nursing son the hundred-mile round-trip to school. He would then sit in an empty classroom with Mark so I could nurse during breaks.

When our nursing babies cried at night, Barry would get up, change their diapers, and bring them to me to nurse. He could hardly remember getting up, but when I got up I had difficulty going back to sleep.

After Mary was born (three years later), Barry and I both considered going back to school for advanced degrees. It was obvious that we could not both go to school since we had two children under the age of five. It was Barry's decision that I should go since I loved school and he didn't, and that he would prefer to be home every evening (after his full-time job as a civil engineer) with the kids while I pursued my Ed.D.

People often ask me how I am able to do all that I do. Now you know—and you have a taste of why I love and appreciate him so much.

CONTENTS

FOREWORD

For thousands of years parents and teachers learned the art of raising children through grandmothers, grandfathers, aunts, uncles, and neighbors who lived together under relatively stable circumstances for generations.

When changes became necessary, the value of sharing wisdom and experiences was instinctively understood by the pilgrims and pioneers who traveled together and settled communities with common values and community goals.

Suddenly, at the end of World War II there was a mass migration from small towns and farm communities into urban and suburban environments. An entire culture was dislocated due to the combined effects of the Industrial Revolution, the GI Bill, reaction to the Depression, and technology. The wisdom and support of extended family and longtime friends was lost. Soon after this dramatic shift to urban communities, nearly eleven million couples began giving birth to an average of 4.2 children each and became urban pioneers, crossing a frontier of lifestyle and technology without networks and support systems to offer an accumulation of wisdom to guide them.

Not knowing they were pioneers, these couples forgot the basic strategy that had enabled other pioneers to successfully colonize a new continent. They forgot that pioneers got together with strangers around the campfire to compare notes on the journey so that everyone didn't have to perish learning the same lessons. Instead of following the wisdom of generations who relied on learning from one another, they became isolated.

Those who did not replace family and community support systems with networks of fellow travelers often covered feelings of inadequacy and lack of knowledge about what to do with a false sense of pride in "handling their own problems." They adopted the belief that people shouldn't discuss family business with strangers. It became important to them to hide their problems and handle them, often very ineffectively, behind closed doors. They traded in wisdom and principles acquired over centuries for books and theories untried and untested.

At the same time a national fantasy grew up that the only thing between Americans and a generation of perfect, super children was perfect, super parents. What a shock when many children did not turn out perfectly. The guilt, stress, and denial tore people apart. Parenting, which was once the cumulative work of generations, became a grim, part-time struggle for two or more relatives who did not have much experience in what they were trying to do.

Statistics show that the approximately 4.3 million children born in 1946 overpowered urban schools in 1951. They took the achievement tests in 1963 and reversed a three-hundred-year upward trend. In all areas of achievement, children had been improving up until this time. The children who were born after World War II started a downward trend in achievement and an upward trend in crime, teenage pregnancy, clinical depression, and suicide. Clearly, our understanding of and resources for raising and educating children was compromised by urbanization and technology.

In her book *Positive Discipline,* Jane Nelsen has gathered up the wisdom of many pioneers ahead of her and has created a warm campfire for parents and teachers who desire timeless principles that work, instead of theories that do not. In this book, Jane gives a very practical set of guidelines for parents and teachers who wish to help their children develop self-discipline, responsibility, and positive capabilities and attitudes.

I think enough of Jane's book that it has been adopted as a text in our internationally recognized training program, Developing Capable People, which is used throughout North and Central America and Africa. The principles work and provide a wonderful basis for the enrichment of the family experience.

H. STEPHEN GLENN
www.empoweringpeople.com
November 1985

Author's Note: H. Stephen Glenn died in 2004. He is greatly missed, and it is a blessing that his Developing Capable People program continues to help thousands.

PREFACE AND ACKNOWLEDGMENTS

Positive Discipline is based on the philosophy and teachings of Alfred Adler and Rudolf Dreikurs. I was not privileged to study under either of these great men, but I would like to acknowledge the people who introduced me to the Adlerian approach. It has changed my life and greatly improved my relationships with children at home and in the classroom.

I am the mother of seven children, and grandmother of eighteen (as of 2006). Many years ago, when I had only five children, including two teenagers, I was frustrated by the same child-rearing problems experienced by so many parents today. I did not know how to get my children to stop fighting with one another, to pick up their toys, or to complete the chores they had promised to do. I had problems getting them to bed at night—and then getting them up in the morning. They didn't want to get into the tub—and then didn't want to get out.

Mornings were miserable, for it seemed impossible to get them off to school without constant reminders and irritating hassles. After school was a continuation of battles over homework and chores. My "bag of tricks" included threatening, yelling, and spanking. These methods felt terrible to me and to my children—and they didn't work. I was threatening, yelling, and spanking for the same misbehaviors over and over again. This became clear to me one day as I heard myself repeating, "I've told you a hundred times to pick up your toys." It suddenly dawned on me who the real "dummy" was—and it wasn't my children. How ridiculous that it took me one hundred times to realize that my approach wasn't working! And how frustrating because I didn't know what else to do.

Compounding my dilemma was my status as a senior in college, majoring in child development. I was reading many wonderful books that expounded the many fantastic things I should be accomplishing with my children, but none of them explained how to achieve these lofty goals. Imagine my relief when, on the first day of a new class, I heard that we were not going to learn many new theories, but would thoroughly investigate the Adlerian approach, including skills for practical application to help children stop misbehaving—and to teach them self-discipline, responsibility, cooperation, and problem-solving skills.

To my delight, it worked. I was able to reduce fighting among my children by at least 80 percent. I learned to eliminate morning and bedtime hassles and to achieve much greater cooperation in the completion of chores. The most important change was that I found that I enjoyed being a mother—most of the time.

I was so enthusiastic that I wanted to share these ideas with others. My first opportunity was with a group of parents of educationally, physically, and mentally challenged children. At first the parents of these children were reluctant to try these methods. They were afraid that their children would not be able to learn self-discipline and cooperation. Many parents of challenged children do not understand how clever all children can be at manipulation. The parents in this group soon learned how disrespectful they were being to their children by pampering them rather than helping them develop their full potential.

I was subsequently employed as a counselor in the Elk Grove Unified School District in Elk Grove, California, where many parents, teachers, psychologists, and administrators were supportive of Adlerian concepts to increase effectiveness with children at home and in the classroom. I am especially grateful to

Dr. John Platt, psychologist, whom I adopted as my mentor. He taught me a great deal.

Dr. Don Larson, assistant superintendent, and Dr. Platt were responsible for obtaining a Title IV-C grant and received federal funding to develop an Adlerian counseling program. I was fortunate to be chosen as the director of this program. During the three years of developmental funding, the program was so effective in teaching parents and teachers to help children change their misbehavior that the program achieved recognition as an exemplary project and received a three-year grant for dissemination to school districts in California. We adopted the name Project ACCEPT (Adlerian Counseling Concepts for Encouraging Parents and Teachers). Through this experience I had the opportunity to share Adlerian concepts with thousands of parents and teachers. It was exciting to hear them share their stories of how they used the skills they had learned in the Project ACCEPT training workshops. I learned more than I taught. I gratefully acknowledge those who gave me permission to share their examples with others.

Special thanks go to Frank Meder for his contributions in the area of class meetings. He was able to grasp and implement an important principle—that freedom is impossible in a social environment without equal emphasis on order.

Acknowledgment and sincere appreciation go to those who worked as paraprofessionals for Project ACCEPT. Judi Dixon, Susan Doherty, George Montgomery, Ann Platt, Barbara Smailey, Marjorie Spiak, and Vicky Zirkle worked tirelessly as leaders of parent study groups while organizing and developing materials used in the project. They all shared many examples of the effectiveness of the principles with their own families and the families with whom they worked.

Lynn Lott is the special friend and colleague who helped me get back on track when one of my children experimented with drugs. I was ready to stop using Positive Discipline concepts and instead use control and punishment. I attended a workshop she facilitated on working with teenagers at a NASAP (North American Society of Adlerian Psychology) convention and knew immediately that she could get me back on track. I asked her to write a book with me because I have learned that if I can make something work for me, then it is worth sharing with others. We have since written four books together, and she has had considerable influence on my growth and development of Positive Discipline concepts.

My children have always been sources of inspiration, opportunity, and love. I refer to them as my before, during, and after children. Terry and Jim were already teenagers when I learned about these concepts. Kenny, Bradley, and Lisa were seven, five, and three, respectively. Mark and Mary were born after I had been teaching parent study groups for a while. They have been the inspiration for many opportunities to keep learning, and taught me over and over that the only time I thought I was an expert was *before* I had children.

The greatest benefit of all has come from the understanding of principles and skills that increase mutual respect, cooperation, enjoyment, and love. Every time I stray from the concepts taught in this book, I create a mess. The positive aspect of that is that all I have to do is go back to the methods and skills and I can not only clean up the mess, but can make things better than they were before. Mistakes truly are wonderful opportunities to learn.

Over the years I have been blessed to have many people come into my life because of their love for Positive Discipline. The Positive Discipline Association (www.posdis.org), a nonprofit organization, has been formed for the training of Certified Positive Discipline Associates, research, workshops, scholarships, demonstrations, schools, and quality assurance. It would take many pages to list all the people who have been responsible for creating this organization, so I won't do that. However, I do want them to know how much I love and appreciate them.

I would like to thank Jody McVittie, M.D., Mike Shannon, M.D., and Marti Monroe, Ph.D., for taking the time to read this third edition and giving many valuable suggestions.

Johanna Bowman, my Ballantine project editor, was fabulous to work with. After thinking I had made as much improvement as I could, Johanna pointed out details and made suggestions that improved this edition even further. Thanks, Johanna.

INTRODUCTION
TO THE THIRD EDITION

I am thrilled that *Positive Discipline* has been in print for twenty-five years and is now considered a classic. I am even more thrilled that I have heard from so many parents and teachers about how much it has improved their lives in homes and classrooms. The following two comments are representative of the hundreds I have heard: "After twenty-five years, I was ready to get out of teaching. Kids have changed so much. However, *Positive Discipline* helped me adjust to and work with the changes and I now enjoy teaching again." "My kids aren't perfect, and neither am I, but I sure do enjoy parenting now."

So, you may wonder, with this kind of success, why would I want to make any changes? Doesn't it make sense that I would learn even more over the past twenty-five years? I have been fortunate to work with thousands of parents and teachers during workshops and lectures. They have shared their successes and their struggles. I have learned what worked, what needed some fine-tuning, what needed more emphasis, and some new ideas that needed to be included.

In the very first chapter you will be introduced to the Four Criteria for Effective Discipline. Parents and teachers have found these criteria helpful to understand the different approaches to discipline and what makes sense for long-lasting, positive effects for children. The four criteria help them eliminate discipline practices that are not respectful to children and are not effective in the long term.

I sometimes wonder if the battle between punishment and permissiveness will go on forever. It seems that many think in terms of these two extremes. People who think punishment is valid usually do so because they think that the only alternative is permissiveness. People who don't believe in punishment often go to the other extreme and become too permissive. Positive Discipline helps adults find a respectful middle ground that is neither punitive nor permissive. Positive Discipline advocates tools that are both kind and firm and that teach valuable social and life skills.

In this edition you will find an increased emphasis on the importance of being kind and firm at the same time. Parents and teachers still seem to struggle with this concept. Part of the reason is thinking in terms of either/or. I have found it helpful to use the analogy of breathing. What would happen if we breathed in but not out—or out, but not in? The answer is obvious. Being either kind or firm isn't a matter of life or death, but being kind *and* firm can make the difference between success and failure. It also helps to know that being kind can offset all the problems of being too firm (rebellion, resentment, damaged self-esteem), and that being firm can offset all the problems of being too kind (permissiveness, manipulation, spoiled brats, damaged self-esteem) when you are both kind and firm at the same time.

I have shared more about using Positive Time-out as a life skill that is effective for both adults and children. Parents and children find it helpful and humorous to remember that, during times of conflict, we revert to our reptilian brains (and reptiles eat their young), where the only option is fight (power struggles) or flight (withdrawal and poor communication). All the more reason to take some Positive Time-out until we feel better and can then solve problems based on closeness and trust instead of distance and hostility.

Sometimes it is easier to be both kind and firm at the same time "after" calming down, apologizing, and then using a Positive Discipline tool. For this reason I have included more emphasis on the importance of the kind of Positive Time-out that helps children and adults *feel* better so they can *do* better.

Speaking of Positive Time-out, many adults struggle with the idea of making time-out a positive experience. They mistakenly believe that it is "rewarding" the misbehavior. However, when they truly understand the long-term effects of punishment and the reptilian brain, they see the benefits of Positive Time-out.

Focusing on solutions is a major theme of this edition. For years I was discouraged as I kept hearing about the focus on logical consequences. It seemed that parents and teachers thought there were only two discipline tools to use: logical consequences and time-out. Time-out was always the "punitive" kind, and logical consequences were usually poorly disguised punishments. Adults really struggle with giving up punishment.

One of my most popular statements is, "Where did we ever get the crazy idea that in order to make children *do* better, first we have to make them *feel* worse." When confronted with this idea, parents and teachers can see that it really is a crazy idea, yet when confronted with misbehavior, they slide into old punishment habits.

Focusing on solutions came as an epiphany for me. I was visiting a class meeting where the kids were focusing on a "consequence" for a student who was tardy from recess. I noticed that all their suggested "consequences" were punitive. I called for a time-out and asked, "What do you think would happen if you focused on solutions to this problem instead of consequences?" The kids "got it" right away. From then on, all of their suggestions were helpful solutions. I started sharing the idea of focusing on solutions with parents and teachers and would later hear that they were amazed at how much power struggles diminished in their homes and classrooms.

Another change you'll find in this book is my emphasis on

adult responsibility for many behavior problems. Before I say any more, I want to share that my biggest hesitation in writing about this was that I didn't want it to sound in any way like blame—just awareness and responsibility. That said, I kept noticing that many of the behavior challenges parents and teachers felt frustrated about could be changed if the adults changed first. Frankly, I got tired of always hearing complaints from adults about what the child did.

I started asking, as gently as possible, what the adults did to help create the problem. It seemed to me that some "misbehaviors" were "set up" by adults. One example was how many children "rebelled" when parents and teachers made demands. These same children might be very cooperative if the adults in their lives involved them in solutions during family or class meetings, or helped them create routine charts and then asked, "What was our agreement?" or "What do you need to be doing now?" Of course this won't work in every situation; that is why there are so many different Positive Discipline tools.

"Personality: How Yours Affects Theirs" is a new chapter that helps adults understand what they invite from children—both assets and liabilities—from their own personalities. Many adults are not aware of the personalities they formed based on decisions they made as children that now affect their children. The information in this chapter can be a fun way to learn how to overcome behaviors that invite poor decisions as children form their personalities. Again, this information should never be used to place blame, labels, or judgments. Awareness is the key to change.

There have been many changes in parenting over the past twenty-five years. A huge change is that more fathers now attend my lectures and workshops—and are much more engaged in the parenting role. Some of the changes (such as materialism and "superparenting") can be remedied if parents pay close attention to some of the suggestions that have always been in *Positive Dis-*

cipline, such as how damaging it is to children when adults do too much for them, overprotect them, rescue them, don't spend enough time with them, purchase too many things for their children, do homework for their children, nag, demand, bawl out, and then bail out.

The foundation for healthy self-esteem is the development by children of the belief "I am capable." Children don't develop this belief when parents do any of these things. Nor do they develop the skills that help them feel capable when they are always told what to do without the experience of focusing on solutions where they are respectfully involved and can practice the skills parents hope they will develop.

Family meetings and class meetings have become more popular, yet we have a long way to go. It is during these meetings that children have the opportunity to develop all of the Significant Seven Perceptions and Skills mentioned in chapter one, yet too many parents and teachers seem to think that children can develop them without any experience or practice.

Recently I was interviewed for a magazine article by an editor who thought that most people today know that punishment doesn't work with children. I only wish that were true. Until it is true, there is much to be done. It is still my dream to create peace in the world through peace in homes and classrooms. When we treat children with dignity and respect, and teach them valuable life skills for good character, they will spread peace in the world.

Some books on discipline are written for parents. Others are written for teachers. This book is written for both because:

- The concepts are the same for parents and teachers. The only difference is the setting in which they are applied. Many teachers are also parents who would like to use these concepts at home and at school.
- Understanding and cooperation between home and school are increased when parents and teachers are united in their

methods of helping children and one another in positive ways.

Positive Discipline principles can be compared to a puzzle with many concepts (pieces). It is difficult to see the whole picture until you have all or most of the pieces. Sometimes one concept does not make sense until you combine it with another concept or attitude.

A Few Pieces of the Puzzle

Understanding the Four Goals of Misbehavior
Kindness and Firmness at the Same Time
Mutual Respect
Mistakes as Opportunities to Learn
Social Responsibility
Family and Class Meetings
Involving Children in Problem Solving
Encouragement

When something isn't working, check to see if one of these pieces is missing. For example, problem solving may not be effective if adults or children do not understand that mistakes are opportunities to learn. Family or class meetings may not be effective until people have learned mutual respect and social responsibility. Too much kindness without firmness may become permissiveness, and too much firmness without kindness may become excessive strictness. Sometimes we have to stop dealing with the misbehavior and heal the relationship first. Often the healing involves encouragement that removes the motivation for misbehavior without dealing directly with the misbehavior. Encouragement may not seem to work until adults understand the belief behind the behavior by understanding the mistaken goals. Throughout this book examples are given of how Positive

Discipline principles have been used effectively in homes and schools. Once you understand the principles, your common sense and intuition will enable you to apply them in your own life. Thousands of parents and teachers have supported one another in learning Positive Discipline concepts through parent and/or teacher study groups. In these study groups no one is the expert, everyone feels free to share their mistakes, and they help one another learn. We all know how easy it is to see solutions to the problems of others—then we have perspective, objectivity, and creative ideas. With our own problems we often become emotionally involved and lose all perspective and common sense. In study groups parents and teachers learn they are not alone, that no one is perfect and everyone has similar concerns. The universal reaction of parents and teachers who attend study groups is, "What a relief to know I'm not the only one who is experiencing frustration!" It is comforting to know that others are in the same boat.

In study groups, group facilitators make it clear that they are not experts. Groups are much more effective if no one assumes the role of an expert. A group leader or coleaders take responsibility for asking the questions and keeping the group on task, not for providing the answers. If no one in the group knows the answer to a question, allow time to find it in the book *Positive Discipline*.

The appendixes offer some guidelines for successful group facilitation. A group may consist of as few as two people or as many as ten. If the group gets larger than that, there is less opportunity for individual involvement. The responsibility of group members is to read the chapters, be prepared to discuss the questions, and cooperate with the leaders by staying on task. If a group member has not found time to read the assigned chapter, he or she can nevertheless benefit from listening to the discussion and participating in experiential activities.

It is not necessary to accept all the principles at once. Use only what makes sense to you at the time. And if you hear something that does not seem right to you, don't throw out the baby with the bathwater. Some concepts that seem difficult to accept or understand now might make more sense later. One group member said that she tried some of the principles on her son, just to prove that they were wrong, and was surprised to see the positive change in their relationship. She later became a parent study group leader because she wanted to share these concepts that had helped her so much.

It is helpful to have patience with yourself and with your children as you try to change old habits. As your understanding of the underlying principles deepens, practical application becomes easier. Patience, humor, and forgiveness enhance your learning process.

One more word of caution: Try only one new method at a time. You will be learning many new concepts and skills that will take practice for successful application. It can be confusing and discouraging to expect too much of yourself. Apply one method at a time and move ahead slowly, remembering to see mistakes as opportunities to learn.

Many parents and teachers have found that even though their children don't become perfect, they enjoy them much more after applying these concepts and attitudes. This is my wish for you.

POSITIVE DISCIPLINE

Chapter One

THE POSITIVE APPROACH

If you are a teacher, have you been teaching long enough to re-member when children sat in neat rows and obediently did what they were told? If you are a parent, do you remember when chil-dren wouldn't dare talk back to their parents? Maybe you don't, but perhaps your grandparents do.

Many parents and teachers today are feeling frustrated be-cause children don't behave the way they used to in the good old days. What happened? Why don't today's children develop the same kinds of responsibility and motivation that seemed more prevalent in children many years ago?

There are many possible explanations, such as broken homes, too much television, video games, and working mothers. These factors are so common in our society today that the situation would seem rather hopeless if they really explained our current challenges with children. (And we all know of many single and working parents who are doing a great job raising their children because they use effective parenting skills.) Rudolf Dreikurs[1] had another theory.

There are many major changes that have taken place in society over the past few years that more directly explain the differences in children today. The outlook is very encouraging because, with awareness and desire, we can compensate for these changes and in doing so can also eliminate some of the problems that many think are caused by broken homes, too much television, and working mothers.

The first major change is that adults no longer give children an example or model of submissiveness and obedience. Adults forget that they no longer act the way they used to in the good old days. Remember when Mom obediently did whatever Dad said, or at least gave the impression she did, because it was the culturally acceptable thing to do? In the good old days few people questioned the idea that Dad's decisions were final.

Because of the human rights movement, this is no longer true. Rudolf Dreikurs pointed out, "When Dad lost control of Mom, they both lost control of the children." All this means is that Mom quit giving the children a model of submissiveness. This is progress. Many things about the good old days were not so good.

In those days there were many models of submission. Dad obeyed the boss (who was not interested in his opinions) so he wouldn't lose his job. Minority groups accepted submissive roles at great loss to their personal dignity. Today all minority groups are actively claiming their rights to full equality and dignity. It is difficult to find anyone who is willing to accept an inferior, submissive role in life. Children are simply following the examples all around them. They also want to be treated with dignity and respect.

It is important to note that equality does not mean *the same.* Four quarters and a dollar bill are very different, but equal. Children obviously do not deserve all the rights that come with greater experience, skills, and maturity. Adult leadership and guidance are important. However, children deserve to be treated with dignity and respect. They also deserve the opportunity to develop the life skills they need in an atmosphere of kindness and firmness instead of an atmosphere of blame, shame, and pain.

Another major change is that in today's society children have fewer opportunities to learn responsibility and motivation. We no longer *need* children as important contributors to economic survival. Instead children are given too much in the name of love without any effort or investment on their part and they develop an entitlement attitude. Too many mothers and fathers believe that good parents protect their children from all disappointment. They rescue or overprotect—thus robbing their children of the opportunity to develop a belief in their capability to handle the ups and downs of life. Skill training is often neglected because of busy life schedules or a lack of understanding of how important it is for children to contribute. We often rob children of opportunities to feel belonging and significance in meaningful ways through responsible contributions and then complain and criticize them for not developing responsibility.

Children do not develop responsibility when parents and teachers are too strict and controlling, nor do they develop responsibility when parents and teachers are permissive. Children learn responsibility when they have opportunities to learn valuable social and life skills for good character in an atmosphere of kindness, firmness, dignity, and respect.

It is important to emphasize that eliminating punishment does not mean that children should be allowed to do whatever they want. We need to provide opportunities for children to experience responsibility in direct relationship to the privileges they enjoy. Otherwise, they become dependent recipients who feel that the only way to achieve belonging and significance is by manipulating other people into their service. Some children develop the belief, "I'm not loved unless others take care of me." Others may develop the belief that they shouldn't try because they can't do very much that doesn't invite shame and pain. It is saddest when they develop the belief "I'm not good enough" because they don't have opportunities to practice proficiencies that would help them feel capable. These children spend a great deal of energy in rebellion or avoidance behaviors.

When all of their intelligence and energy is directed toward manipulation, rebellion, and avoidance, children do not develop the perceptions and skills needed to become capable people. In the book *Raising Self-Reliant Children in a Self-Indulgent World,*[2] H. Stephen Glenn and I identify the Significant Seven Perceptions and Skills necessary for developing capable people.

Significant Seven Perceptions and Skills

1. Strong perceptions of personal capabilities—"I am capable."
2. Strong perceptions of significance in primary relationships—"I contribute in meaningful ways and I am genuinely needed."
3. Strong perceptions of personal power or influence over life—"I can influence what happens to me."
4. Strong intrapersonal skills: the ability to understand personal emotions and to use that understanding to develop self-discipline and self-control.
5. Strong interpersonal skills: the ability to work with others and develop friendships through communicating, cooperating, negotiating, sharing, empathizing, and listening.
6. Strong systemic skills: the ability to respond to the limits and consequences of everyday life with responsibility, adaptability, flexibility, and integrity.
7. Strong judgmental skills: the ability to use wisdom and to evaluate situations according to appropriate values.

Children developed these perceptions and skills naturally when they were allowed to work side by side with their parents, receiving on-the-job training while making meaningful contributions to the family lifestyle. The irony is that in the good old days children had opportunities to develop strong life skills, but had few opportunities to use them. Now the world is full of opportunities for which too many children are not prepared. Today children do not have many natural opportunities to feel needed and significant, but parents and teachers can thoughtfully provide these opportunities. A wonderful fringe benefit is that most behavior problems can be eliminated when parents and teachers learn more effective ways to help their children and students develop healthy perceptions and skills. Most misbehavior can be traced to a lack of development in these Significant Seven Perceptions and Skills.

Understanding why children do not behave the way they used to is the first step for parents and teachers who are facing child-discipline challenges. We need to understand why controlling methods, which worked so well many years ago, are not effective with children today. We need to understand our obligation to provide opportunities, which were once provided by circumstances, for children to develop responsibility and motivation. And most important, we need to understand that cooperation based on mutual respect and shared responsibility is more effective than authoritarian control (see Table 1.1).

TABLE 1.1
THREE MAIN APPROACHES FOR ADULT–CHILD INTERACTION

STRICTNESS (excessive control)	• Order without freedom • No choices • "You do it because I said so."
PERMISSIVENESS (no limits)	• Freedom without order • Unlimited choices • "You can do anything you want."
POSITIVE DISCIPLINE (authoritative; kindness and firmness at the same time)	• Freedom with order • Limited choices • "You can choose within limits that show respect for all."

The attitude of parents or teachers who choose between each of the three approaches is very different.

Strictness—"These are the rules by which you must abide, and this is the punishment you will receive for violation of the rules." Children are not involved in the decision-making process.

Permissiveness—"There are no rules. I am sure we will love each other and be happy, and you will be able to choose your own rules later."

Positive Discipline—"Together we will decide on rules for our mutual benefit. We will also decide together on solutions that will be helpful to all concerned when we have problems. When I must use my judgment without your input, I will use firmness with kindness, dignity, and respect."

As a fun way to illustrate the extreme differences between the three approaches, Dr. John Platt[3] tells the story of three-year-old Johnny at breakfast time in each home. In a strict home, where Mom knows what is best, Johnny does not have a choice regarding breakfast. On a cold, rainy day, controlling mothers all over the world know that Johnny needs some kind of hot mush to get him through the day. Johnny, however, has different ideas. He looks at the mush and says, "Yuck! I don't want this stuff!" One hundred years ago it was much easier to be a strict, controlling mother. She could just say, "Eat!" and Johnny would obey. It is more difficult today, so Mom goes through the following four steps in her effort to get obedience.

Step one: Mom tries to convince Johnny why he needs hot mush to get him through the day. Remember what your mother told you hot mush would do inside your body? "It will stick to your ribs!" Have you ever thought about what a three-year-old thinks when he is told hot mush will stick to his ribs? He is not very impressed.

Step two: Mom tries to make the mush taste better. She tries all kinds of concoctions—brown sugar, cinnamon, raisins, honey, maple syrup, and even chocolate chips. Johnny takes another bite and still says, "Yuck! I hate this stuff!"

Step three: Mom tries to teach him a lesson in gratitude. "But Johnny, think of all the children in Africa who are starving to death." Johnny is still not impressed and replies, "Well, send it to them."

Step four: Mom is now exasperated and feels that her only alternative is to teach him a lesson for his disobedience. She gives him a spanking and tells him he can just be hungry.

Mom feels good about the way she handled the situation for about thirty minutes before she starts feeling guilty. What will people think when they find out she couldn't get her child to eat? And what if Johnny is really suffering from hunger?

Johnny plays outside long enough to build up *guilt power* before he comes in and claims, "Mommy, my tummy is so hungry!"

Mom now gets to give the most fun lecture of all—the "I told you so" lecture. She doesn't notice that Johnny is staring into space while he waits for her to finish so he can get on with life. Mom feels very good about her lecture. She has now done her duty to let him know how right she was. She then gives him a cracker and sends him out to play again. To make up for the nutritional loss suffered from the lack of a good breakfast, she goes into the kitchen and starts fixing liver and broccoli. Guess what lunch will be like?

The next scene takes place in a permissive home, where Mom is training a future anarchist. When this Johnny comes into the kitchen, Mom says, "What would you like for breakfast, sweetheart?"

Since Johnny has had three years of training, he is a real "sweetheart" and proceeds to run Mom through his training routine. Johnny first requests a soft-boiled egg on toast. He makes Mom cook nine eggs before she gets it just right. Then he decides he doesn't really want a soft-boiled egg, he wants French toast. Mom has three eggs left, so she whips up French toast. Meanwhile Johnny has been watching television. During the commercial he sees that athletes can do marvelous things if they eat the Breakfast of Champions. He says, "I want Wheaties, Mom!" After he tastes the Wheaties, he changes his mind and asks for Sugar Crispies. Mom doesn't have Sugar Crispies, but runs to the store to get some. Johnny doesn't ever have to build up guilt power. He has Mom running on it twenty-four hours a day.

These stories are not exaggerations. They are examples of true situations. One mother told me that her child wouldn't eat anything except potato chips. I asked her where he got them. She exclaimed, "Well, I buy them because he won't eat anything else!" Many children are being raised to be tyrants who feel they are significant only if they can manipulate other people into fulfilling their demands.

We will now go into a home where Positive Discipline is used. There are two significant differences before breakfast starts. First, Johnny will be dressed and have his bed made before he even comes to breakfast. (Later, you will learn how to accomplish this.) The second difference is that Johnny will do something to make a contribution to the family routine, such as setting the table, making the toast, or scrambling the eggs. (Yes, three-year-old children can scramble eggs, as you will see when we discuss chores.)

This morning is a cereal day. Mom gives Johnny a limited choice. "Would you like Cheerios or Wheaties?" (She doesn't buy sugar-coated cereals.)

This Johnny has also been watching television commercials about what the great athletes eat, so he chooses Wheaties. After one taste, he changes his mind and says, "I don't want this stuff!"

Mom says, "Fine. We can't recrisp the Wheaties. Go outside and play, and I'll see you at lunchtime." Notice that Mom skipped all the steps the controlling mom went through. She didn't try to convince him or tell him about starving children or try to make it taste better. She didn't even have to spank him. She simply allowed him to experience the consequences of his choice.

Since Mom is new at this, Johnny tries to build up guilt power. Two hours later when he tells Mom that his tummy is so hungry, she respectfully replies, "I'll bet it is." Mom avoids her "I told you so" lecture and instead reassures Johnny, "I'm sure you can make it until lunch."

It would be nice if the story could end here with understanding and cooperation from Johnny; however, it doesn't happen that quickly. Johnny is not used to Mom behaving this way. He is frustrated because he didn't get what he expected and has a temper tantrum. At this point it would be natural for most mothers to think, this Positive Discipline stuff doesn't work. Johnny's mom knew about the following illustration, which explains what often happens when we change our approach.

Children are used to getting certain responses from adults. When we change our responses, they will probably exaggerate their behavior (get worse) in their effort to get us to respond like we are supposed to. This is the kick-the-soda-machine effect. When we put money in the soda machine and a soda doesn't come out, we kick and pound to try to get it to do what it is *supposed* to do.

The problem with "strictness" is that when misbehavior is

met with punishment, the behavior stops immediately but soon begins again—and again and again.

Although misbehavior might get worse when Positive Discipline skills are first used, you will notice that there is a leveling off before the child misbehaves again. When a child experiences that his manipulation tactics don't work, he or she will probably test again—just to make sure. Misbehavior becomes less intense, with longer leveling-off periods, when Positive Discipline is used consistently.

When we use firmness with dignity and respect, children soon learn that their misbehavior does not get the results they expect, and they are motivated to change their behavior, with their self-esteem intact. Once we realize this, going through the times when behavior gets worse for a short period is not as bad as the constant hassles of power struggles that occur with an excessively controlling approach.

When Johnny has a temper tantrum, Mom can use the technique of a cooling-off period (explained later) and go to another room until they both feel better. It is not much fun to have a temper tantrum without an audience. Or she might try the I-need-a-hug approach (explained in chapter seven) so they both feel better. They can then work together on a solution to the problem if the child is old enough to participate in problem solving. For younger children, just feeling better or a simple distraction is often enough to change the behavior.

This story illustrates and provides many examples of the difference between the three approaches to adult–child interaction, and how much more effective it is to use Positive Discipline for effective long-term results. However, there is still much work to be done to convince some adults of the long-term benefits of Positive Discipline.

Many adults refuse to give up their attempts to make excessive control work because of their mistaken belief that the only alternative is permissiveness, which is very unhealthy for children and adults. Children who are raised permissively grow up thinking that the world owes them a living. They are trained to use all their energy and intelligence to manipulate and hassle adults into taking care of their every wish. They spend more time trying to get out of responsibility than developing their independence and capabilities.

BEWARE OF WHAT WORKS

Many people feel strongly that strictness and punishment work. I agree. I would never say that punishment does not *work*. Punishment does *work* in that it usually stops *misbehavior* immediately. But what are the long-term results? We are often fooled by immediate results. Sometimes we must *beware of what works* when the long-term results are negative. The long-term results of punishment are that children usually adopt one or all of the Four R's of Punishment:

The Four R's of Punishment

1. Resentment—"This is unfair. I can't trust adults."
2. Revenge—"They are winning now, but I'll get even."
3. Rebellion—"I'll do just the opposite to prove I don't have to do it their way."
4. Retreat:
   a. Sneakiness—"I won't get caught next time."
   b. Reduced self-esteem—"I am a bad person."

Children are not usually consciously aware of the decisions they are making in response to being punished. However, future behavior is based on these subconscious decisions. For example: a child might decide, "I'm a bad person," and will continue to act the part. Another child, who makes the same decision, might become a pleaser (an approval junkie) to seek the love he doesn't believe he deserves. For this reason adults need to be more aware of the long-term effects of their actions instead of being fooled by the short-term results.

Where did we ever get the crazy idea that in order to make children do better, first we have to make them feel worse? Think of the last time you felt humiliated or treated unfairly. Did you feel like cooperating or doing better? Take the time to close your eyes and remember a recent time (or a time during your childhood) when someone tried to motivate you to do better by trying to make you feel bad. Remember exactly what happened. Get in touch with how you felt. Be aware of what you were deciding about yourself, about the other person, and about what to do in the future (even though, most likely, you were not aware that you were making decisions at the time). Did you feel motivated to do better? If so, was it a good feeling, or was it based on negative feelings about yourself or the other person? Did you feel motivated to give up or to *cover up* so you could avoid future humiliation? Or, did you want to become an approval junkie—giving up a big part of yourself in order to please others? Children do not develop positive characteristics based on the feelings and subconscious decisions they make as a result of punishment.

Parents and teachers who don't like excessive control or permissiveness, but don't know what else to do, may switch back and forth in confusion between two ineffective alternatives. They may try excessive control until they can't stand themselves for sounding so tyrannical. They then switch to permissiveness until they can't stand how spoiled and demanding the children get—so they go back to excessive control.

What is the price when excessive control seems to work with some children? Research has shown that children who experience a great deal of punishment become either rebellious or fearfully submissive. Positive Discipline does not include any blame, shame, or pain (physical or emotional) as motivators. On the other hand, permissiveness is humiliating to adults and children and creates unhealthy codependence instead of self-reliance and cooperation. The purpose of Positive Discipline is to achieve positive long-term results, as well as responsibility and cooperation now.

Since many parents and teachers believe that the only alternative to giving up excessive control and strictness is permissiveness, it is important that we define discipline. *Discipline* is a word that is often misused. Many people equate discipline with punishment—or at least believe that punishment is the way to help people achieve discipline. However, discipline comes from the Latin word *discipulus* or *disciplini,* which means a follower of truth, principle, or a venerated leader. Children and students will not become followers of truth and principle unless their motivation comes from an internal locus of control, that is, until they learn self-discipline. Both punishment and reward come from an external locus of control.

IF NOT STRICTNESS, AND
NOT PERMISSIVENESS—THEN WHAT?

Positive Discipline is an approach that does not include excessive control or permissiveness. How is it different from other discipline methods? One difference is that Positive Discipline is not humiliating to children or to adults.

Positive Discipline is based on mutual respect and cooperation. Positive Discipline incorporates kindness and firmness at the same time as the foundation for teaching life competencies based on an inner locus of control.

When excessive control is used, children depend on an "external locus of control." It is the adult's responsibility to be constantly in charge of children's behavior. The most popular form of excessive control used by parents and teachers is a system of *rewards* and *punishment.* With this system, adults must catch children being *good* so they can give rewards and catch them being *bad* so they can dole out punishment. Who is being responsible? Obviously it is the adult; so what happens when the adult is not around? Children do not learn to be responsible for their own behavior.

It is interesting to note how often controlling adults complain about irresponsibility in children without realizing that they are training children to be irresponsible. Permissiveness also teaches irresponsibility because both adults and children relinquish responsibility.

One of the most important concepts to understand about Positive Discipline is that children are more willing to follow rules that they have helped establish. They become effective decision-makers with healthy self-concepts when they learn to be contributing members of a family, a classroom, and society. These are important long-term effects of the Positive Discipline approach. They can be summarized as follows.

The Four Criteria for Effective Discipline

1. Is it kind and firm at the same time? (Respectful and encouraging)
2. Does it help children feel a sense of belonging and significance? (Connection)
3. Is it effective long-term? (Punishment works in the short term, but has negative long-term results.)
4. Does it teach valuable social and life skills for good character? (Respect, concern for others, problem solving, accountability, contribution, cooperation)

Punishment does not meet any of these criteria. Every method taught in Positive Discipline does. The first criterion, kindness and firmness at the same time, is a cornerstone concept for Positive Discipline.

KINDNESS AND FIRMNESS AT THE SAME TIME

Rudolf Dreikurs taught the importance of being both kind and firm in our relations with children. Kindness is important in order to show respect for the child. Firmness is important in order to show respect for ourselves and for the needs of the situation. Authoritarian methods usually lack kindness. Permissive methods lack firmness. Kindness and firmness are essential for Positive Discipline.

Many parents and teachers struggle with this concept for many reasons. One is that they often don't feel like being kind when a child has "pushed their buttons." Again I want to ask, "If adults want children to control their behavior, is it too much to ask that adults learn to control their own behavior?" Often, it is the adults who should take some Positive Time-out (more on this in chapter six) until they can "feel" better so they can "do" better.

Another reason adults have difficulty being kind and firm at the same time is that they don't know what kind and firm look like. They may be stuck in the vicious cycle of being too firm when upset—or because they don't know what else to do; and then being too kind to make up for being too firm.

Many parents and teachers have mistaken notions about kindness. One of the biggest mistakes some parents and teachers make when they decide to do Positive Discipline is becoming too permissive because they don't want to be punitive. Some mistakenly believe they are being kind when they please their children, or when they rescue them and protect them from all disappointment. This is not being kind; it is being permissive. Being kind means to be respectful of the child *and* of yourself. It is not respectful to pamper children. It is not respectful to rescue them from every disappointment so they don't have the opportunity to develop their "disappointment muscles." It is respectful to validate their feelings: "I can see that you are disappointed (or angry, or upset, etc.).” Then it is respectful to have faith in children that they can survive disappointment and develop a sense of capability in the process.

Now let's take a look at being respectful to you. It is not kind to allow children to treat you (or others) disrespectfully. This is where it gets a little tricky. Not allowing children to treat you or others disrespectfully does not mean handling this situation in a punitive manner. Punishment is very disrespectful. So how do you handle it?

Let's suppose a child talks back to you. One kind and firm way to handle this is to leave the room. Oh, I can hear the objections: “But isn't that allowing the child to ‘get away with it’? Let's take a closer look. You can't make another person treat you with respect, but you can treat yourself with respect. Walking away is treating yourself with respect—and is a strong model for children. You can always follow up later, when everyone has had a chance to calm down to *feel* better so they can *do* better.

Follow-up might look like this: “Honey, I'm sorry you were so angry. I respect your feelings, but not how you handled them. Whenever you treat me disrespectfully, I will just leave for a while. I love you and want to be with you, so when you are ready to be respectful you can let me know and I'll be happy to help you figure out other ways you can deal with your anger. Then we can focus on finding a solution that is respectful to both of us.” It is best to let a child know what you are going to do in advance when everyone is calm.

It bears repeating that too many parents think they need to deal with the problem at the time of upset. This is the worst time to deal with a problem. When people are upset, they access their primitive brains, where the only option is fight (power struggles) or flight (withdraw and fail to communicate). It is not possible to think rationally when coming from our primitive brains. We say things we are later sorry for. It only makes sense to calm

down until you can access your rational brain before you deal
with a problem. This is a great skill to teach children. Sometimes it is better to "decide what you will do" (a tool you will
learn more about in chapter five) than to try to make a child do
something—at least until you can invite cooperation instead of
a power struggle. So remember: kind equals respect.

Now let's tackle firmness. Most adults are used to thinking
that firmness means punishment, lectures, or some other form of
control. Not so. Firmness, when combined with kindness, means
respect for the child, for you, and for the situation.

Let's take the situation of limits. Most parents decide what
the limits should be and then take responsibility for enforcing
them. But let's consider the purpose of limits. The purpose is to
keep children safe and socialized. When adults set the limits and
then enforce them with punishment, lectures, and control, they
often invite rebellion and power struggles. This does not keep
children safe or socialized. Instead, involve children when setting
and enforcing limits. For example, you can brainstorm together
what the limits should be for TV viewing, curfews, playtime
away from home, or homework. Include children in a discussion
(which means they talk at least as much, if not more, than you
do) of why the limits are important, what they should be, and
how everyone can be responsible to follow them. For example,
when you ask children why homework is important, they will
tell you ("so I can learn," "so I will get a better grade"). They can
then decide how much time they need and when is the best time
for them. (Parents usually want their children to do their homework as soon as they get home from school. Children would
usually like some downtime first. When children get some
choice, they feel empowered.) Once they decide on the time that
works best for them, you can both set some limits such as "TV
for only one hour and only after homework is done. I will be
available to help only between seven and eight, and will not give

in to last-minute pleas for help during other times." Children are much more willing to follow limits they have helped create based on their understanding of why they are necessary and how to be responsible for them.

Of course, limit setting is different for children under the age of four. Parents need to set limits for younger children, but they can still be enforced with kindness together with firmness.

When a limit is broken, don't lecture or punish. Continue respectful involvement with the child. Avoid telling what happened and what should be done about it. You might ask curiosity questions: "What happened? What do you think caused that to happen? What ideas do you have to solve the problem now? What did you learn that will help you next time?"

A word of warning: if children are used to lectures and punishment, they may say, "I don't know." This is the time for you to say, "You are such a good problem solver. Why don't you think about it and we'll get together in thirty minutes and you can let me know what you have come up with."

Parents and teachers habitually lecture and make demands. Children often respond by resisting or rebelling. The following "kind and firm" phrases will help you avoid disrespectful language and increase cooperation:

- Your turn is coming.
- I know you can say that in a respectful way.
- I care about you and will wait until we can both be respectful to continue this conversation.
- I know you can think of a helpful solution.
- Act, don't talk. (For example, quietly and calmly take the child by the hand and show him or her what needs to be done.)
- We'll talk about this later. Now it is time to get in the car.
- (When child is having a temper tantrum.) We need to leave the store now. We'll try again later (or tomorrow).

When you decide to stop being punitive, you will need to practice new skills. And you will need to take time for training to help children learn mutual respect and problem-solving skills.

OPPOSITES ATTRACT: WHEN ONE PARENT IS KIND AND THE OTHER IS FIRM

It is interesting to note that two people with these opposing philosophies often get married. One has a tendency to be just a little too lenient. The other has a tendency to be just a little too strict. Then the lenient parent thinks he or she needs to be just a little more lenient to make up for the mean old strict parent. The strict parent thinks he or she needs to be just a little more strict to make up for the wishy-washy lenient parent—so they get further and further apart and fight about who is right and who is wrong. In truth they are both being ineffective.

One way to help children and parents learn effective communication is to have regular family meetings where they have an opportunity, on a weekly basis, to brainstorm for solutions to problems and to choose the solutions that are respectful to everyone. Focusing on solutions is one of the best ways for "opposites" to get closer together and be supportive of each other and their children. This is discussed in more detail in chapter six.

HELPING CHILDREN FEEL A SENSE OF BELONGING AND SIGNIFICANCE (CONNECTION)

Belonging and significance are the primary goals of all people—especially children. It is so important that a sense of connection (or lack thereof) is a primary indicator of how well children will do in school—both academically and socially. None of the students who killed other students and teachers felt a sense of belonging and significance.

Punishment does not help children feel a sense of belonging

and significance. That is one reason why punishment is not effective in the long term. Positive Discipline methods do help children feel a sense of belonging and significance and is an ongoing theme of this book. Chapter four presents details of why and how children misbehave when they don't feel a sense of belonging and significance.

IS IT EFFECTIVE LONG-TERM?

One of the primary reasons parents and teachers continue to use punishment is that it works—in the short term. Punishment will usually stop the misbehavior for the moment. The problem is that adults don't understand the long-term effects of punishment. Children who have been punished are not thinking, "Oh thank you. This is so helpful. I can hardly wait to seek your help with all my problems." Instead, they are thinking about rebelling (as soon as they get a chance) or complying at great loss to their sense of self.

Other reasons adults use punishment are that they are afraid that the only alternative is permissiveness; they are afraid that they will be giving up control and will not be doing their jobs as parents and teachers. And punishment is easier. You never have to tell adults how to use punishment. They know. Punishment is often a "reactive" response, but it takes effort and skills to use effective discipline.

The final reason adults use punishment even though it is not effective in the long term is that they don't know what else to do. This book is filled with alternatives to punishment that are effective in the long term—and that teach the last criterion for effective discipline.

TEACHING VALUABLE AND SOCIAL LIFE
SKILLS FOR GOOD CHARACTER

This is a new idea for most parents and teachers. They just haven't thought about the possibility that discipline could teach social and life skills. If you care to check out the research on the long-term effects of punishment, you will find that it teaches violence, sneakiness, low self-esteem, and many other negative skills. As you study Positive Discipline methods, you will notice that all of the discipline tools not only stop misbehavior; they also teach social and life skills for good character.

THE POSITIVE DISCIPLINE JOURNEY

When embarking upon the journey into Positive Discipline, it helps to have a destination in mind. What is it that you really want for your children? When parents and teachers are asked to make a list of characteristics they would like to help children develop, they think of the following qualities:

positive self-concept	interest in learning
responsibility	courtesy
self-discipline	honesty
cooperation	self-control
open-mindedness	patience
objective thinking skills	sense of humor
respect for self and others	concern for others
compassion	problem-solving skills
acceptance of self and others	inner wisdom
enthusiasm for life	integrity

Add any characteristics to the list that you feel have been left out. Keep these characteristics in mind as you study the concepts of Positive Discipline. It will be evident that children develop these characteristics when they are actively involved in the Positive Discipline model of mutual respect, cooperation, and focusing on solutions.

REVIEW

Positive Discipline Tools

1. Eliminate punishment.
2. Eliminate permissiveness.
3. Use kindness and firmness at the same time.
4. Provide opportunities for children to develop strength in the Significant Seven Perceptions and Skills.
5. Beware of what works (punishment has negative long-term results).
6. Give up the crazy idea that in order to make children do better, first you have to make them feel worse.
7. Involve children in setting limits.
8. Ask curiosity questions
9. Use kind and firm phrases.

Questions

1. What are the two main reasons children don't behave the way they used to in *the good old days*?
2. What are the Significant Seven Skills and Perceptions? How could a lack of these lead to *misbehavior* in children?
3. What are three approaches to child discipline, and what are the differences among them?
4. Discuss the two main differences between Positive Discipline and other methods and why these differences are important for long-term results.

5. What is meant by "beware of what works"?

6. What are the Four R's of Punishment? Share personal experiences of times you felt any of the Four R's and why.

7. What are the long-term effects for children who learn through strict methods, and why?

8. What are the long-term effects for children who learn through Positive Discipline, and why?

9. Why do things sometimes get worse before they get better?

10. Which characteristics would you like to see children internalize as a result of their interaction with you as a parent or teacher?

11. What are the Four Criteria for Effective Discipline, and how do they fit with punishment? Why are they effective in the long term?

12. What are some phrases that include kindness and firmness at the same time?

Chapter Two

SOME BASIC CONCEPTS

This book contains hundreds of practical application ideas for nonpunitive discipline. However, before getting into "how to," it's important to know "why to." Too many parents and teachers use methods that don't produce effective long-term results for children because they don't understand essential concepts of human behavior. The basic Adlerian concepts described in this and the next two chapters (along with many practical application suggestions) help parents and teachers understand more about human behavior, why children misbehave, and why Positive Discipline methods work to help children learn the important life skills and attitudes they need to become happy, contributing members of society.

Alfred Adler was a man with ideas ahead of his time. During his popular lectures and public seminars in Vienna (after breaking away from Freud), he advocated equality for all people, all races, women, and children long before it was popular to do so. Adler, an Austrian of Jewish descent, had to leave his native land during the Nazi persecution in order to continue his work.

Rudolf Dreikurs worked closely with Adler and continued to develop Adlerian psychology after Adler's death in 1937. Dreikurs authored or coauthored books to help parents and teachers understand the practical application of Adlerian theory in order to improve their relationships with children at home and at school (see "Suggested Readings").

Dreikurs was concerned because so many adults who attempted to practice his suggestions did not understand some of the basic concepts. This lack of understanding caused them to distort many of the techniques and use them to win over children rather than to win children over. Adults win over children when they use controlling, punitive methods. Adults win children over when they treat them with dignity and respect (kindness and firmness at the same time) and have faith in their abilities to cooperate and contribute. This requires that adults use lots of encouragement and take time for training in essential life skills.

Winning over children makes them losers, and losing generally causes children to be rebellious or blindly submissive. Neither characteristic is desirable. *Winning children over* means gaining their willing cooperation.

An example of how adults misunderstand the basic concepts of Positive Discipline is the common practice of adding humiliation to a logical consequence in the mistaken belief that children won't learn unless they *suffer* for their mistakes. It is true that humiliation may motivate children to do better, but at what cost to their sense of self-worth? Will they become "pleasers" or approval junkies—always thinking that their worth depends on the approval of others? Will they do better but be afraid to take risks for fear of failure? Will their learning include blame, shame, and pain and the kind of adult-generated discouragement that invites lowered self-esteem? Or will their learning be based on adult empathy, encouragement, unconditional love, and empowerment that invites life-skill training and a healthy sense of self-worth?

SELF-ESTEEM—AN ILLUSIONARY CONCEPT

Since self-esteem and self-worth have been mentioned, it is important to define these terms—even though experts don't agree on a definition. I was a member of the California Self-esteem Task Force, and it was interesting to listen to the task force members debate over a definition of self-esteem.

I believe we have done children a disservice by thinking we can give them self-esteem. There has been a movement to give children self-esteem through praise, happy stickers, smiley faces, and making them "very important person of the day." All of this could be fun and harmless, unless a child decides that his or her self-worth depends on the outside opinion of others. When this happens, children may become pleasers or approval junkies. They learn to look to others to decide if what they are doing is okay instead of learning to self-evaluate and reflect on right action internally. They develop "other" esteem instead of self-esteem.

Have you noticed how illusive self-esteem can be? One day you may feel great about yourself. Then you make a mistake and criticize yourself, or hear criticism from someone else—and, suddenly, your self-esteem goes down the tubes.

We perform the greatest service to children when we teach them self-evaluation (discussed in more detail in chapter seven) instead of being dependent on praise and the opinion of others. Adults can help by teaching that mistakes are wonderful opportunities to learn. By allowing them to experience failure, kids will figure out for themselves how to solve problems when they arise. They will benefit greatly from learning to be resilient so they know how to handle the ups and downs of life. Children benefit by having many opportunities to feel good about themselves when they make a meaningful contribution in their home, school, and community. A sense of belonging and significance is the key.

One of my favorite *Peanuts* cartoons shows Lucy asking Linus, "How was school today?"

Linus answers, "I didn't go. I opened the door and asked, 'Does anyone in there need me?' No one answered so I went home." Children need to feel needed.

When children develop strength in all of the Significant Seven discussed in chapter one, they will have a strong sense of self-worth and will be able to deal with the illusive nature of self-esteem. Adults can start by creating a positive learning environment by *winning children over* instead of trying to *win over children*.

WINNING CHILDREN OVER

Children feel encouraged when they think you understand their point of view. Once they feel understood, they are more willing to listen to your point of view and to work on a solution to the problem. Remember that children are more likely to listen to you *after* they feel listened to. Using the following Four Steps for Winning Cooperation is a great way to create an atmosphere where children feel ready to listen and to cooperate.

Four Steps for Winning Cooperation

1. Express understanding for the child's feelings. Be sure to check with him or her to see if you are right.
2. Show empathy without condoning. Empathy does not mean you agree or condone. It simply means that you understand the child's perception. A nice touch here is to share times when you have felt or behaved similarly.
3. Share your feelings and perceptions. If the first two steps have been done in a sincere and friendly manner, the child will be ready to listen to you.
4. Invite the child to focus on a solution. Ask if he has any

ideas on what to do in the future to avoid the problem.
If he doesn't, offer some suggestions until you can reach
an agreement.

An attitude of friendliness, caring, and respect is essential to
these steps. Your decision to win cooperation will be enough to
create positive feelings in you. After the first two steps, the child
will be won over, too. The child will now be ready to hear you
when you use the third step (even if you may have expressed
your feelings many times before without being heard). The
fourth step is likely to be effective now that you have created an
atmosphere of respect.

Mrs. Martinez shared the following experience. Her daughter, Linda, came home from school complaining that her teacher
had yelled at her in front of the whole class. Mrs. Martinez put
her hands on her hips and asked Linda in an accusing voice,
"Well, what did you do?"

Linda dropped her eyes and angrily replied, "I didn't do anything."

Mrs. Martinez said, "Oh, come on, teachers don't yell at students for nothing. What did you do?"

Linda flopped on the couch with a sullen look on her face and
just glared at her mother. Mrs. Martinez continued in her accusing tone. "Well, what are you going to do to solve this problem?"

Linda belligerently replied, "Nothing."

At this point Mrs. Martinez remembered the Four Steps for
Winning Cooperation. She took a deep breath, changed her attitude, and commented in a friendly tone of voice, "I'll bet you
felt embarrassed to have the teacher yell at you in front of the
others." (Step one. Express understanding.)

Linda looked up at her mother with suspicious interest. Mrs.
Martinez then shared, "I can remember once in the fourth grade
that happened to me just because I got up to sharpen my pencil
during a math test. I was so embarrassed and angry that my

teacher would yell at me in front of the whole class." (Step two. Show empathy without condoning—and share a similar experience.)

Linda was interested now. "Really?" she said. "All I did was ask to borrow a pencil. I certainly didn't think it was fair for my teacher to yell at me for that."

Mrs. Martinez said, "Well, I can certainly understand how you must have felt. Can you think of anything you might do to avoid that kind of embarrassing situation in the future?" (Step four. Invite child to focus on a solution. Step three was not necessary in this case.)

Linda responded, "I suppose I could be sure I had more than one pencil, so I would not have to borrow."

Mrs. Martinez said, "That sounds like an excellent idea."

One of Mrs. Martinez's goals was to help Linda behave in ways that would not invite her teacher's anger and disapproval. Notice that the first time she invited Linda to think about what she could do to solve the problem, Linda was feeling too hostile to cooperate. Once her mother used encouragement (through the Four Steps for Winning Cooperation), Linda felt closeness and trust instead of distance and hostility, and was willing to think of a solution. When her mother was able to see things from Linda's point of view, Linda no longer felt the need to be defensive.

Mrs. Jones also used the Four Steps for Winning Cooperation when she learned that her six-year-old son, Jeff, had been stealing. She found a quiet time when no one else was around and asked Jeff to come sit on her lap. She then told Jeff she had heard about him stealing a pack of gum from the store. (Notice she didn't "set him up" by asking him if he had done something when she already knew he had.) Next she shared a time when she was in the fifth grade and had stolen an eraser from a store; she knew she shouldn't have done it, and it made her feel very guilty, so she decided it wasn't worth it. Jeff said defensively, "But the store has so much gum." Mrs. Jones then led Jeff in a discussion exploring how much gum and other merchandise the store owner had to sell in order to pay his rent, pay employees, pay for inventory, and earn enough money to live on. Jeff admitted he had never thought of that. They also discussed how they wouldn't like to have others take their things. Jeff confided he did not want to steal things anymore and that he would pay for the gum he had stolen. Mrs. Jones offered to go with him for moral support.

Mrs. Jones was able to win Jeff over by not accusing, blaming, or lecturing. Jeff did not have to feel he was a bad person for what he had done, and he was willing to explore socially responsible reasons for not doing it again. Also, he was able to participate in a solution that, although embarrassing for him, would be a very valuable life lesson for future behavior. He was able to do this because his mother created a feeling of support rather than attack and defensiveness.

THE FEELING BEHIND WHAT WE DO OR SAY

The feeling behind what we do or say is more important than what we do or say. What we do is never as important as how we do it. The feeling and attitude behind what we do will determine the *how*. An adult can ask, "What did you learn from this?" with a tone of voice that is blaming and shaming or with a tone of voice that shows empathy and interest. An adult can create an atmosphere that invites closeness and trust, or an atmosphere that creates distance and hostility. It is amazing how many adults believe they can have a positive influence on children after creating distance and hostility instead of closeness and trust. (Do they really believe this—or are they simply reacting without thinking?)

The feeling behind words is often most evident in our tone of voice. Adding humiliation violates the basic concept of mutual respect. It also changes what could be a logical consequence into punishment, which won't achieve positive long-term effects. If a child spills milk on the floor, the logical consequence (or solution) would be for her to clean it up. It remains a logical consequence (or solution) so long as the adult engages the child through kind but firm words, such as "Whoops, what do you need to do about that?" Notice how much more engaging it is to *ask* the child what needs to be done instead of *telling* her. *Asking* instead of *telling* is one of the most effective Positive Discipline methods you will learn and is discussed in more detail in chapter six. Telling invites resistance and rebellion. Respectfully involving children invites them to feel capable to use their power in contributing ways. A request becomes a punishment when adults don't use a tone of voice that is kind and respectful or adds humiliation, such as, "How can you be so clumsy? Clean that up right now, and let me pour the milk from now on since you can't seem to get it right."

Adlerian psychology provides a set of basic concepts that offer a wealth of knowledge to help us increase our understanding of children and of ourselves, but it is so much more than just theory. The basic concepts are lost without attitudes of encouragement, understanding, and respect. If these attitudes are not understood, the techniques will be reduced to disrespectful manipulation. We will be more effective with children if we always ask ourselves, "Is what I am doing empowering or discouraging?"

BASIC ADLERIAN CONCEPTS

1. Children Are Social Beings

Behavior is determined within a social context. Children make decisions about themselves and how to behave, based on how they see themselves in relationship to others and how they think others feel about them. Remember that children are constantly making decisions and forming beliefs about themselves, about the world, and about what they need to do to survive or thrive. When they are "thriving" they are developing strength in all of the Significant Seven discussed in chapter one. When they are in their "survival" mode (trying to figure out how to feel a sense of belonging and significance), adults often interpret this as misbehavior. Does misbehavior seem different to you when you think of it as "survival mode" behavior?

2. Behavior Is Goal Oriented

Behavior is based on a goal to be achieved within a social context. The primary goal is to belong. Children are not consciously aware of the goal they hope to achieve. Sometimes they have mistaken ideas of how to achieve what they want and behave in ways that achieve just the opposite of their goal. For example, they may want to belong, but they act obnoxious in their awkward attempts to achieve this goal. It can become a vicious cycle. The more their behavior invites annoyance or anger, the more obnoxious they may act because they want to belong.

Dreikurs explained: "Children are good perceivers, but poor interpreters." Children are not the only ones with this problem. The following situation is an example of how it begins.

When the mother of two-year-old Adele comes home from the hospital with a new baby brother, Adele perceives how much attention Mother gives to the baby. Unfortunately, Adele *interprets* this to mean that Mother loves the baby more than her. This is not true, but the truth is not as important as what Adele believes. Her behavior will be based on what she believes is true rather than on what is true. Adele's goal is to regain her special place with Mother, and she mistakenly believes that the way to achieve this goal is to act like a baby, so she may want a bottle, poop her pants, and cry a lot. She achieves just the opposite of her goal when Mother feels frustrated and rejecting rather than loving and affectionate.

3. A Child's Primary Goal Is to Belong and to Feel Significant

The first two concepts are brought together here as we see that the goal of all behavior is to achieve a sense of belonging and significance within the social environment. Misbehavior is based on a mistaken belief about how to achieve belonging and significance, as in the previous example.

4. A Misbehaving Child Is a Discouraged Child

A misbehaving child is trying to tell us, "I don't feel I belong or have significance, and I have a mistaken belief about how to achieve it." When a misbehaving child acts obnoxious, it is easy to understand why it is difficult for most adults to get past the misbehavior and remember the real meaning and message behind it: "I just want to belong." Understanding this concept is the first step for adults to be more effective in helping misbehaving children. It helps to be a "code breaker." When a child misbehaves, think of the misbehavior as a code and ask yourself, "What is she really trying to tell me?" Remember, the child is not consciously aware of her coded message, but will feel deeply understood when you deal with her hidden belief instead of reacting just to the behavior. You will feel differently about misbehavior if you remember that behind the misbehavior is a child who just wants to belong and is confused or unskilled about how to accomplish this goal in a socially useful way. Also, it will be helpful if you look closely to see if your behavior is inviting the child to believe she doesn't belong or have significance. These first four concepts are discussed in greater detail in chapter four.

5. Social Responsibility or Community Feeling

Another important contribution of Alfred Adler is the concept of *Gemeinschaftsgefühl,* a beautiful German word coined by Adler. There is not a good English translation, but Adler finally chose social interest (and I use social responsibility). It means having real concern for one's fellow person and a sincere desire to make a contribution to society. The following story was shared by Kristin R. Pancer in the December 1978 issue of *The Individual Psychologist* to convey the meaning of social responsibility.

Once there were two brothers who owned a farm together. They had a difficult time making a living because of the rocky soil and drought, but they shared all profits equally. One of the brothers had a wife and five children. The other was a bachelor. One night the married brother could not sleep. He tossed and turned as it occurred to him how unfair their arrangement was. He thought, "My brother does not have any children to go home to, or to take care of him in his old age. He really needs more than half. Tomorrow I will offer him two thirds of our profits. Surely that will be more equitable." That same night the other brother also had difficulty sleeping, because he also decided that their fifty-fifty arrangement was not fair. He thought, "My brother has a wife and five children to feed. They also contribute more labor to the farm than I do. My brother deserves more than half. Tomorrow I will offer him two thirds." The next day the brothers met and each shared his plan for a more equitable arrangement. This is an example of social responsibility in action.

Adler had what he called his Fourteen-Day Cure Plan. He claimed he could cure anyone of mental illness in just fourteen days if they would just do what he told them to do. One day a woman who was extremely depressed came to see Adler. He told her, "I can cure you of your depression in just fourteen days if you will follow my advice."

She was not very enthusiastic as she asked, "What do you want me to do?"

Adler replied, "If you will do one thing for someone else every day for fourteen days, at the end of that time your depression will be gone."

She objected. "Why should I do something for someone else, when no one ever does anything for me?"

Adler jokingly responded, "Well, maybe it will take you twenty-one days." He went on to add, "If you can't think of anything you are willing to do for someone else, just think of what you could do if you felt like it." Adler knew that if she would even think about doing something for someone else, she would be on her way toward improvement.

It is extremely important to teach social responsibility to children. What good is academic learning if young people do not learn to become contributing members of society? Dreikurs often said, "Don't do anything for a child that a child can do for herself." The reason for this is that we rob children of opportunities to develop the belief that they are capable, through their own experience, when we do too much for them. Instead they may develop the belief that they need to be taken care of or that they are "entitled" to special service.

The first step in teaching social responsibility is to teach self-reliance. Then children are ready to help others, and feel extremely capable when they do. When adults take the role of supermoms and superteachers, children learn to expect the world to serve them rather than to be of service to the world. These are the children who think it is unfair if they don't get their own way. When others refuse to serve them they feel sorry for themselves or seek revenge in some hurtful or destructive way. When they seek revenge, they always hurt themselves as much or more than they hurt others.

At the other extreme are parents and teachers who are too busy to take the time to teach children social and life skills for good character. These same adults become upset when children don't "behave themselves." I'm not sure where they think these children learn respectful behavior. Too many adults are "blaming" children for their misbehavior instead of taking responsibility (not blame) for their part in the misbehavior equation.

Positive Discipline helps children and adults end these vicious cycles by encouraging social responsibility. Parents and teachers are usually not aware of how much they are doing for children that children could be doing for themselves. They don't take time to teach children how to make a contribution to the home or classroom. Take an inventory. Teachers, how many things are you doing in the classroom that could be done by children? Parents, how much are you doing for children because it is expedient instead of helping them feel capable by contributing?

In the book *Positive Discipline in the Classroom*[1] my co-authors and I talk about the importance of getting students involved in brainstorming about all the jobs that need to be done in the classroom. The teacher can participate in the brainstorming, but it is amazing how many things children can think of when they are invited to do so. After the list is completed, ask for volunteers for each job. Make sure there is at least one job for every student. There can even be a "job monitor." It is important to establish (with student input) a job rotation system so that no one gets stuck with the less enticing jobs for too long. It is obvious how job sharing can increase belonging, teach life skills, and allow children to experience social responsibility.

6. Equality

Many people today do not have trouble with the concept of equality until it comes to children. Then many objections are raised. "How can children be equal when they don't have the same experience, knowledge, or responsibility?" they ask.

As emphasized in chapter one, equality does not mean "the same." Adler meant by equality that all people have equal claims to dignity and respect. Most adults are willing to agree that children are equal to them in value. This is one reason why Positive Discipline does not include humiliation. Humiliating techniques are contrary to the concepts of equality and mutual respect.

7. Mistakes Are Wonderful Opportunities to Learn

In our society we are taught to be ashamed of mistakes. We are all imperfect. What we need to achieve is the courage to change our debilitating beliefs about imperfection. This is one of the most encouraging concepts, and yet one of the hardest to achieve in our society. There isn't a perfect human being in the world, yet everyone is demanding it of themselves and others— especially children.

Close your eyes and remember the messages you received from parents and teachers about mistakes when you were a child. What were those messages? To make this exercise more powerful, you may want to write them down. When you made a mistake, did you receive the message that you were stupid, inadequate, bad, a disappointment, a klutz? Close your eyes again and let yourself remember a specific time when you were being berated for a mistake. What were you deciding about yourself and about what to do in the future? Remember, you were not aware that you were making a decision at the time; but when you look back it is usually obvious what decisions you were making. Some people decide they are bad or inadequate. Others decide they should not take risks for fear of humiliation if their efforts fall short of perfection. As discussed above, too many decide to become approval junkies and try to please adults, at great cost to their self-esteem. And some decide they will be sneaky about their mistakes and do everything they can to avoid getting caught. Are these healthy messages and decisions that encourage productive life-skill development? Of course not.

When parents and teachers give children negative messages about mistakes, they usually mean well. They are trying to motivate children to do better "for their own good." They haven't taken time to think about the long-term results of their methods. So much parenting and teaching is based on fear. Adults fear they aren't doing a good job if they don't "make" children do better. Too many are more concerned about what the neighbors will think than about what their children are learning. Others are afraid that children will never learn to do better if they don't instill them with fear and humiliation. Most are afraid because they don't know what else to do—and fear that if they don't inflict blame, shame, and pain, they will be acting permissively. Often adults cover up their fear by acting more controlling.

There is another way. It is not permissive, and it truly motivates children to do better without paying the price of a lowered sense of self-worth. We need to learn and teach children to be excited about mistakes as opportunities to learn. Wouldn't it be wonderful to hear an adult say to a child, "You made a mistake. That is fantastic. What can we learn from it?" And I do mean "we." We are partners in most of the mistakes made by children. Many mistakes are made because we haven't taken time for training and encouragement. We often provoke rebellion instead of inspiring improvement. Model the courage to accept imperfection so that children will learn from you that mistakes truly are an opportunity to learn.

Children learn to see and practice mistakes as opportunities to learn during family and class meetings (discussed in chapters eight and nine). Many families have found it helpful during dinnertime to invite everyone to share a mistake of the day and what they learned from it. Once a week during a class meeting (held on a daily basis) some teachers allow time for every student to share a mistake and what they learned from it. Children need daily exposure to the value of mistakes—and learning from them in a safe environment.

A primary theme of this book, one that you will hear over and over, is learning how to use discipline challenges as opportunities to learn. First, however, adults need to change any negative beliefs about mistakes they may have so they can model what Rudolf Dreikurs called the courage to be imperfect. Using the Three R's of Recovery is an excellent way to model the courage to be imperfect.

The Three R's of Recovery from Mistakes

1. Recognize—"Wow! I made a mistake."
2. Reconcile—"I apologize."
3. Resolve—"Let's work on a solution together."

It is much easier to take responsibility for a mistake when it is seen as a learning opportunity rather than as something bad. If we see mistakes as bad we tend to feel inadequate and discouraged and may become defensive, evasive, judgmental, or critical—of ourselves or others. On the other hand, when mistakes are seen as opportunities to learn, recognizing them will seem like an exciting venture. "I wonder what I will learn from this one." Self-forgiveness is an important element of the first R of Recovery.

Have you ever noticed how forgiving children are when we are willing to apologize? Have you ever said you were sorry to a child? If so, how did that child respond? I ask this question during lectures all over the world, and the response is universal. When adults sincerely apologize, children almost always say, "That's okay, Mom" (or Dad, or Teacher). Children can be feeling angry and resentful in response to disrespectful behavior one minute (and adults probably deserve it) and switch to total forgiveness as soon as the adult says, "I am sorry."

The first two R's of Recovery—recognize and reconcile—create a positive atmosphere for the third R, working on solutions. Trying to work on solutions while the atmosphere is hostile is totally nonproductive.

Just like most adults and children, even when I know better, I don't always do what I know. As human beings it is common for us to become emotionally hooked and lose our common sense (revert to our reptilian brains). We then thoughtlessly react instead of acting thoughtfully. One thing I love about the Positive Discipline principles is that no matter how many mistakes I make, and no matter how many messes I create with my mistakes, I can always go back to the principles, learn from my mistakes, clean up the mess I made—and make things better than they had been before the mistakes.

Since I make so many mistakes, the Three R's of Recovery is one of my favorite concepts. My signature example is the time I said to my then eight-year-old daughter, "Mary, you are a spoiled brat." (Does that sound like kindness, firmness, dignity, and respect?)

Mary, who is very familiar with the Three R's of Recovery, retorted, "Well, don't tell me later that you are sorry."

In total reaction, I said, "You don't have to worry, because I'm not."

Mary ran to her bedroom and slammed the door. I soon reverted back to my rational brain, realized what I had done, and went to her bedroom to apologize. She was still angry, and was not ready for an apology. She had her copy of an early edition of *Positive Discipline* and was very busy underlining with a big, black marking pen. I looked over her shoulder and saw that she had scribbled "phony" in the column.

I left the room thinking, "Oh dear, there will probably be another *Mommie Dearest* book hitting the market any day." I knew I had made a huge mistake.

In about five minutes Mary came to me, timidly put her arms around me, and said, "I'm sorry, Mama."

I said, "Honey, I'm sorry too. In fact, when I called you a spoiled brat, I was being one. I was upset at you for losing control of your behavior, but I had lost control of my own behavior. I am so sorry."

Mary said, "That's okay, I was acting like a brat."

I said, "Well, I can see what I did to provoke you to act that way."

Mary said, "Well, I can see what I did."

I have seen this happen over and over. When adults take responsibility for what they did to create a conflict (and any conflict takes at least two), children are usually willing to follow this modeling and take responsibility for their part. Children learn accountability when they have models of accountability.

A few days later I overheard Mary on the phone saying to her friend, "Oh Debbie, you are so stupid!" Mary quickly realized what she had done and said, "I'm sorry, Debbie. When I call you stupid, that means I am being stupid."

Mary had internalized the principles of Recovery and learned that mistakes are nothing more than wonderful opportunities to learn.

8. Make Sure the Message of Love Gets Through

Mrs. Smith, a single parent, called for help with a problem she was having with her daughter, Maria. Mrs. Smith was afraid Maria might be getting into drugs. She had found a six-pack of beer on the floor in Maria's closet. She confronted Maria with the six-pack of beer in her hand and asked, "What is this?"

Mrs. Smith's tone of voice clearly indicated that she was not really interested in an answer to her question. It was a setup question designed to trap and humiliate. The question immediately created distance and hostility.

Maria replied with sarcasm, "It looks like a six-pack of beer to me, Mom."

The battle escalated. Mrs. Smith said, "Don't get smart with me, young lady. You tell me about this."

Maria said, with total innocence, "Mom, I don't know what you are talking about!"

Mrs. Smith was now ready to spring the trap. "I found this beer on the floor of your closet, young lady, and you'd better explain."

Maria did some fast thinking and said, "Oh, I forgot all about that. I was hiding it for a friend of mine."

Mrs. Smith sarcastically said, "Oh, sure! Do you think I'm going to believe that?"

Maria angrily replied, "I don't care if you believe it or not," as she went into her bedroom and slammed the door.

I wanted to help Mrs. Smith get to the bottom-line message of love by asking, "Why were you upset about finding the beer?"

I could tell she thought that was a stupid question as she indignantly replied, "Because I don't want her to get into trouble."

"Why don't you want her to get into trouble?" was the next question.

I could tell Mrs. Smith was sorry she had called as she answered with total irritation, "Because I don't want her to ruin her life!"

Since she still hadn't discovered her bottom-line message, I persisted. "And why is it that you don't you want her to ruin her life?"

She finally got it. "Because I love her!" Mrs. Smith exclaimed.

The final question was asked gently. "Do you think she got that message?"

Mrs. Smith felt chagrined as she realized she had not come even close to conveying her message of love to Maria.

The next week Mrs. Smith called to report how she had used a combination of the Three R's of Recovery and the Four Steps for Winning Cooperation. The next night, when Maria came home she greeted her at the door, and coming from an attitude of love she asked, "Maria, can we talk?"

Maria asked belligerently, "What do you want to talk about?" (It is important to note that it may take a while for children to hear and trust a change in attitude by adults.)

Mrs. Smith understood this. Instead of reacting to the belligerence, she got into Maria's world and made a guess about how she might be feeling: "I'll bet that when I started yelling at you about the six-pack of beer last night, you probably thought I didn't even care about you."

Maria felt so understood that she started to cry. With accusation and a tremor in her voice she said, "That's right. I've been feeling like I'm nothing but a bother to you—and that only my friends really care about me."

Mrs. Smith said, "I can see how you might feel that way. When I come at you with my fear and my anger instead of my love, how could you feel anything else?"

Maria visibly relaxed her belligerent attitude. Her mother's attitude of love was finally getting through to her. When Mrs. Smith could see this she continued. "I'm really sorry for the way I blew up at you yesterday."

The distance and hostility had changed to closeness and trust. Maria responded by saying, "That's okay, Mom. I really was hiding it for a friend."

Mrs. Smith then shared, "Maria, I really do love you. Sometimes I get scared that you might do things that could hurt you. I go overboard with my fears, and I forget to tell you that it is only because I love you." Mrs. Smith put her arms around Maria and said, "Will you give me another chance? Can we start talking with each other and solve problems together with love and concern for each other?"

Maria said, "Sure, Mom. Sounds good to me."

Mrs. Smith reported that they started having family meetings that night. She felt grateful because an atmosphere of love and cooperation had been established that totally changed their relationship.

You'll notice that the examples in this chapter illustrate how adult misbehavior (lack of knowledge or skills) contributes to the misbehavior of the children. When the adults change their behavior, so do the children. And, in every case, the adults experience more joy, as well as positive results, when they remember to make sure that the message of love gets through.

These eight basic Adlerian concepts provide the foundation for understanding behavior and developing the attitudes and methods necessary to implement the Positive Discipline approach. The methods will help adults learn the attitudes and skills to help children develop the life skills and characteristics they need when they venture out into the world.

REVIEW

Positive Discipline Tools

1. Win children over instead of using your power to win over children.
2. Provide opportunities for children to develop and practice the Significant Seven Perceptions and Skills to increase their sense of self-worth.
3. Stop "telling" and start "asking" in ways that invite children to participate in problem solving.
4. Use the Four Steps for Winning Cooperation.
5. Remember that the feeling behind what you do or say is more important than what you do or say.
6. Involve children in brainstorming the chores that need to be done and a plan for doing them.

7. Avoid pampering so children can develop a belief in their own capabilities.
8. Teach and practice that mistakes are wonderful opportunities to learn.
9. Teach and practice the Three R's of Recovery from Mistakes.
10. Make sure the message of love gets through.

Questions

1. What is the difference between winning over the child and winning the child over?
2. What are the Four Steps for Winning Cooperation? Think of a behavior challenge you are experiencing with a child. How could you use these steps in this situation?
3. What are the important attitudes necessary for the positive approach to be effective with children?
4. What does it mean to be a social being?
5. What is the primary goal toward which all behavior is oriented?
6. Why do children often behave in ways that are counterproductive to achieving their primary goal?
7. What are misbehaving children trying to tell us with their misbehavior?
8. How might we behave differently if we remember the hidden message behind children's misbehavior?
9. What is social responsibility and why is it important for children to develop it?
10. What does Adler mean by equality?
11. Why is humiliation out of place in a positive approach?
12. What is the purpose of mistakes?
13. Why is it important to have the courage to be imperfect?
14. Why would it be helpful to teach children that mistakes

are opportunities to learn rather than something to be ashamed of?

15. What are the Three R's of Recovery? Discuss.

16. What is the key concept that unlocks all doors? Share an example of how something you did with a child might have been different if you had started with the message of love.

Chapter Three

THE SIGNIFICANCE OF BIRTH ORDER

An understanding of birth order can increase your understanding of how children might develop misperceptions about themselves based on their interpretations of their birth-order position in the family. It is another way to "get into the child's world" in order to increase your understanding of his or her reality.

Children are always making decisions and forming beliefs about themselves, about others, and about their world based on their interpretation of their life experiences. Their behavior is then based upon those decisions and what they believe they need to do in order to survive or thrive. It is very common for children to compare themselves to their siblings and decide that if a brother or sister is doing well in a certain area, their only survival choice is one of the following:

- to develop competence in a completely different area;
- to compete and try to be better than other siblings;
- to be rebellious or revengeful;
- to give up because of a belief that they can't compete.

Being in a family is like being in a play. Each birth-order position is like a different part in the play, with distinct and separate characteristics for each part. Therefore, if one sibling has already filled a part, such as the "good child," other siblings may feel they have to find other parts to play, such as rebellious child, academic child, athletic child, social child, and so on.

We may ask, "Why is this? It doesn't make sense. Why can't two children understand that they can both be good at something?" First, it is important to note that there are exceptions to every general rule. Sometimes all children in a family will choose to excel in the same area—especially when the family atmosphere is one of cooperation instead of competition. However, most children believe they need to be different in order to feel a sense of belonging and significance. It doesn't help to try making sense of this. It does help to simply understand that children usually form certain conclusions based on their birth-order position.

It may seem more logical for children to have similarities because they come from the same family than because they share the same-position birth order, but the opposite is true. Children in the same family are often extremely different, even though they have the same parents, the same home, and the same neighborhood. Of course, the environment cannot be totally the same for children in the same family, but the factor that makes the biggest contribution to differences within families is the interpretation each child gives to the environment that he or she perceives. Most interpretations are based on how children compare themselves with their siblings.

As we saw in chapter two, children are good perceivers but poor interpreters. This becomes very apparent in the study of birth order. The truth of a situation is not as important as the child's interpretation of a situation. Behavior is based on the latter. Children of the same birth order often make similar interpretations about themselves and how they think they need to behave in order to find belonging and significance in life. This is why people of the same birth order often have similar characteristics and behaviors.

Birth order isn't the only explanation for personality development, but it is one important factor. There are many other theories that can help us understand similarities and uniqueness in people, such as an understanding of the Nine Temperaments theory studied by Chess and Thomas.[1] They found that children are born with certain characteristics that last their whole lives. These characteristics and how they relate to Positive Discipline are discussed in *Positive Discipline for Preschoolers*.[2] Lifestyle Priority theory, developed by Israeli psychologist Nira Kefir, explains another factor that influences the personalities of children. This theory describes how adults choose a lifestyle priority of control, pleasing, superiority, or comfort that motivates their behavior when they are under stress. How these lifestyle priorities may invite certain decisions and behaviors from children is discussed in chapter ten.

The purpose of learning about birth order (or any of the personality theories mentioned) is not to label and stereotype. It is rather to help us increase our knowledge and understanding of ourselves and children so we can become more effective in our relationships.

OLDEST CHILDREN

The most predictable similarities are found among oldest children, because this is the one position that has the fewest variables. For instance, there are many ways to be a middle child, such as the middle of three or one of the middles of seven. Youngest children have almost as many predictable similarities as do oldest children. Only children will be more similar to oldest or youngest, depending on whether they were pampered like a youngest or given more responsibility like an oldest.

All oldest children will not form the exact same conclusions and be exactly alike, nor will all middle children, all only children, or all youngest children. We are all unique and have as many differences as we do similarities, but those of the same birth order often adopt some similar characteristics.

Before you read further, close your eyes and think of several adjectives that come to your mind to describe the oldest, youngest, and middle children you know. It is easy to come up with descriptions of oldest children, such as responsible, leader, bossy (even though in their minds they want others to do better for their own good), perfectionist, critical (of self and others), conformist, organized, competitive, independent, reluctant risk-takers, and conservative. Because oldest children are the first-born, they often adopt the mistaken interpretation that they must be first or best in order to be important. This can be mani-fested in many different ways. For some it may seem important to get their schoolwork done first, even though it is sloppy. Others may be the last to hand in their work because they take so much time making it the best.

YOUNGEST CHILDREN

The characteristic we think of first to describe youngest children is spoiled. Many youngest children are pampered, both by parents and by other siblings. This makes it easy for them to adopt the mistaken interpretation that they must continue to manipulate others into their service in order to be important. Youngest children are often skilled in using their charm to inspire others to do things for them. Youngest children are often creative and fun-loving. Much of their creativity, energy, and intelligence may be channeled into achieving significance through charming manipulation.

Often youngest children are put in the confusing position of being favored by parents and resented by their siblings. The greatest danger for children who have been pampered is that they often interpret life as unfair whenever they are not taken care of or given whatever they want. They often feel hurt by these unfair conditions and think they have a right to have temper tantrums, feel sorry for themselves, or seek revenge in some way that is destructive or hurtful to others. They may develop the belief, "I feel loved when others take care of me."

Youngest children may have difficulty adjusting to school. They may feel not only that the teacher should continue the service they have received at home, but that the teacher should also learn for them. Consciously they say, "Teacher, please tie my shoes for me." Subconsciously, and by their actions, they are saying, "And while you are at it, please learn for me." "I can't" and "Show me" are often simple demands meaning "Do it for me."

As an elementary school counselor, I talked with many children who had difficulty adjusting to the learning environment. I always asked these children, "Who dresses you in the morning?" As you might guess, there is usually someone else who is still taking the responsibility to dress them. If it isn't Mom or Dad, it may be an older sibling.

As a child development instructor at a community college, I had many students who worked in preschools and day care centers. For ten years these students did surveys among the children with whom they worked. Rarely did they find a child who dressed himself or herself in the morning.

Children can dress themselves from the time they are two or three years old if they have clothes that are easy to put on and have been taught how to do it. When parents continue to dress their children after the age of three, they are robbing them of developing a sense of responsibility, self-sufficiency, and self-confidence. They are less likely to develop the belief that they are capable. Instead they feel a sense of belonging when others do things for them. Without a belief in their own capability, they are less likely to be good learners in school and may not develop the skills they need for success in life.

Since pampering is so damaging to children, why do parents do it? Many parents really think it is the best way to show love for their children. I have heard some argue that children have plenty of time to adjust to the cold, cruel world, so why not let them have it easy and pleasurable for as long as possible? These parents are not aware of how difficult it is to change beliefs, habits, and characteristics once they are established. The beliefs we develop as children become our "blueprint for living" as adults, even when those beliefs no longer make sense.

Other reasons parents might pamper are because it is easier, it fills their need to be needed, they think that is what "good" parents are supposed to do, they want to be sure their children do not experience the difficult childhood they feel they had, or they feel pressure from friends and family. Parents are not really thinking about long-term effects when they rob their children of the opportunity to practice valuable life skills because they can do it more easily, faster, and better. It never ceases to amaze me when parents tell me they "just don't have time" to let children do things for themselves. These same parents will later be disappointed and frustrated when they discover that their children never developed better life skills and attitudes. Do they think skills are developed automatically? Parents who want the best for their children will be more effective if they reevaluate their time priorities.

We need to understand that "supermoms" are not good for children. It is important to educate parents on what a great disservice they do their children when they pamper them. This is why, as was mentioned in chapter two, Dreikurs said, "Never do anything for a child that the child can do for himself." This does not mean that you can never do anything for a child. It does mean that children are shortchanged when they don't learn how capable they can be when they aren't pampered.

Children learn valuable life skills when parents take time for training, and then allow children to develop responsibility and self-confidence by practicing these life skills. It is a mistake to think children can always learn to take care of themselves later. The longer they wait, the more difficult it is to change their interpretations of what they think they need to do to find belonging and significance.

Some youngest children choose an entirely different interpretation of life and become speeders. They often adopt the mistaken interpretation that they must catch up with and outdo everyone ahead of them in order to be important. They become adults who are overachievers still trying to prove their significance.

MIDDLE CHILDREN

It is more difficult to generalize about the characteristics of middle children because of the many different positions. They usually feel squeezed in the middle, without the privileges of the oldest or the benefits of the youngest. This provides good reason to adopt the mistaken interpretation that they must be different in some way in order to be significant. This difference may take the form of overachieving or underachieving, "social butterfly" or "shy wallflower," "rebel with a cause" or just plain "rebel." Many are more easygoing than their siblings. Most middle children have a great deal of empathy for the underdog, with whom they identify. They are often good peacemakers, and others seek them out for sympathy and understanding. They are usually much more liberal than their oldest, conservative sibling.

ONLY CHILDREN

As explained earlier, only children may be similar to oldest or youngest children, with some important differences. If they are like the oldest, it will be with less intensity for perfectionism, because they haven't felt the pressure from someone coming up behind them to threaten their position. However, lessened perfectionism does not remove this trait entirely. Only children usually have the same high expectations of themselves that they felt from their parents. Because they have been the only child in the family, they usually desire and appreciate solitude—or they may fear loneliness. It may be more important for them to be unique than to be first.

All of the original astronauts were either oldest, psychological oldest (as explained on page 57), or only children. Neil Armstrong, an only child, had the unique experience of being the first man to walk on the moon.

How does birth-order information help us to understand children and be more effective with them? Being aware of a child's birth order will allow us to make some intelligent guesses about the child's world and point of view. Hopefully this awareness will help parents and teachers understand the importance of avoiding pampering, of providing oldest children with opportunities to feel okay about losing and not always being first, of helping middle children feel less squeezed, and generally of getting into each child's world.

EXCEPTIONS TO THE RULES

There are many factors that explain exceptions to general rules. One is gender. If the first and second child are different sexes, they may both develop characteristics of an oldest child, especially if there is a definite division of sex roles in their family. Each will assume oldest-child responsibilities within their sex role. For instance, if the oldest is a boy, he will have oldest-child characteristics in the masculine role. If the second child is a girl, she will still develop oldest-child characteristics in the female role.

However, if the two oldest children of three or more siblings are of the same sex, the differences between the two oldest are likely to be extreme. The two oldest children of the same sex are usually complete opposites. The closer they are in age, the more pronounced the differences, which brings us to the second factor accounting for exceptions to general rules.

When there are four years or more between children, they are less influenced by each other. They feel less competition when there is an age gap. If there are five children in a family with more than four years between each child, each may develop characteristics closer to an only or oldest child. They become a "psychological oldest" or a "psychological youngest." In one family where there are seven children ages nineteen, seventeen, fifteen, nine, seven, three, and one, there is one actual oldest. The children who are nine and three are psychologically oldest children, because the sibling before them is four or more years older. There is also one actual youngest and two psychological youngest—the children who are fifteen and seven—because they were youngest children for four or more years before the next sibling was born. When a child has had an opportunity to be in a position for more than four years, he has already formed many interpretations about life and himself and how to find belonging and significance. These may be modified when the family constellation changes but usually are not changed entirely. It is interesting to observe what sometimes happens when an older sibling leaves for college. The second child may change considerably—taking on more responsibility, but without the intensity of perfectionism. The dynamics in blended families can be better understood when there is a knowledge of birth order. It can be very upsetting for an oldest or youngest to be dethroned from their positions when other children join the family. A child who was once the oldest can suddenly become a youngest or a middle child. A youngest may suddenly lose her position as the "pampered one" when a younger child joins the family. It will help a lot if these children feel understood and are involved in family meetings (see chapter nine) so they can feel a sense of belonging and significance by being respectfully involved in solving problems.

Another exception to the rule is that children sometimes arbitrarily switch typical position characteristics. A second child may become an "Avis child"—one who tries harder and overtakes the first. The oldest may then give up and relinquish the typical characteristics of a first child. A sure sign of perfectionism is giving up. This child has decided, "If I can't be the best or first, why try?" An oldest child who has "given up" to make room for a younger "Avis child" may become a life "dropout." Many parents have shared how this explanation helped them understand the plight of their oldest child, who had been dethroned by a second-born. This understanding gave them a basis for encouragement (instead of anger and frustration) with their oldest child.

A youngest who becomes a speeder leaves the role of the pampered vacant. The child who is second from the youngest may move in to fill this role and adopt characteristics of a youngest.

FAMILY ATMOSPHERE

Another factor that accounts for exceptions to the general rule is the family atmosphere. The family atmosphere can either increase or decrease differences. In families where competition is valued and modeled (as in many American families), differences will be increased. In families where cooperation is valued and modeled, differences will be decreased. Many parents don't realize that they create a competitive family atmosphere when they disagree about parenting methods. Parents who agree on parenting methods create a cooperative family atmosphere.

As stated earlier, one general rule that can almost always be counted on is that the two oldest children will be very different from each other if they are the same sex and close in age. However, I had an opportunity to experience a vivid exception to this general rule. While doing an Adlerian lifestyle interview with one lady who had a sister only eighteen months older, my first guess was that they would be extreme opposites in characteristics. The interview proved this guess to be wrong. They were very similar. When we came to the question regarding what her parents were like, I asked if I could guess before she told me. I guessed that her parents were very loving and cooperative with each other, they agreed on child-rearing techniques, and the children felt they were loved and treated fairly. She asked me how I knew. I based my guess on my knowledge of the effects of family atmosphere. When two sisters only eighteen months apart are similar in characteristics, instead of opposites, we can guess that the parents created an atmosphere of cooperation rather than competition.

USING BIRTH-ORDER INFORMATION TO ENCOURAGE

In one school district birth-order information was used to help staff members become aware of the high number of youngest or psychologically youngest children in educationally disabled classes. This raised a valid question about educational disabilities. Are they physiological or behavioral? Do youngest children learn to use challenges to obtain more special service? If they are physiological, are we missing many educational challenges in older children because they learn to overcompensate?

*Remember, this information is not to be used to create labels and stereotypes, so we can feel smug about being "right" about others. It is simply to aid us in understanding why children often have mistaken interpretations about how to find belonging and significance, so we can be aware of more effective ways to help (or know when we should refrain from helping). It can also be used to focus on strengths. We should always remember to look for and appreciate the many ways each individual is unique.

In one elementary school, a group of students seemed to be driving every teacher crazy. When this group was in the second grade, their teacher considered retiring. When they were in the third grade, their teacher could hardly wait for summer. Finally, the fourth-grade teacher took a birth-order survey and learned that 85 percent were youngest children. Many of them spent a great deal of time displaying helplessness and seeking special attention. Through the use of class meetings, the fourth-grade teacher was able to achieve significant improvement as the children learned to help one another and themselves by improving their problem-solving skills.

Judy Moore, a fifth-grade teacher, did her master's thesis on birth order and reading groups. She found that there were a high percentage of oldest and only children in top reading groups and youngest children in lowest reading groups. Mrs. Moore took tape recordings of the dynamics in each group while she asked questions. In the top group all the children would raise their hands in eager competition to be the first to answer. The middle group was more easygoing, but someone would usually have an answer. In the lowest group there was a greater tendency for the children to express lack of understanding and need for further help.

Mrs. Moore had one student in her class (I'll call him John) who was her very lowest reader. She was concerned about the possibility of a low IQ, so her first step toward helping was to request psychological testing. She then did a lifestyle interview with John and learned that he was the youngest. Even more interesting, he had three older sisters named Georgia, Roberta, and Paula. She learned that everyone in the family called John "King John." With this information, Mrs. Moore could make some educated guesses about the value of boys in this family and the possibility of extreme pampering. Why should John want to do anything for himself, including learning, if he had never had much experience with responsibility? Mrs. Moore's hunches were confirmed when she received the report from the psychologist that John was gifted. He had been using all his intelligence to sharpen his charming manipulation skills.

Mrs. Moore kindly confronted John and told him she now knew he was a very capable young man who could do well in a top reading group. She moved him to a top group, and he lived up to her expectations. He knew he could no longer fool Mrs. Moore. The biggest problem was for John's sisters, who thought Mrs. Moore was being unreasonable to expect and insist on so much from their little brother.

It is important to note the attitude of Mrs. Moore when she informed John that the game was up. She did not say, with a lecturing tone, "I know you can do better." Instead she said, "John, I have discovered what a capable young man you are. I'm moving you to the top reading group because I have every confidence in your ability to do well there."

How many of us just hated it when our parents said, "You could do better if you would just try"? The attitude behind this statement was usually one of lecturing and disappointment. This attitude is discouraging to all children. It would be devastating to tell most oldest children they could do better if they tried. The reason oldest children might not be doing as well as possible is that trying too hard for perfection often causes them to be too tense to perform well. It might be discouraging to tell middle children they could do better if they tried because of their mistaken interpretation that they cannot do as well as older siblings who already have that area all sewed up. Youngest children often do not like being told they could do better because of their mistaken interpretation that they have more belonging and significance when others are taking care of them. Mrs. Moore's approach worked with John because of the way it was done—with an attitude of encouragement instead of disappointment.

Knowledge of birth order can help you as a parent or teacher get into the child's world. Just letting another person know that you can see, understand, and respect his or her point of view is one of the most encouraging things you can do. To be able to say "I can understand how you must feel" is quite different from the accusation and blame of "Well, no wonder you act that way, since you are an oldest (middle, youngest, only)."

Understanding birth order helped one dad stop the cycle of perfectionism that his son Mark was developing. Mark is an oldest child who could not stand to lose at games by the time he was eight years old. Dad was contributing to Mark's attitude by always letting him win at chess because he didn't like to see Mark get upset and cry. After learning about birth order, Dad realized it was more important to allow Mark some experience with losing, so he started winning at least half the games. Mark was upset at first, but soon began to win and lose with more grace. Dad felt a milestone had been reached one day when he was playing catch with Mark and threw a bad ball. Instead of getting upset about missing the ball, Mark was able to use his sense of humor and commented, "Nice throw, Dad. Lousy catch, Mark."

BIRTH ORDER AND MARRIAGE

Birth-order knowledge can also help parents understand and encourage each other. It is interesting to contemplate the implications of birth-order information as it relates to marriage. As you might guess, there is often an attraction between oldest and youngest children. Youngest like to be taken care of, oldest like to take care of, so it seems like a perfect match. However, as Adler said, "Tell me your complaint about your spouse and I will tell you why you married that person in the first place." The very characteristics that attract in the beginning often irritate later.

In this case the oldest may later get tired of always being the responsible partner and may criticize the more irresponsible spouse, forgetting that this very trait seemed attractive in the beginning. The youngest may also get tired of being taken care of and told what to do—except when they decide they want it. The problem is that when the spouse wants it is often not when the oldest wants to give it.

When two oldest children marry, it is often because of admiration for the traits they also respect in themselves; the trouble begins when they can't agree on who is in charge or who really knows the best way to do things.

Two youngest may marry because they recognize how much fun they can have together, but later may resent the other for not taking better care of them.

It may be easiest or hardest for middles to adjust to any situation, depending on how rebellious or easygoing they have become.

All combinations can be successful with understanding, mutual respect, cooperation, and a sense of humor. A good friend of mine is a youngest married to a youngest. They started off on a vacation. He turned to her and asked if she had made motel reservations. She replied, "No, didn't you?" They both laughed and had a good time finding a motel.

BIRTH ORDER AND TEACHING STYLES

Teaching styles may vary because of birth order. Teachers who are oldest children often like to be in charge. They are often willing to organize interesting and complicated projects for their students. They prefer structure and order and are happiest when children are sitting in neat rows doing as they have been told. Since this scene is not as typical as it used to be, many of these teachers are frustrated, until they learn methods to help them achieve order without being authoritarian. They are quick to see the long-range benefits of a positive approach for children and for themselves.

Teachers who are middle children are often as interested in the psychological well-being of their students as they are in academic achievement. They are drawn to the rebellious students and hope to influence them in a more positive direction. These teachers try to achieve order through mutual respect and understanding.

Teachers who are youngest children are often creative and fun-loving and have the easiest time adjusting to noise and disorder. These teachers are often willing to allow children to take more responsibility so that they won't have to do everything themselves.

Information about birth order can help parents and teachers increase their understanding of children and of themselves.

GROUP EXERCISE

The following exercise is an excellent way to experience the similarities and differences of people in the same birth-order position.

Have the group divide into smaller groups of the same birth-order position. Supply each group with felt-tip pens and butcher paper. Give them the following instructions: "Each member of the group should think of adjectives that describe you as a person. Share these adjectives with your group. If the majority agrees that characteristic fits them also, write it down on the butcher paper."

Allow about ten minutes for this exercise and then have each group use masking tape to hang their butcher paper on the wall. You can then have a discussion about how well their findings match the information given in this chapter. Be sure to discuss the following points:

- Factors that account for exceptions and uniqueness
- The importance of stressing the positive traits of each birth-order position
- Ways in which the information can be used to increase understanding of children and ourselves
- The destructiveness of using this to label or stereotype

Also ask the group if anyone gained insight about why they might have formed certain interpretations regarding themselves and mistaken beliefs about what they need to do to find belonging and significance.

Consider playing Wayne Frieden and Marie Hartwell-Walker's songs on birth order.[3] They have written a song for seven different birth-order positions. An example of one verse from "Number One" is:

> *Oh it's hard to be number one.*
> *And lately it's just no fun at all.*
> *Life was so nice, when there were three,*
> *Mommy and Daddy and Me.*
> *And now there's another.*
> *And I don't like it one bit.*
> *Send it back to the hospital*
> *And let's just forget about it.*

REVIEW

Questions

1. What is the main purpose of understanding birth order and how might it help you in working with children?
2. What are some common choices children make when they compare themselves to their siblings?

3. What are some ways we can misuse knowledge about birth order?
4. What are the typical characteristics of each birth-order position?
5. What are the dangers of pampering and why do some parents do it?
6. What are the factors that account for exceptions to general rules about birth order?

Chapter Four

A NEW LOOK AT MISBEHAVIOR

One of my favorite scenes from the movie *Kramer vs. Kramer* shows Seth shouting in anger at his Dad, "I hate you."

Dad picks him up and carries him to his room, throws him on his bed, and shouts back, "I hate you too, you little shit."

Did this father and son really hate each other? Of course not. They loved each other very much. So what was going on?

Seth was feeling *hurt* because his father was busy working and wasn't paying attention to him. The father had a deadline and got very upset when a drink was spilled all over his project. He reacted by scolding Seth with some blame, shame, and pain. At a subconscious level Seth felt like he didn't belong; he felt insignificant. So he told his father that he hated him. Dad reacted with some revenge of his own. They became engaged in a "revenge cycle." Dad played a big part in this misbehavior episode. He was equally, if not more, responsible.

RESPONSIBILITY DOES NOT EQUAL BLAME OR SHAME

As we take a new look at misbehavior, the results can be encouraging for children and adults if you do not equate responsibility with blame or shame. It is more helpful if you see responsibility as liberating—something based on awareness that you can change if you choose, not something to feel guilty about. When you realize that you may be part of the misbehavior equation of your child or student, you will have information about how to change your part, and thus help the child change his or her part.

WHAT IS MISBEHAVIOR?

When you look closely you'll see that misbehavior is nothing more than a lack of knowledge (or awareness), a lack of effective skills and developmentally appropriate behavior, discouragement—or, often, a matter of some incident that invites us to revert to our primitive brains where the only option is power struggles or withdrawal and poor communication. Adults often are just as lacking in knowledge, awareness, and skills, and engage in as much primitive brain behavior as children. This is why power struggles between adults and children are so common—it takes at least two people for a power struggle to exist. And adults are often just as discouraged as children. Would misbehavior (yours and your child's) seem different if you saw it as "discouraged behavior," "lack of skills behavior," "reptilian brain behavior," or "age-appropriate behavior"?[1]

Most of the time, young children are just "acting their age," not misbehaving. Many parents and teachers don't have enough knowledge about human behavior and child development, and thus treat age-appropriate behaviors as misbehavior. It is truly sad to think of the many young children who are being punished for behavior that is developmentally appropriate. For example, toddlers are punished for being "naughty" when their brains have not yet developed sufficiently to comprehend what is expected of them. They don't have the language or social skills to get what they want—especially when what they want seems irrational, inconvenient, or inappropriate to the adults in their lives. It is heartbreaking to see toddlers punished by being given time-out when they have not yet developed the capability to truly understand cause and effect.

How often do children misbehave because they are tired or hungry? Who is responsible for this? (Often it is due to circumstances that can't be helped, which is all the more reason to have compassion for your child and yourself instead of using the label of misbehavior). Perhaps children have not been respectfully included in creating routines. Perhaps adults have not realized that demands are an invitation to rebellion and power struggles, while curiosity questions (and other Positive Discipline methods) might invite cooperation. It can be very exciting to think in terms of responsibility and focusing on solutions (and mistakes as opportunities to learn) instead of misbehavior and punishment.

It may sound as though I'm advocating that parents and teachers don't do anything about developmentally appropriate behavior that is socially inappropriate (usually called misbehavior). That is not what I'm saying. What I'm saying is that parents and teachers are the adults. We want children to learn to control their behavior so we should learn to control our own behavior. With awareness, we can be the ones to take responsibility for our behavior and change in ways that invite improved behavior in children without damaging their sense of self-worth. We can be the ones to take some time out to regather ourselves until we can act thoughtfully instead of reacting thoughtlessly. I'm suggesting that we take at least equal responsibility for our misbehavior and learn to use methods that are encouraging and effective in the long term because they meet all of the Four Criteria for Effective Discipline described in chapter one.

The better we understand behavior—our own as well as children's—the more effective we can be as parents and teachers. A good start is to get into the child's world to understand more about discouragement behavior.

As Rudolf Dreikurs said so many times, "A misbehaving

child is a discouraged child." Dreikurs discovered four inappropriate or mistaken goals children adopt when they feel discouraged. They are called mistaken goals because they are based on mistaken beliefs about how to achieve belonging and significance.

When Rudolf Dreikurs explained the four mistaken goals, people often asked, "How can you keep putting children in these boxes?" He would reply, "I don't keep putting them there, I keep finding them there."

The Four Mistaken Beliefs and Mistaken Goals of Behavior

1. Undue Attention—The mistaken belief: I belong only when I have your attention.
2. Misguided Power—The mistaken belief: I belong only when I'm the boss, or at least when I don't let you boss me.
3. Revenge—The mistaken belief: I don't belong, but at least I can hurt back.
4. Assumed Inadequacy—The mistaken belief: It is impossible to belong. I give up.

The primary goal of all human beings is to feel a sense of belonging and significance. Children (and many adults) adopt one or more of the four mistaken goals because they believe that:

• Undue attention or misguided power will help them achieve belonging and significance.
• Revenge will give some satisfaction for the hurt experienced in not feeling a sense of belonging and significance.
• Giving up is their only option because they really believe they are inadequate.

MISTAKEN GOAL CHART

The CHILD'S GOAL is:	If the PARENT/ TEACHER feels:	And tends to REACT by:	And if the CHILD'S RESPONSE is:	The BELIEF behind the CHILD'S BEHAVIOR is:	PARENT/TEACHER PROACTIVE AND ENCOURAGING RESPONSES include:
Undue Attention (to keep others busy or to get special service)	Annoyed Irritated Worried Guilty	Reminding Coaxing Doing things for the child he/she could do for himself/herself	Stops temporarily, but later resumes same or another disturbing behavior	I count (belong) only when I'm being noticed or getting special service. I'm only important when I'm keeping you busy with me.	Redirect by involving child in a useful task. "I love you and ___." (Example: I care about you and will spend time with you later.) Plan special time. Set up routines. Take time for training. Use family/class meetings. Touch without words. Set up nonverbal signals.
Power (to be boss)	Provoked Challenged Threatened Defeated	Fighting Giving in Thinking "You can't get away with it" or "I'll make you" Wanting to be right	Intensifies behavior Defiant compliance Feels he/she's won when parent/teacher is upset Passive power	I belong only when I'm boss or in control, or proving no one can boss me. "You can't make me."	Acknowledge that you can't force her and ask for help. Don't fight and don't give in. Withdraw from conflict and calm down. Be firm and kind. Act, don't talk. Decide what you will do. Let routines be the boss. Develop mutual respect. Give limited choices. Get help from child to set reasonable and few limits. Practice follow-through. Encourage. Redirect to positive power. Use family/class meetings.
Revenge (to get even)	Hurt Disappointed Disbelieving Disgusted	Retaliating Getting even Thinking "How could you do this to me?"	Retaliates Hurts others Damages property Gets even Escalates the same behavior or chooses another weapon	I don't think I belong so I'll hurt others as I feel hurt. I can't be liked or loved.	Deal with the hurt feelings. "Your behavior tells me that you must feel hurt. Can we talk about that?" Avoid punishment and retaliation. Use reflective listening. Make amends. Encourage strengths. Use family/class meetings.
Assumed Inadequacy (to give up and be left alone)	Despair Hopeless Helpless Inadequate	Giving up Doing for Overhelping	Retreats further Passive No improvement No response	I don't believe I can belong, so I'll convince others not to expect anything of me. I am helpless and unable; it's no use trying because I won't do it right.	Show faith. Take small steps. Stop criticism. Encourage any positive attempt, no matter how small. Focus on assets. Don't pity. Don't give up. Set opportunities for success. Teach skills/show how. Enjoy the child. Build on his/her interests. Encourage, encourage, encourage. Use family/class meetings.

Children are not aware of their mistaken belief. If you ask them why they misbehave, they will tell you they don't know or will give some other excuse. Later I will explain how you can use goal disclosure to help children become aware of their mistaken goal without feeling ashamed or threatened.

Everyone wants attention. There is nothing wrong with that. The problem occurs when children want undue attention. In other words, they seek belonging in annoying ways rather than useful ways. The behavior is annoying because it comes from children's subconscious mistaken belief that "I belong only when I'm the center of attention." This out-of-awareness belief adds a sense of urgency and persistence to the behavior that others find annoying. It can be very encouraging to children seeking undue attention, to redirect them in ways to get attention in contributing ways. This invites children to reexperience the sense of belonging that they were seeking and simultaneously teaches them how to get that sense of belonging in a more constructive manner.

If students are pestering you, give them a job (such as collecting papers, calling on other people who have their hand raised, or being the job monitor). One mother found a way to redirect her four-year-old daughter's annoying behavior of interrupting her while she was on the phone. The next time the phone rang, she interrupted the caller long enough to give her daughter her watch and said, "See this second hand that is moving around? Watch it until it goes all the way around three times, and then I'll be done."

The little girl watched the second hand intently, occasionally glancing at her mother. Her mother hung up the phone before the three minutes were up and her daughter said, "Mommy, you had more time, you had more time."

Everyone wants power. Power is not a bad thing, depending on how it is used. When children have the mistaken belief (again subconscious) that they belong only when they're the boss, their use of power looks like misbehavior. When children operate from the mistaken goal of misguided power, they are not learning to use their power in useful ways and need redirection to use their power in socially useful ways.

When teachers or parents find themselves in a "power struggle" with a child, it is most effective to back out of the struggle. Admit what is happening. "It looks to me as though we are in a power struggle. I can see what I'm doing to contribute to this problem. My guess is that you are feeling overpowered. I don't want to do that, but I do need your help. Let's take some cooling-off time and then see how we can work this out in a way that is respectful to both of us."

Just like the father in *Kramer vs. Kramer,* it seems to be human nature to strike back when we feel hurt. This is why revenge cycles are so common. Again, it is ironic that adults want children to control their behavior when the adults have difficulty controlling their own behavior. However, controlling your own behavior is important to break the revenge cycle. Notice when you are feeling hurt and avoid striking back. Instead, validate the child's feelings. "You must be feeling very hurt right now. I can understand. I would probably feel the same way in your shoes." Validating feelings is a powerful way to defuse a revenge cycle, but may need to be followed up with problem solving. "When we both feel better, why don't we get together and talk about this."

It is important to note that you may not have been the one to hurt this child—or that the child has the perception of being hurt when you meant to be helpful, not hurtful. It is also important to understand that the punishment (even when poorly disguised as a logical consequence) only perpetuates a revenge cycle.

Children who operate from the mistaken goal of assumed inadequacy (because of a mistaken belief about their capabilities) may not cause you many problems during the day, but may haunt you at night when you have time to think about how they seem to have given up. Unlike children who say, "I can't," just to get you to pay attention, children operating from assumed inadequacy really believe they can't. With increased awareness about the mistaken belief, you might say to children operating from undue attention, "Honey, I have faith in you to figure it out." However, for children operating from the mistaken belief and goal of assumed inadequacy, you need to take time to show them a small step. Don't do all the steps. Having too much done for them could be what gave them the impression that they are inadequate. An example is to say, "I'll draw one half of the circle, and you can draw the other half," or, "I'll show you how to tie one shoe, and then you can show me what you have learned and let me know if you need more help."

Why is it important to identify the mistaken goal? It is helpful to know the mistaken goal (and belief) so that you can know the most effective action you can take to help children achieve their true goal of a sense of belonging and significance.

Identifying the belief behind the behavior and the mistaken goal is not always easy, because children may use the same behavior to achieve any of the four mistaken goals. For example, children may refuse to do their homework in order to gain attention ("Look at me, look at me"), to show power ("You can't make me"), to seek revenge ("It hurts that my grades are more important to you than I am, so I will hurt you back"), or to express their sense of inadequacy ("I really can't"). Understanding the goal is important because effective intervention and encouragement will be different for each goal.

Note the word *encouragement*. This is very important since a misbehaving child is a discouraged child. The discouragement comes from discouraging beliefs and a sense of not belonging or feeling significant. It does not matter whether the beliefs are based on facts or children's perception of the situation. Behavior is based on what children think is true, not what is true.

CLUES TO HELP IDENTIFY MISTAKEN BELIEFS AND GOALS

There are two clues adults can use to help them identify the mistaken goal.

Clue Number One

The adult's feeling reaction to the behavior. This may seem strange at first. You may wonder why your feelings let you know the child's mistaken goal. Practice noticing your feelings and you'll catch on to how this works.

The primary feelings adults experience when confronted with behavior for each of the four mistaken goals are as follows (see the second column of the Mistaken Goal chart on page 71): If you are feeling irritation, worry, guilt, or annoyance, the child's goal is likely to be undue attention. If you are feeling threatened (you want to be the boss as much as the child does), challenged, provoked, or defeated, the child's goal is likely to be power. If you react with power, you will become involved in a power struggle. If you are feeling hurt (How could the child do such a thing when you try so hard to be a good parent or teacher?), disappointed, disbelieving, or disgusted, the child's goal is likely to be revenge. If you are feeling inadequate (How can I possibly reach and inspire this child?), despair, hopeless, or helpless, the child's goal is likely to be assumed inadequacy. If you give in to your feeling, you will be giving up just as the child has.

When asked for their feeling reactions to behavior, many adults respond with the words *anger* and *frustration,* which are both secondary responses to a primary feeling reaction. There is a good reason for this. Feeling threatened, hurt, or inadequate are such helpless feelings that we quickly cover them with the secondary response of anger. With anger we at least have a sense of pseudopower—we can do something, even though that *something* is merely to rant and rave or lash out. Frustration and anger are both secondary responses to being unable to control the situation that causes our more primary feelings. If you cover your primary feelings with anger, instead of validating the child's feelings, you are likely to become involved in a revenge cycle.

You need to ask yourself, "What is underneath my anger or frustration? Am I feeling hurt, defeated, threatened, scared?" Look at the Mistaken Goal chart on page 71 and check the feelings column to see which one fits you. Many parents and teachers have reported that they keep a copy of this chart on their desk or refrigerator as a useful resource. It helps them remember the basis for most behavior and to be more effective in helping their children during these times of stress.

Clue Number Two

The child's response when you tell him or her to stop the behavior. (See the fourth column of the Mistaken Goal chart, page 71.)

Undue Attention: The child stops for a while, but usually soon resumes the same behavior or some other behavior to get your attention.

Misguided Power: The child continues misbehaving and may verbally defy or passively resist your request to stop. This often escalates to a power struggle between you and the child.

Revenge: The child retaliates by doing something destructive or saying something hurtful. This often escalates to a revenge cycle between you and the child.

Assumed Inadequacy: The child usually is passive, hoping you will soon give up and leave him or her alone. Sometimes this child will "act out" (perhaps being the class clown) to cover up feelings of inadequacy in academics.

These clues help us "break the code" of what our children are really saying with their behavior. Even when we understand this, it may not be easy. When we encounter a child who is misbehaving, it is much easier (and normal) to react from our secondary feelings of anger and frustration than it is to stop and wonder: What is this child trying to tell me?

In the Positive Discipline workshops we do an experiential activity called "The Jungle," adapted from an activity by John Taylor from his book, *Person to Person*.[2] In this activity some adults stand on chairs while other adults role-play children who look up at them and say, "I'm a child, and I just want to belong." The "adults" are instructed to pretend the "children" are misbehaving and to make punitive, discouraging statements such as "Stop interrupting me. Can't you see I'm busy? Why can't you be more like your brother? How can you act so selfish? Then why don't you clean your room or do your homework? How many times have I told you?"

Later we process the activity by asking everyone how they were feeling, what they were thinking, and what they were deciding as children and adults in the role-play. It is an emotional experience. We wouldn't put people through it except that nothing we do is more powerful in helping adults see, hear, and experience the immediate and long-term effects of reacting to the behavior instead of breaking the code and understanding what the child really needs.

After the activity we ask, "What did you learn from this activity?" The group expresses many lessons they learned, the most important one being that a misbehaving child is really saying, "I'm a child and I just want to belong." When we don't understand the mistaken beliefs and goals of behavior, we react to the behavior instead of responding to the belief behind the behavior.

Once adults really understand that a misbehaving child is a discouraged child, they are ready to work on ways to encourage the child. Encouragement is the most effective way to change behavior. An encouraged child does not need to misbehave.

To repeat—an encouraged child does not need to misbehave. This is the most difficult concept for parents and teachers to understand. We are so used to trying to motivate children to do better through punishment, lectures, and other forms of blame, shame, and pain.

Recently I received a phone call from a dear friend who feels so bad that she raised her eleven children believing that the way to motivate them to do better was to put them down when they made mistakes or didn't do things as well as they should have. She is now trying to undo the results of low self-esteem and anger churning in several of her children.

Encouragement is not rewarding the misbehavior, as so many believe. Encouragement removes the need to misbehave.

EFFECTIVE ENCOURAGEMENT METHODS
FOR EACH MISTAKEN GOAL

There is never just one way to solve a behavior challenge. In parent and teacher study groups, participants can brainstorm to come up with several possible suggestions based on the principles you are learning in this book. The parent or teacher seeking help can then choose the most acceptable suggestion.

Many problems can best be solved in a family or class meeting because children develop a sense of belonging and significance while learning to focus on respectful solutions. However,

Positive Discipline includes many alternative tools and skills when more immediate action is desired or necessary. The following general guidelines for effective responses to each mistaken goal are discussed in more detail in later chapters. They are outlined here to emphasize how many different solutions there are to any one problem or mistaken goal of behavior.

After you have read the entire book and understand the concepts of Positive Discipline, you may want to refer back to this outline as a reminder of effective methods for each goal. All methods are effective only when based on the basic attitudes of encouragement, understanding, and mutual respect, as discussed in previous chapters.

Undue Attention

Remember that everyone needs attention. It is undue attention that is not encouraging to children.

- Redirect children into contributing behavior. Give them a job that gives them positive attention in the classroom or that is helpful, such as giving them a stopwatch to time your phone conversation at home.
- Do the unexpected. (A big hug is often very effective.)
- Set up a schedule for spending special time with children on a regular basis. At school, a few minutes once in a while is sufficient.
- Smile in a knowing way that communicates you are not going to get hooked into this, and then say, "I'm looking forward to our special time at six o'clock."
- Set up nonverbal signals with children in advance: a hand over your heart to signal "I love you" or a hand cupped to your ear to signal you are ready to listen when the whining stops.
- Avoid special service.

- Give reassurance and show faith. ("I love you, and I know you can handle this yourself.")
- Ignore the behavior while placing your hand on the child's shoulder in a caring manner. (Continue your conversation—ignoring the behavior, but not the child.)
- During pleasant times take time for training and role-play other ways to behave, such as using words instead of whining.
- Shut your mouth and act. For example, stop coaxing, get off the couch, take your children by the hand, and lead them to the bathroom to brush their teeth. You might try a little tickle to keep the mood firm but playful.
- Verbalize love and caring.

Misguided Power

Remember that power is not a bad thing. It can be used constructively instead of destructively.

- Withdraw from the power struggle to allow for a cooling-off period, then do one or more of the following:
- Admit that you can't make children do anything and ask for their help in finding a solution that works for both of you.
- Use the Four Steps for Winning Cooperation (see chapter two).
- Follow up with a one-to-one problem-solving session.
- Redirect children to use their power constructively.
- Get children involved in finding solutions.
- Decide what you will do, not what you will try to make the child do. ("I will continue the lesson when everyone is ready." "I will wash clothes that are in the hamper, not those that are thrown on the floor." "I will pull over to the side of the road until you stop fighting.") It is very

important that these actions be done with kindness as well as firmness. It is especially effective to keep your mouth shut—avoid reminders and lectures.

- Set up a schedule for spending special time with your children on a regular basis or occasionally at school.
- Get children involved in creating routines and then let the routines be the boss.
- Offer limited choices.
- Invite children to put problems on the class meeting or family meeting agenda.
- Verbalize love and caring.

Revenge

Remember that children cover up hurt feelings (which make them feel powerless) by seeking revenge (which gives them a sense of control).

- Withdraw from the revenge cycle by avoiding retaliation.
- Remain friendly while waiting for the cooling-off period.
- Make a guess about what has hurt the child, and show empathy. Validate children's hurt feelings.
- Use emotional honesty to share your feelings: I feel _____ about_____ because_____, and I wish _____.
- Use reflective listening: Get into the child's world by reflecting back what you are hearing: "You sound very hurt." Reflective listening can include curiosity questions: "Can you tell me more? Then what happened? How did that make you feel?" The point is to avoid sharing your point of view and to understand the child's point of view.
- Use the Three R's of Recovery if you caused the hurt (chapter two).
- Use the Four Steps for Winning Cooperation (chapter two).

• Engage children in one-to-one problem solving.
• Show you care and use encouragement.
• Set up a schedule for spending special time with children
  on a regular basis or occasionally at school.
• Verbalize love and caring.

Assumed Inadequacy

Remember that children are not inadequate, but will continue
to act inadequate until they give up their belief that they are.

• Take time for training, making the steps as basic as is
  necessary for children to experience success.
• Demonstrate a small step that children can duplicate. "I'll
  draw half the circle, you draw the other half."
• Arrange for small successes. Find out anything children can
  do, and give them many opportunities to share their
  expertise.
• Acknowledge any positive attempt, no matter how small.
• Eliminate all expectations of perfection.
• Focus on children's assets.
• Do not give up.
• Spend regular, special time with children.
• In classrooms encourage children to choose a buddy or
  peer tutor for help.
• Verbalize love and caring.

To emphasize that the same behavior could represent all four
mistaken goals, we will go back to the example of children who
will not do their homework.

If the children's goal is undue attention, you feel annoyed.
When you tell the children to do their work, they will do it for a
while. To help these children you might simply ignore their un-

finished work and show appreciation in areas where they cooperate. This allows them to learn that not doing their work is not
a good way to get attention. You could give them a choice about
when they want to do it—now or after school. You could redirect their behavior by asking them to help you with some task as
soon as they are finished with their work. Or you could tell them
you will wink at them and smile every time you see that they are
not doing their work. It is especially effective if you make this
arrangement with them after you have done goal disclosure (see
page 86). It may seem that winking and smiling will reinforce
their bid for attention, but instead it helps children feel belonging and significance so that they soon do not feel the need to get
attention in this way. You could let children experience the consequences of not doing their work and then follow up with curiosity questions: "What happened? How do you feel about the
results? What did you learn from this? How would you like it to
be? What could you do to get what you want?"

If children's mistaken goals are misguided power, you feel
your power is threatened or defeated and want to show them you
can make them do what you want. When you tell these children
to do their work, they may tell you they won't or may passively
ignore you. If you insist on winning by imposing some punishment, they may dig in with more power to prove "You can't
make me." Or they may shift to the goal of revenge. (It hurts to
be the loser.) The way to help these children is to back away
from the power struggle.

Children who are into power are sometimes inspired by an
adult who is into power. It is the adult's responsibility to change
this atmosphere. When you truly want mutual respect and cooperation based on mutual understanding and shared decision
making, children will know the difference. When they trust this
difference (which may take some time), they are more likely to
cooperate.

During a one-to-one problem-solving discussion, admit that you have been participating in a power struggle. State that you would really like to change your relationship with the child and start solving problems with mutual respect and understanding. Tell her you would like her help in letting you know whenever she feels you are trying to overpower or control her. Share your willingness to work together toward solutions that would satisfy both of you. Remember that children are more willing to follow solutions when they have been involved in the decision.

Family meetings and class meetings are effective in solving power issues. Children who are into power often have good leadership qualities. You could let this child know you appreciate these qualities and ask for help in some leadership task. One counselor trained students to be peer counselors (see Appendix II) to help other students who were referred to the office due to behavior challenges.

Teachers may simply act by giving the child a poor grade for unfinished work. An attitude of kindness and firmness instead of power is important. You could then follow up with curiosity questions (as mentioned above) to help the child understand that she has power over what happens to her and power to change it if she wants.

If the child's goal is revenge, you may feel hurt or disgusted. You can't understand why the child won't do his work when you have tried so hard as a parent or teacher. When you tell this child to do his work, he may say something hurtful, such as, "I hate you." Or he may do something destructive, such as tearing up his paper.

To help this child, do not retaliate. Validate the hurt feelings. Remain friendly by saying, "I can see that you are upset, so we can't discuss this now, but I would like to talk to you later." After a cooling-off period you can use the Four Steps for Winning Cooperation or you can ignore the problem and share special interests, as described in chapter seven. You may need to use goal disclosure to get to the hurt feelings.

If the child's goal is assumed inadequacy, you may feel inadequate about your ability to help her. When you ask her to do her work, she looks dejected and hopes you will soon leave her alone. (This is an important difference between assumed inadequacy and attention. An attention-seeking child may act inadequate, but is delighted when you pay attention. A child who believes she is inadequate wants to be left alone.)

To help this child, be sure she knows how to do the work. Take time for training, even if you feel the child should understand because you have already explained it many times. The difference between a child who won't do her work in order to gain attention and the child who won't do her work because of assumed inadequacy is that the former really does know how to do it and is just trying to manipulate you into helping because of the mistaken belief that she doesn't *belong* unless you are paying attention to her. The latter is discouraged because she really does not think she can do it and does not want your attention. Since the behavior can be similar for children in these two goals, it is important to sharpen your awareness so that you can feel when a child is simply trying to keep you busy or when a child would really prefer that you stay away.

Another option is to ask this child if she would like your help or if she would like to choose another student to help her. Or you might try finding a level where she does feel adequate and let her work at that level. Be sure to arrange the situation so that she will be successful.

Don't give up. This child may do some work just to get you off her back. Whatever the reason, if she does some work, she will have some success and feel encouraged. Spending special time with this child is very important.

GOAL DISCLOSURE

Since children are not aware of their mistaken goals, goal disclosure is one way to help them become aware of their mistaken belief.

Goal disclosure may be conducted by teachers, counselors, or trained parent educators. It is essential to be objective and friendly during the process. It is almost impossible for parents to be objective with their own children, so goal disclosure may not work for them.

Since objectivity and friendliness are essential, goal disclosure should not be done at the time of conflict. It is best to talk to the child alone when you are learning this procedure. Trained people often do goal disclosure in groups or in front of an audience. Adler and Dreikurs were famous for doing goal disclosure with a child in front of an audience so that everyone, including the child, could learn from the process. I recommend, however, that when you do this with children, choose a private time when both of you are feeling calm.

First ask the child if she knows why she is engaging in a certain behavior. You should name the behavior specifically, such as, "Mary, do you know why you keep wandering around the room when you are supposed to be in your seat?"

Children will usually say, "I don't know." It is true that they don't know at a conscious level. Goal disclosure helps them understand what is happening. Even if they give some reason, it is not the *real* reason.

If they give a reason, you say, "I have some other ideas. Would it be okay with you if I guess? You can tell me if I'm right or wrong."

If they say they don't know, ask if you can guess as above. If your manner is objective and friendly, the child will be intrigued to have you guess. Then ask what Dreikurs called "could it be" questions, waiting for the child to respond to each question.

- "Could it be that the reason you wander around the room is to get my attention and keep me busy with you?" (Undue Attention)
- "Could it be that the reason you wander around the room is to show me you can do whatever you want?" (Misguided Power)
- "Could it be that the reason you wander around the room is because you feel hurt and want to get even with me or someone else?" (Revenge)
- "Could it be that you wander around the room because you don't feel you can succeed so you don't even want to try?" (Assumed Inadequacy)

There are two responses that will let you know if your guess is correct and the child has become aware of her goal. The first is a recognition reflex. This means that the child involuntarily smiles, even while saying no. If the answer is no, without the recognition reflex, go on to the next question. However, the recognition reflex (a spontaneous smile while saying no) tells you your guess is correct. The other response is a simple yes. Once you have a recognition reflex or an affirmative response, there is no need to go on to another question. You can then engage the child in a discussion of other ways to feel belonging and significance. If the goal is attention, explain to the child that everyone wants attention. Then redirect the child into constructive ways of seeking attention. For example, "Can you help me think of some other ways for you to get attention in ways that will also help others?"

You could also agree to give the child attention for her behavior and let her know you will wink and smile to let her know she has your attention an agreed-upon number of times. Make this a special conspiracy between the two of you. To many this seems like rewarding the misbehavior. Actually, it is what Dreikurs called "spitting in the soup." Awareness makes it less appetizing.

If the goal is power, admit that you are powerless to force her to behave differently. Then ask for her help in designing a plan of mutual respect and cooperation. "You are right. I can't make you. How could we both use our power in respectful ways to solve this problem?" Asking for help is an important phrase to use when the goal is to redirect both adult and child from power struggle to contributing power.

If the goal is revenge, you can show your interest in understanding what you or someone else might have done to hurt her. "I'm sorry I didn't realize I had hurt you. Will you forgive me?" or, "I'm sorry you felt hurt by that situation. I would probably feel the same if it happened to me." Caring enough to listen, without judgment, can be the most encouraging procedure for this goal. Do not rationalize, explain, or try to change her perception. Reflective listening might help. After the child feels understood, she may be more willing to hear your point of view and then work on solutions.

If the goal is assumed inadequacy, reassure her that you can understand how she might feel because you feel discouraged yourself sometimes. Follow this with expressions of faith in her ability and work on a plan of small, achievable steps to ensure success. "I know you don't believe you can, but I know you can; and I'm willing to do whatever it takes to help you be successful."

Goal disclosure can be your third clue to identifying the mistaken goal. There is a film of Dreikurs interviewing a child when he seems certain that the child's goal is power. He keeps trying to get a recognition reflex by asking the "could it be" question in many different ways to indicate power, but he continuously gets a negative response and no recognition reflex. Dreikurs finally goes on to ask the question for revenge, and the child agrees that he felt hurt by what his parents had done.

Teachers can use goal disclosure to increase their understanding and to show interest in the child. Once you know the goal, you can use it as a basis for discussion and problem solving.

DEGREE OF DISCOURAGEMENT

Children do not necessarily start with the first goal of attention and work their way down through assumed inadequacy. Children who are more passive might go directly to assumed inadequacy if treated harshly or for some other reason believe they lack belonging and significance.

Children who are spunky enough to choose power might never go to assumed inadequacy, but they are often pushed to revenge by adults who insist on winning the power struggle.

Mrs. Smith shared why she was so grateful to learn about the Four Mistaken Goals of Behavior and corrective remedies. Her oldest child, Seth, was a challenging child. He often did hurtful or destructive things, as in the following example.

One day the whole Smith family (Mr. and Mrs. Smith, Seth, his younger brother, Scott, and baby sister, Maria) spent the day looking at properties. Seth and Scott complained constantly about how bored and hot they were. They kept requesting to go home. Two-year-old Maria was content, napping on Mother's lap when she got tired.

The Smiths wanted to continue their search for property the next day, but decided to do Seth and Scott a favor by leaving them home with a neighbor. It was a nice day, and they were old enough to play with their friends in the neighborhood. Since Maria had not been any trouble and was too young to play in the neighborhood, they decided to take her with them. When they got ready to go, Seth said he wanted to go. Mrs. Smith reminded him how hot and bored he had been and tried to convince him he would be happier staying home. Seth insisted he wanted to go. Mrs. Smith was firm in her decision and even gave Seth and Scott a quarter for Popsicles as a treat (bribe). Seth was still not satisfied, but they left him anyway.

When they came home, Mrs. Smith was dismayed to see that

Seth had taken a knife and slashed the vinyl on Maria's high-chair. Mrs. Smith's first reaction was to feel hurt as she wondered, "How could he do such a thing?" She quickly covered her hurt with anger, spanked Seth, and sent him to his room.

At the time this incident occurred, Mrs. Smith was also attending a parent study group and keeping a journal to remind her of situations she would like to work on with the group. As soon as she started writing in her journal, she was able to be objective enough to see things from Seth's point of view and she understood why his mistaken goal was revenge. She used the Four Steps for Winning Cooperation (explained in chapter two) as follows:

Mrs. Smith went into Seth's room and asked, "Did you think the reason we wanted to take Maria and not you is because we loved her more than you?"

Seth tearfully replied, "Yes."

Mrs. Smith said, "I can understand how it might seem that way to you. I'll bet that didn't make you feel very good." Seth started to cry.

Mrs. Smith put her arms around him and waited for him to stop crying. She then said, "I think I can understand what you felt. When I was thirteen, my mother took my sixteen-year-old sister to New York City. I wanted to go but was told I was too young. I didn't believe that. I really thought it was because my mother loved my sister more than me." Seth was very sympathetic. Mrs. Smith then asked Seth, "Would you like to know why I wanted to leave you home?" Seth nodded. Mrs. Smith told him, "I felt bad yesterday because you were so hot and bored. It was not very enjoyable for us to look at property when you were so miserable. I really thought we would all be happier if you stayed home and played with your friends so you wouldn't be bored. Can you understand why I thought I was doing you a favor?"

Seth said, "I guess so."

Mrs. Smith added, "I can see why you might have thought we loved Maria more, since we took her and not you, but that is not true. I love you very much. I would have preferred to leave Maria home too, but I knew she couldn't go out and play with her friends the way you could."

Mrs. Smith continued to hold Seth for a while and then asked, "What do you think we should do to fix the highchair?"

Seth said with enthusiasm, "I can fix it."

Mrs. Smith said, "I'll bet you can."

They worked out a plan to use some of his allowance to buy a piece of vinyl. They cut out a pattern and together stapled it to the chair. The highchair was better than before—and so was their relationship. (This is another example that shows how mistakes can provide opportunities to make things better than they were before the mistake.)

Mrs. Smith realized that she and Seth had been engaging in a revenge cycle. He had adopted the mistaken belief that he was not loved (lacked belonging and significance). This hurt and inspired the mistaken goal of wanting to hurt back. Seth would do something hurtful or destructive, but Mrs. Smith tended to cover her hurt with anger and would retaliate against Seth with more punishment.

Mrs. Smith realized now that the chair was already damaged and that punishment would not fix it. She also knew she couldn't ignore such behavior. Punishment gave her the feeling that she had not let him "get away with it," but she now understood that it did not produce the long-term goals she wanted.

After recognizing Seth's mistaken goal of revenge, Mrs. Smith was able to handle it effectively to produce positive long-term results. When Seth would do something destructive, she would acknowledge that she could see he was hurt and upset, and they would talk about it later. After a cooling-off period she would go through the Four Steps for Winning Cooperation, as she did in the above example, and they would end up with a solution that brought them closer together, rather than continuing the revenge cycle—and the misbehavior.

This all happened several years ago. Mrs. Smith reports that she and Seth now have an excellent relationship. Seth is never hurtful or destructive anymore. She hates to think of how things would have been if they had continued their revenge cycle.

WORKING WITH TEENAGERS

As you look at the Four Mistaken Goals of Behavior, I am sure you will recognize that even adults often adopt these mistaken goals and beliefs. However, it is not quite so simple to find children in one of these four boxes after they reach the age of eleven or twelve. Many misbehaving teenagers have the mistaken goals of undue attention, misguided power, revenge, or assumed inadequacy, but other factors are involved too.

Peer pressure is extremely important to teenagers. Younger children are influenced by peer pressure, but adult approval is even more important to them. Peer approval is more important to teenagers than adult approval and becomes one of their mistaken goals. Teenagers also go through a major individuation process. They are exploring who they are separate from their parents. This often translates into rebellion as they test parental values. This rebellion seldom lasts into the twenties unless parents become controlling and punitive.

The latest brain research by David Walsh and Nat Bennett[3] shows that during the teen years there may be rapid brain growth in the prefrontal cortex that results in some confusion for teens. Teens often misinterpret the body language of those around them as being aggressive when it isn't. As if being a teen isn't hard enough, the brain wires kids for misperception and miscommunication. It is helpful for parents to recognize that the prefrontal cortex doesn't mature until twenty-five (insurance companies have it right) and that extra care in being clear, and not making assumptions, is required when parenting teens.

Excessively controlling methods can be disastrous with teenagers, who are usually even less willing than younger children to assume an inferior, submissive position. When teenagers have been subjected to controlling behavior from adults, they are very suspicious of the word *cooperation*. They interpret it to mean "give in." They are often right—that is what many adults mean by cooperation.

Encouragement, which is covered more thoroughly in chapter seven, is just as important to teenagers as to younger children. When Lynn Lott and I wrote *I'm on Your Side: Resolving Conflict with Your Teenaged Son or Daughter,* it sold only moderately well for two years. Then the book title was changed to *Positive Discipline for Teenagers,*[4] and it sold more copies in two months than it had in two years under the old title. What could this mean? We don't know for sure, but it seems obvious that parents don't realize how important it is to convey to teenagers that they are on their side. Many parents and teenagers have drawn the battle lines and parents seem more interested in trying to control their teenagers. We are saddened by this, because we know it is absolutely impossible to control teenagers—it is too late. The more you try to control them, the more defiant and/or devious they get.

The best way to win the cooperation of teenagers is through mutual respect and equality in problem solving. Family meetings and class meetings teach social responsibility and get teenagers involved in the decision-making process. When treated with kindness, firmness, dignity, respect, and lots of joint problem-solving, teenagers usually fall back on parental values in their twenties—and they will have learned more of the important life skills they need when they are no longer under the authority of adults.

REVIEW

The four goals discussed in this chapter are called mistaken goals because they lead to misbehavior due to mistaken beliefs about how to find belonging and significance. The four mistaken goals represent four mistaken beliefs children adopt when they feel they do not have belonging and significance.

Sometimes it is difficult for us, as parents and teachers, to remember that misbehaving children are speaking to us in code—that they are trying to tell us they want to belong when their behavior inspires frustration rather than love and caring. Some experts believe we will reinforce the behavior if we respond positively to a child who is misbehaving. If, however, we understand that a misbehaving child is a discouraged child, it is obvious that the best way to remove the motivation for misbehavior is to find a positive way to help the child feel belonging and significance.

Accepting this concept intellectually is one thing, but it is quite another to put it into practice for the following reasons:

1. Most adults do not feel like being positive when a child is misbehaving.
2. Most adults don't fully understand how their own misbehavior can invite misbehavior from children and therefore are reluctant to accept responsibility for their part of the "show"—how they may be misbehaving in a way that invites misbehavior from a child. Awareness without blame is a huge step in resolving conflict.
3. The rare adult who is able to respond to misbehavior with positive encouragement will often be rejected by the child. This is because children (like most of us) are not always receptive to encouragement when they need it the most. They are too emotionally upset to accept it. Wait for a cooling-off period and try again with encouragement.

The child who needs love the most is often the child who acts the most unlovable.

Understanding the Four Mistaken Goals of Behavior helps adults remember what children are really saying with their misbehavior: "I just want to belong." It also helps adults know what to do to help resolve the problem in ways that are encouraging while teaching children life skills.

Remember that punishment may stop the misbehavior momentarily, but will not solve the problem permanently. Only helping the child feel belonging and significance through encouragement will have long-term positive effects.

If encouragement cannot be given or accepted at the time of the problem behavior, it should always be considered essential as a follow-up after a cooling-off period. Also, keep in mind that it takes two for a power struggle or a revenge cycle. You might want to take a look at your own mistaken goals and work on changing them for more encouraging attitudes and behavior.

Positive Discipline Tools

1. Accept responsibility (without blame) for your part in the misbehavior equation.
2. Understand and respond with encouragement to the Four Mistaken Goals of Behavior.
3. Be a "code breaker" to understand what the child is really saying with misbehavior—"I'm a child, and I just want to belong."
4. Use the clues to help you understand the mistaken goal of behavior. What do you feel? What does the child do in response to what you do?
5. For Undue Attention: Review all the tools suggested on pages 79–80.
6. For Misguided Power: Review all the tools suggested on pages 80–81.

7. For Revenge: Review all the tools suggested on pages 81–82.

8. For Assumed Inadequacy: Review all the tools suggested on page 82.

9. Use goal disclosure in a friendly manner to help children be aware of their mistaken goals.

10. Four Steps for Winning Cooperation.

Questions

1. In what ways might adults be "responsible" for what is referred to as "child misbehavior"?

2. What are some other terms that could be used for what is now called misbehavior?

3. What are the Four Mistaken Goals of Behavior?

4. What is the child's mistaken belief for each goal?

5. Why is it important to identify the goal?

6. What are the two clues that help adults identify the goal?

7. What is the adult's primary feeling reaction to behavior in response to each of the four goals? Answer this question for each goal, one at a time.

8. How do children respond when misbehaving within each of the four goals when you tell them to stop their misbehavior? Answer for each goal.

9. What are some effective responses or actions you can take to help correct the misbehavior at each goal?

10. Why are the four goals called mistaken goals?

11. Children do not base their behavior on what is true but rather on what?

12. What is a child trying to tell you with his misbehavior?

13. Why is it difficult to remember what the child is trying to tell you?

14. Why might children reject your attempts to be positive when they are misbehaving?
15. What kind of child usually needs love the most?
16. What is the most important thing you can do to help a child overcome his or her motivation to misbehave?

Chapter Five

BEWARE OF LOGICAL CONSEQUENCES

For years I advocated the use of logical consequences. However, I was continually frustrated when I heard parents and teachers give me examples of the consequences they imposed. They sounded like punishment to me.

Some parents and teachers seem to think they can disguise a punishment by calling it a logical consequence. However, when I point out that most logical consequences are poorly disguised punishments, they agree. I thought I was the first to discover this phenomenon until I reread *Children the Challenge* and found the following quote by Dreikurs[1]: "When we use the term 'logical consequences,' parents so frequently misinterpret it as a new way to impose their demands upon children. This children see for what it is—disguised punishment."

Have you ever wondered what children are thinking about when they are being punished (even if it is called a logical consequence)? Some may be deciding they are bad or worthless. Some children decide not to repeat the behavior that caused the punishment, but they do so because of fear and intimidation, not because they have adopted principles regarding right and wrong. These are the children who may become approval junkies, always trying to prove they are worthwhile because deep down they have decided they are not good enough. Others may be thinking about how to defeat you later, or how to avoid getting caught in the future. Many are thinking about revenge. Punished children often do something to get even very soon. After children experience punishment, some are left with a sense of unfairness. Instead of focusing on the behavior that inspired the punishment, they focus on anger toward the adult who imposed the punishment or shame about themselves.

Some adults make the mistake of thinking that children continue to misbehave because the punishment wasn't severe enough to teach them a lesson. So they punish again, more severely—and children find more clever ways to get even. A revenge cycle is perpetuated. Parents may not recognize the severity of the revenge cycle until their children are teenagers and rebel totally by running away, getting involved in the drug scene, getting pregnant, or some other extremely hurtful event. The irony is that these children hurt themselves through revenge as much or more than they hurt their parents.

I am not saying that punishment (even when called a logical consequence) doesn't work. Anyone who has been involved with children knows they will stop misbehaving when punished, at least for a while. For this reason adults may think they are winning many discipline battles. However, they have inevitably lost the discipline war when children are inspired to get even, avoid detection, or conform out of fear or a sense of worthlessness.

Again, we must beware of what works and consider the long-term results. As long as it is important for adults to win, they will make losers out of children.

Most parents are shaken when they think about the long-term results of punishment. It was never their intention to create circumstances where their children would develop a sense of worthlessness or rebellion. They really thought punishment would inspire their children to do better and to become better people. Thinking about the long-term results is a totally new concept to many parents. However, those who take the time to think about the long-term effects of what they do are thrilled when they discover more encouraging discipline methods that are effective in the long term to help children develop a sense of personal capability and learn valuable social and life skills.

Because I have seen natural and logical consequences misused more often than I have seen them used effectively, I now advocate not using logical consequences—at least hardly ever. I would eliminate them entirely except that I know logical consequences, when properly used, can be an effective and encouraging method to use with children. However, logical consequences would now be close to the bottom of my tool list in nine out of ten cases. Many families and teachers have told me that the atmosphere in their homes and classrooms changed dramatically when they stopped focusing on consequences and instead focused on solutions (see chapter six).

There are three reasons to discuss logical (and natural) consequences, even after saying they are close to the bottom of my tool list. Actually, it is only logical consequences that are at the bottom of my tool list. Natural consequences provide an excellent learning experience for children when adults don't interfere as they usually do.

1. There are times when natural and logical consequences are appropriate, helpful, and effective.
2. Logical consequences are one of the most widely used discipline tools in homes and schools. Parents and teachers may find it very useful to know what a true logical consequence is and how to use it appropriately.
3. Natural and logical consequences can be respectful and encouraging to children, yet they too often are misused or underused. When properly used, children can learn a great deal from natural and logical consequences to help

them develop responsibility and accountability with dignity and respect.

NATURAL CONSEQUENCES

A natural consequence is anything that happens naturally, with no adult interference. When you stand in the rain, you get wet. When you don't eat, you get hungry. When you forget your coat, you get cold. No *piggybacking* allowed. Adults *piggyback* when they lecture, scold, say "I told you so," or anything else that adds more blame, shame, or pain than the child might experience *naturally* from the experience. Piggybacking actually lessens the learning that can occur from experiencing a natural consequence because the child stops processing the experience and focuses on absorbing or defending against the blame, shame, and pain. Instead of piggybacking, show empathy and understanding for what the child is experiencing: "I'll bet it was hard to go hungry (get wet, get that bad grade, lose your bicycle)." When it seems appropriate, rather than patronizing, you could add, "I love you and have faith in you to handle this." It can be difficult for parents to be supportive without rescuing or overprotecting, but it is one of the most encouraging things you can do to help your children develop perceptions of capability. Let's look at an example of how natural consequences work.

Billy, a first grader, forgot his lunch every day. His mother would interrupt her busy schedule to drive to school with his lunch. After learning about natural consequences, she decided that Billy might learn to remember his lunch if he experienced the natural consequence of forgetting. She first discussed this with Billy, letting him know she was confident that he could be responsible for remembering his lunch. She also told him she would no longer bring his lunch to school if he forgot it because she knew he could learn from his mistakes. It is important and respectful to discuss, in advance, when you plan to change your behavior and allow your children to experience the natural consequences of their choices.

Her intentions were sabotaged for a while because Billy's teacher took over and loaned him money for lunch when he forgot. It was not until Billy's mother and teacher got together on a plan to allow Billy to learn from the natural consequences of his behavior that he became responsible for remembering his lunch.

Billy tested the plan. The next time he forgot his lunch, he asked his teacher if he could borrow some lunch money. She said, "I'm sorry, Billy, but we agreed that you could handle your lunch problem by yourself." Billy then phoned his mother and demanded that she bring his lunch. She also kindly but firmly reminded him that he could handle the problem. Billy pouted for a while, even though one of his friends gave him half a sandwich.

After that, Billy seldom forgot his lunch. When he did forget it, he managed to find someone who would share some food with him. By the time Billy reached the second grade, he added the responsibility of making his own lunch, as well as remembering to take it.

Many adults don't have much tolerance for the whining, pouting, and disappointment. Billy's mother did not find it easy to listen to her child be demanding, and it was difficult for her to allow him to experience being upset. She noticed some guilty feelings because he was hungry, but reminded herself that forgetting his lunch was really just a small mistake, one of many Billy would make in his lifetime. If she did not follow through on her plan, he would not be learning the life skill of getting a little more organized in the morning, and the good feelings of handling a problem himself. Instead he would be learning that whenever things didn't work out for him, he could whine or complain and get someone else to take care of his problems. Looking at it that way, Billy's mother was able to stay calmer.

DECIDE WHAT YOU WILL DO

This example of a natural consequence could also be called "deciding what you will do instead of what you will make your child do." Because natural and logical consequences are so often misused and abused, I will give several examples of a *consequence by some other name* that increases the respectful use of consequences.

Another mom found that it was effective to decide what she would do to help eleven-year-old Julie be responsible for her own clean clothes. She was constantly nagging Julie to put her dirty clothes in the hamper. Julie did not respond to the nagging, but constantly complained because the clothes she wanted to wear were not clean. Her mother would often give in and hurriedly do a special wash to rescue Julie from suffering.

When Julie's mother learned that she was hurting Julie more than helping her, she allowed Julie to experience a natural consequence by *deciding what she would do.* She kindly but firmly told Julie she had confidence in her ability to be responsible for her own clothes. She explained that from now on she would wash only the clothes that were in the hamper on wash days. By deciding what she would do instead of trying to make Julie do something, Mom allowed Julie to experience the natural consequences of not having her clothes in the hamper before wash time.

Julie tested this plan. A few days later she wanted to wear some pants that she had neglected to put in the hamper to be washed. When Julie complained, her mother empathetically said, "I'll bet you are really disappointed that they are not clean." When Julie pleaded with her to do a special wash, her mother said, "I'm not willing to do that. I'm sure you can figure out another solution." She then got into the shower to avoid further discussion during this time of conflict. Julie was upset that she had to wear something else that day, but it was a long time before she forgot to put her clothes in the hamper.

Some people might call this a logical consequence because the mom is involved. However, you'll notice that her involvement is to "stay out of it" except to show empathy and encouragement, and allow her daughter to experience the "natural consequences" of what happens when her clothes aren't in the hamper.

Even though natural consequences are often one way to help a child learn responsibility, there are times when natural consequences are not practical:

1. *When a child is in danger.* Adults cannot allow a child to experience the natural consequences of playing in the street, for example.

   When this point is made, someone inevitably uses it as a reason for spanking, using the argument, "I have to spank my toddler to teach her not to run in the street." I ask this parent if she would be willing to let her toddler play near a busy street unsupervised after she has been spanked to "teach" her to stay out of the street. The reply is always, "Of course not." I then ask how many times she would need to spank before she would feel it is safe to let her child play unsupervised near a busy street. Most parents agree that they would not let their toddlers play unsupervised near a busy street until they are somewhere between six and eight years of age, no matter how many spankings they have had to "teach" them to stay out of the street. This illustrates the fact that maturity, or readiness to learn certain responsibilities, is the key—not spankings.

2. *Take time for training.* Adults still need to take time for training while children are maturing, but it is more effective and less humiliating to use logical consequences instead of punishment as one way to help children develop responsibility. The logical consequence in this

case would be to kindly and firmly put the child in the house or backyard every time she runs into the street (again deciding what you will do). Some people may call this *distraction*. Supervision, distraction, and redirection are three of the best tools you can use with small children. Meanwhile, you can take time for training until the child's brain matures enough for her to understand cause and effect. Taking time for training would involve teaching her about dangers every time you cross the street together. Before crossing a street, ask your toddler to look up the street and down the street to see if any cars are coming. Ask her what might happen if you tried to cross the street when a car is approaching. Ask her to let you know when she thinks it is safe to cross the street. She will actually learn more from this than from a spanking, but will still not be ready for unsupervised play until she is older.

3. *When natural consequences interfere with the rights of others.* Adults cannot allow the natural consequences of allowing a child to throw rocks at another person, for example. This is one reason why supervision is especially important with children under the age of four. The only way you can prevent potentially dangerous situations for children this age is to supervise so you can rush in and prevent a dangerous occurrence.

4. *When the results of children's behavior do not seem like a problem to them, natural consequences are ineffective.* For example, it does not seem like a problem to some children if they don't take a bath, don't brush their teeth, don't do their homework, or eat tons of junk food.

LOGICAL CONSEQUENCES

Logical consequences are different from natural consequences in that they require the intervention of an adult—or other children in a family meeting or a class meeting. It is important to decide what kind of consequence would create a *helpful learning experience* that might encourage children to choose responsible cooperation.

For example, Linda liked to tap her pencil while doing desk work. This disturbed the other children. Her teacher gave her the choice to stop tapping or to give up her pencil and complete the work later. (It is usually a good idea to give children a choice either to stop their misbehavior or to experience a logical consequence.) Of course there are other solutions. Often children are not aware that their behavior is disturbing others. The teacher could simply ask Linda to please stop tapping her pencil. Or the teacher could work out a solution with Linda, or they could agree to ask the class for help during a class meeting. If a consequence feels even close to punishment, choose another Positive Discipline tool.

Dan brought a toy car to school. His teacher called him aside and asked him if he would like to leave it with her or with the principal until after school. Dan chose to leave it with his teacher. (It is a good idea to speak to children about a consequence in private, when possible, so they don't lose face with their peers.)

Giving children a choice and speaking to them in private about the consequences are not the only guidelines for effectively applying logical consequences. If this were so, it would be reasonable to give a child a choice either to stop the misbehavior or to have a spanking. The Four R's for Logical Consequences is a formula that identifies the criteria to help ensure that solutions are logical consequences, rather than punishment.

The Four R's for Logical Consequences

1. Related
2. Respectful
3. Reasonable
4. Revealed in advance

Related means the consequence must be related to the behavior. *Respectful* means the consequence must not involve blame, shame, or pain and should be kindly and firmly enforced. It is also respectful to everyone involved. *Reasonable* means the consequence must not include piggybacking and is reasonable from the child's point of view as well as the adult's. *Revealed in advance* means just that—allowing a child to know what will happen (or what you will do) if he or she chooses a certain behavior. If any of the Four R's is missing, it can no longer be called a logical consequence.

When a child writes on a desk, it is easy to conclude that the *related* consequence would be to have the child clean up the desk. But what happens if any of the other Four R's is missing?

If a teacher is not *respectful* and adds humiliation to the request that the desk be cleaned, it is no longer a logical consequence. Mr. Martin thought he was using a logical consequence when he said to Mary in front of the whole class, "Mary, I'm surprised that you would do such a stupid thing. Now clean up that desk or I'll have to let your parents know how disappointed I am in you." In this example, respect has been eliminated and the teacher did some piggybacking with humiliation.

If a teacher is not *reasonable* and requests that a student clean every desk in the room to make sure the student has learned the lesson, it is no longer a logical consequence. Reasonableness has been eliminated in favor of the power to ensure suffering. This is usually because of the mistaken belief that children learn only if they suffer.

If the consequence is not *revealed in advance,* it is easier to be construed as punishment. Revealing in advance, when possible, adds a dimension of respect and choice.

When a child spills milk, the *related* consequence is to have him clean up the spill. It is not respectful if you say, "How can you be so clumsy? That is the last time I'll let you pour milk." A more *respectful* comment would be, "Whoops. What do you need to do now?" (It is amazing how often the child knows what a logical consequence [solution] would be and how willing he is to do it, when asked respectfully.) If the child doesn't know what to do, it could be because you haven't taken time for training— thus making your expectation or request unreasonable. Handling it *respectfully* also demonstrates that mistakes are wonderful opportunities to learn. It would not be *reasonable* to ensure that children suffer for their mistakes by saying, "To make sure you learn, I want you to scrub the whole floor." The fourth R, *revealed in advance,* does not apply in this example.

Actually, if adults eliminate one of the Four R's so that consequences are not related, respectful, reasonable, and revealed in advance (when appropriate), children may experience the Four R's of Punishment, first explained in chapter one. Here they are again so you can see how they relate to the misuse of consequences.

The Four R's of Punishment

1. Resentment—"This is unfair. I can't trust adults."
2. Revenge—"They are winning now, but I'll get even."
3. Rebellion—"I'll show them that I can do whatever I want."
4. Retreat, in the form of sneakiness—"I won't get caught next time."—or reduced self-esteem—"I am a bad person."

Parents and teachers don't like to admit it, but often the main reason they like to use punishment is to demonstrate their power to win over the child or to gain revenge by making the child suffer. The subconscious thinking behind this idea is, I am the adult and you are the child. You will do what I say—or else you will pay. This concept was depicted in a cartoon showing a mother watching her husband chase their child with a stick. In the caption the mother is calling, "Wait, give him another chance." The father replies, "But he might not ever do it again." Obviously, it is more important for this father (and many adults) to make the child suffer for his misbehavior than to help him change it.

Suffering is not a requirement of logical consequences. For example, a child might enjoy cleaning up his or her desk. (This is fine, since the purpose of a logical consequence is to stop the misbehavior and find a solution, not to get revenge by causing suffering.) Another name for a logical consequence is redirection.

REDIRECTION

A logical consequence is effective when it redirects the child into a useful (contributing) behavior.

Mark was being very disrespectful and disruptive in class by talking when the teacher was trying to teach. Mr. Smith, his teacher, punished him by telling him he had to write "I will use the proper manners and will not be disrespectful while in a classroom" thirty times. Mark did not respond favorably by thinking, Oh great! I really deserve this, and it will teach me not to talk in class anymore. Instead he felt rebellious and resentful, so he didn't write the sentences. Mr. Smith is one of many adults who think that if the punishment doesn't work, it is only because it was not severe enough—so Mr. Smith doubled the sentence to sixty.

Mark felt even more resentful and rebellious and refused to do it. His mother pointed out that if he didn't do it, they would probably be doubled again (whether it was fair or not) and that he would probably be suspended. Mark said, "I don't care. I'm not doing it." The sentence was doubled again to 120, and Mark's mother was called in for a conference. Many teachers also believe that if the punishment is not working, it is because the parents aren't supporting the punishment. In this case the teacher was right. Mark's mother did not believe in the effectiveness of punishment.

At the conference, she established that she certainly agreed that Mark had been disrespectful and disruptive and that this should be corrected. She thought a logical consequence might be more effective, and she made the suggestion, "Since Mark did something to make your job unpleasant, how about having him do something to make up for it that would help make your job be more pleasant?"

Mr. Smith said, "Like what?"

She suggested cleaning the blackboards, emptying the trash, or teaching part of a lesson.

Mark was really interested in this suggestion and chimed in, "Yeah, I could teach about transitives and intransitives."

Mr. Smith said, "Yes, you do understand that, and many of the students haven't grasped it yet." He then looked at Mark's mother and stated, "But he would enjoy that."

Mr. Smith was not willing to follow the suggestion to redirect misbehavior into contributing behavior because he was afraid that would be rewarding misbehavior and would inspire Mark to continue misbehaving.

This is an excellent example of the misconception that in order to make children do better, we first have to make them feel worse. It could be that Mr. Smith also represents those who think it is more important for children to pay for what they have done than to learn from what they have done. I'm going to say it again. The opposite is true. Children do better when they feel better. Many teachers, as you will see in later examples, have found that redirecting misbehavior into contributing behavior has worked to encourage children to stop, or greatly diminish, their misbehavior.

Another reason logical consequences can be difficult to use is that it takes thought, patience, and self-control. It means acting instead of reacting. Many adults find it easier to request self-control of children than to do it themselves.

LOGICAL CONSEQUENCES AND
THE MISTAKEN GOALS OF BEHAVIOR

Another important guideline for the use of logical consequences is to consider the mistaken goal of behavior. Logical consequences may be effective at the time of conflict only if the goal is undue attention. When the goal is misguided power or revenge, logical consequences can be effective during a problem-solving session *after a cooling-off period,* and *after winning the child's co-operation.* Again, this was one of the guidelines taught by Dreikurs (who was the first to introduce and popularize the concept of logical consequences to encourage improved behavior). He said, "Logical consequences cannot be applied in a power struggle except with extreme caution because they usually deteriorate into punitive acts of retaliation. For this reason, natural consequences are always beneficial but logical consequences may backfire."[2]

For example, suppose a child is not doing work in the classroom. The teacher could say to the child, "You'll need to get your work done before recess, or you can go to the workbench during recess." (Notice how respectful it is to have a choice as part of the logical consequence.) If the goal is undue attention, the child is likely to smile and start getting her work done. On the other hand, if the goal is misguided power, the child may refuse to do her work to prove "You can't make me" unless you have won the child's cooperation by discussing this pattern of behavior in advance and asking her what choice would work for her. If the goal is revenge, the child may refuse to do the work in order to hurt your feelings until her hurt feelings are dealt with. If the goal is assumed inadequacy, she needs more time for training, not a logical consequence.

In other words, an understanding of children's behavior and of long-term results is required for the effective use of logical consequences.

Remember, logical consequences may not be appropriate at all no matter what the mistaken goal. Perhaps the work being requested is not meaningful. Perhaps the teacher has not invited the children to be involved in planning the work and finding ways to make it relevant for students. Perhaps the teacher needs to involve students in a discussion about what, how, and why work needs to be done. There is nothing like involving students in problem solving to win their interest and cooperation. Logical consequences are only one tool, and often not the best tool for the situation.

AN ATTITUDE SHIFT MAY BE NECESSARY

When I first learned about these concepts, I was in the midst of psychology classes and believed it was important to be open, honest, and spontaneous. My problem was that the open, honest, spontaneous reaction to my misbehaving children was threatening, yelling, and spanking. I thought it would not be honest or spontaneous to act kind when I felt the need to be firm, since I was usually angry over the misbehavior. Fortunately, I soon realized that it was not too much to ask that I control my behavior, since I was expecting my children to control theirs. It took practice, but the results were worth the effort.

My first experience with logical consequences failed because I had missed the importance of being both kind and firm and I did not know about the Four R's of Logical Consequences. I was firm, but not kind, and added humiliation.

I told my children in advance that if they were late for dinner, they might miss it and have to fix their own and clean up their own mess. I added that I did not want to take the responsibility of finding them or of cooking and cleaning up twice (deciding what I would and would not do). The first time they were late, instead of being kind and firm while following through on this decision, I scolded them for not remembering and added my "I told you so's." I turned what could have been a logical consequence into punishment, and then wondered why it wasn't effective.

If I had understood kind and firm follow-through I would have said, "I'm sorry you missed dinner. What is our rule about what needs to be done if you fix yourself something to eat?" (This could be said only if we had agreed in advance on rules such as cleaning up messes.) Eventually I became more successful in using logical consequences because I learned all the guidelines, including involving my children in advance.

INVOLVING CHILDREN IN ADVANCE

For years I had been nagging my children about getting dressed in the morning. After learning the concepts of natural and logical consequences, we had a family meeting and together decided that breakfast would be served from eight to eight-thirty in the morning. Anyone who was not dressed and ready to eat by then would have to wait until lunch to eat. Because the children had been involved in the decision, they seemed eager to cooperate for the first few weeks. Seven-year-old Kenny even decided to arrange his clothes fireman-style so that he could get dressed quickly in the morning.

Kenny was also the first one to test the plan. One morning he sat on the couch in his pajamas with one eye on the clock. At 8:31 A.M. he came into the kitchen and demanded his breakfast. I said, "Sorry, Kenny, but breakfast is over. I'm sure you can make it until lunch." Kenny argued that he wasn't going to wait and climbed up on the counter to get some cereal. I had to grit my teeth to remain kind while I firmly lifted him down from the counter. He cried and had a first-class temper tantrum for about forty-five minutes, stopping only long enough to try getting up on the counter once in a while. Each time, I kindly and firmly lifted him down. He finally went outside. I wasn't at all sure that it had worked and remembered how much easier it was to punish instead of going through that for forty-five minutes—even though I kept punishing for the same thing over and over and over.

Kind and firm follow-through seemed to be effective. For the next two weeks, everyone was dressed and ready for breakfast on time. Then Kenny decided to test the rule once more. When he came to the table in his pajamas at 8:31, I repeated what I had said the last time: "I'm sorry you missed breakfast. I'm sure you can make it until lunch." I was thinking, "Oh no. I don't think I can take another forty-five minutes of kindness and firmness while he has a temper tantrum."

To my delight, I had to lift him down from the counter only once before he mumbled under his breath as he went out to play, "I didn't want any breakfast anyway."

That was the last time I had a problem with the children getting dressed in the morning before breakfast. It had worked! This example is an illustration of two other concepts discussed earlier:

1. Things often get worse before they get better as children test the plan. It is difficult but effective to remain kind and firm during this testing period.

2. Punishment may get quicker results, but, properly used, logical consequences are one of the many nonpunitive methods that help children develop self-discipline and cooperation.

Even though logical consequences worked in this case, other methods might have been even better. As soon as the enthusiasm for the plan diminished, we could have discussed it again during another family meeting. As I explain in chapter nine on family meetings, this worked quite well for diminished interest in chores. I could have sat down with Kenny and asked curiosity questions to find out his perception of what was happening, how he was feeling about it, and what ideas he had to solve the problem. I could have given him a big hug and told him I really needed his help to follow our plan so we could have a peaceful morning.

Logical consequences are often used when another method would be more effective. One key is to think of the long-term effects. If problem solving would teach your child more than a logical consequence, then use that method. On the other hand, simply allowing your child to experience the consequences of his or her choices can teach valuable life lessons. Following is an example where either a natural or a logical consequence would have been effective, but neither was used.

Gina lost her softball mitt. The natural consequence would have been for her to do without. However, her mother is such a supermom that she can't stand having her child learn from her life experiences. Supermoms want to be in control of everything. Gina's mother used the "bawl 'em out and then bail 'em out" technique. After giving Gina a moralizing lecture (one Gina has heard many times) about how she should take care of her things, and how she could just go without since she was so irresponsible (bawling her out), her mother gave in and bailed her out by driving her to the store (as usual, promising she would never do this again) to purchase another mitt. Not allowing Gina to experience the natural consequence would not have been so bad if Gina's mother had substituted the logical consequence of having Gina earn the money to pay for a new mitt. But Gina's mother is like so many others. Her intervention did not resemble logic. Gina has been well trained to know that she does not have to be the responsible one, even if her mom makes a big fuss about it.

Many parents and teachers use the phrase "I've told you a hundred times." They need to realize that it is not the children who are dense. Children know what works for them. Adults need to accept that telling a hundred times is not effective. Children will never learn to be responsible for their own behavior as long as adults take that responsibility away from them by repeating reminders or by solving problems for them, rather than with them.

Mrs. Silvester had told her children a hundred times to pick up their toys. After learning these concepts she kindly let her children know that from now on if they didn't pick up their toys, she would—again, deciding what she would do. She added, however, that if she picked them up, she would put each one away until they could demonstrate that they would take care of them by picking up their other toys.

Keep in mind that, often, the problem of toys being left out is a problem of too many toys having been purchased by parents. When this is the case, children don't care if you do pick them up and put them away permanently. These parents should own the problem and do something about it (stop buying too many toys) rather than expecting cooperation from their children.

Mrs. Silvester learned which toys her children really cared about and which ones were a result of her problem of buying too many toys. When toys were left out, she would say only once, "Do you want to pick up your toys or do you want me to?" Her children picked up the ones they cared about. The ones she picked up stayed on the top shelf and were forgotten.

When all the toys the children did not want had been put on the top shelf, Mrs. Silvester told her children she would no longer warn them, but would just pick up any toys that had not been put away. She did not have to pick up many toys as the children scrambled to beat her to it. When her children asked for toys she had put away, she would give them back only after they had kept their other toys picked up for a week.

This example illustrates another guideline that is helpful for understanding logical consequences. Children need to learn that there is a responsibility that goes along with privileges. With this understanding, the formula is quite simple.

Privilege = Responsibility

Lack of responsibility = Loss of privilege

Having toys is a privilege. The responsibility that goes along with the privilege is to take care of the toys. The obvious logical consequence of not accepting the responsibility of taking care of the toys is to lose the privilege of having the toys. Mrs. Silvester also demonstrated the effectiveness of deciding what she would do, respectfully letting the children know, and then following through and doing what she said she would do.

Mrs. Silvester added a sequel to this story. The only toys she buys now are those her children want badly enough to save their allowance for until they can pay at least half. She no longer has a serious problem. Children seem to care more about things in which they have an investment.

Even when parents and teachers become convinced of the value of natural and logical consequences, they can still be very difficult methods to use. In rational moments, adults know that their bottom-line goal is to inspire children to be happy, responsible people. However, it is so easy to react and become engaged in power struggles and give in to the temptation to win over children instead of winning children over. Parents and teachers don't like to admit that punishment can feel good to them because it gives them that sense of power they feel is being taken away when children misbehave. Besides, they believe it is their job to make children behave properly. They forget that force is not an effective motivator to instill life skills for good character. They also forget that the main purpose of discipline is to motivate children to do better.

This leads to another guideline to remember. I have said it or implied it many times in this chapter and throughout the book: *Logical consequences are not the best way to handle most problems.* Many parents and teachers get so excited about logical consequences that they try to find a consequence for every misbehavior. I don't know how many times I have heard people ask, "What would a logical consequence be for this situation?" I tell them, "If a logical (related) consequence isn't obvious, then it is probably not appropriate to use a logical consequence in this situation." There are other methods that might be more effective, such as holding a family meeting, focusing on solutions instead of consequences, creating routines, offering limited choices, asking for help, dealing with the belief behind the behavior, deciding what you will do instead of what you will make your child do, following through with dignity and respect, hugging, helping children explore consequences of their choices instead of imposing consequences, and using many other concepts discussed throughout this book.

REVIEW

Positive Discipline Tools

1. Think it through. Are "logical consequences" really poorly disguised punishments?

2. Beware of what works. Consider the long-term effects of your discipline methods.

3. Avoid "piggybacking." Express empathy and understanding for what the child is experiencing.

4. Don't impose natural consequences, but allow children to experience the natural consequences of their choices without adding blame, shame, or pain—and without rescuing them.

5. Decide what you will do instead of what you will make your child do.

6. Offer choices whenever possible.

7. Consider the Four R's of Logical Consequences.

8. Consider the Four R's of Punishment to understand the long-term results of your discipline methods.

9. Remember that it is a crazy idea to think that you have to make children feel worse before they will do better.

10. Children do better when they feel better.

11. Redirect misbehavior into contributing behavior.

12. If you expect children to control their behavior, model self-control.

13. Logical consequences are inappropriate for most mistaken goals.

14. Use kind and firm follow-through.

15. Help children explore the consequences of their choices through curiosity questions.

16. Logical consequences are not the best way to handle most problems.

17. Use the formula: Privilege = Responsibility. Lack of responsibility = Lack of privilege.

18. Focus on solutions for improved family and classroom atmosphere.

Questions

1. How do parents and teachers sometimes try to disguise punishment?
2. What are many children thinking about while they are being punished?
3. What are the immediate results of punishment?
4. What are the long-term results of punishment?
5. Why must we sometimes beware of what works?
6. If adults insist on winning, what position does that leave for children?
7. What is the definition of a natural consequence? Give some examples.
8. What part do adults play in natural consequences?
9. What is the definition of a logical consequence?
10. What are the Four R's of Logical Consequences?
11. How can a logical consequence become a punishment if any one of the Four R's is missing? Give an example.
12. When children don't experience the Four R's for Logical Consequences, what are the other Three R's they may experience?
13. What is the mistaken belief of adults when they use their power to ensure suffering?
14. Why is it important to be both kind and firm at the same time?
15. Why is it difficult to be both kind and firm at the same time?
16. Why is doing nothing sometimes the most effective thing you can do?
17. Why are logical consequences not the best solution for every misbehavior problem?
18. For which mistaken goal are logical consequences usually effective, even during the time of conflict?

19. What are the two things that must take place before logical consequences can be used during a problem-solving session when the mistaken goal is power or revenge?
20. For which mistaken goal should natural and logical consequences not be used?
21. How do you help children explore the consequences of their choices instead of imposing consequences on them?
22. What could you focus on instead of consequences in nine out of ten cases?

Chapter Six

FOCUSING ON SOLUTIONS

The shift to focusing on solutions requires small adjustments in attitude and skills, but the difference is huge. Even small shifts can be difficult when you are used to thinking in a certain way, but once the shift is made you may wonder, "Why didn't I think of that sooner?" It then seems so simple.

Traditional discipline focuses on teaching kids what *not* to do or what to do because someone else "said so." Positive Discipline focuses on teaching children what to do because they have been invited to think through the situation and use some basic guidelines, such as respect and helpfulness, to find solutions. They are active participants in the process, not passive (and often resistant) receivers. Children start making better behavior choices because it makes sense to them and because it feels good to be treated with respect and to treat others with respect.

When we focus on solutions, kids learn how to get along with others and they have tools to bring with them to the next challenge. No, they won't always get it right the next time (adults don't always learn on the first try either), but they do learn. The challenge for adults is to let go of the crazy idea that we learn better when we hurt first. I keep bringing this up because it is so

ingrained in our culture that we have to hurt kids to teach them right from wrong.

Focusing on solutions creates a very different family and classroom atmosphere from focusing on punishment, and even from focusing on logical consequences. Your thinking and behavior will change, and so will the thinking and behavior of your children. Many parents and teachers have reported that power struggles are greatly reduced when they focus on solutions.

The theme for focusing on solutions is: *What is the problem and what is the solution?* Children are excellent problem solvers and have many creative ideas for helpful solutions when adults take time for training and allow many opportunities for them to use their problem-solving skills.

The Three R's and an H for Focusing on Solutions is very similar to the Four R's of Logical Consequences presented in chapter five. In fact, the first three are identical. Only the H is different. However, the focus is very different because the emphasis is on helping people learn how to solve the problem instead of having to *pay* (through punishment) for the problem.

The Three R's and an H for Focusing on Solutions

1. Related
2. Respectful
3. Reasonable
4. Helpful

The following is an excerpt from *Positive Discipline in the Classroom*[1] that illustrates the amazing difference in brainstormed suggestions when students first focus on logical consequences and then focus on solutions:

During a class meeting, students in a fifth-grade class were asked to brainstorm logical consequences for two students who didn't hear the

recess bell and were late for class. Following is their list of conse-
quences:

1. *Make them write their names on the board.*
2. *Make them stay after school the same number of minutes
   they were late.*
3. *Take away from tomorrow's recess the same number of
   minutes they were late today.*
4. *Take away all of tomorrow's recess.*
5. *Yell at them.*

The students were then asked to forget about consequences and
brainstorm for solutions that would help the late students get to class
on time. Following is their list of solutions:

1. *Everyone could yell together, "Bell!"*
2. *The students could play closer to the bell.*
3. *The students could watch others to see when they are
   going in.*
4. *Adjust the bell so it is louder.*
5. *The students could choose a buddy to remind them that it is
   time to come in.*
6. *Someone could tap the students on the shoulder when the
   bell rings.*

The difference between these two lists is profound. The first looks and
sounds like punishment. It focuses on the past and on making children pay for their mistakes. The second list looks and sounds like solutions that focus on helping the students do better in the future. The
focus is on seeing problems as opportunities for learning. In other
words, the first list is designed to hurt, the second is designed to help.

Jody McVittie, a Certified Positive Discipline Associate in Everett, Washington, shared the following story about a class meeting where the students switched from "hurtful" solutions to "helpful" solutions with very little prompting:

I came as an observer to a class meeting and arrived after they had completed their complements and had begun problem solving. The problem they were discussing was that an unnamed student had taken Alex's pencil without asking. The student leader of the meeting passed an object around the class so that class members could give ideas of how to solve the problem. At first the suggestions were consequences: "She could stay in for recess." "The teacher could move her desk."

It rapidly became clear to me that everyone knew who the offender was, though she had not been named. It also seemed clear that she was a "repeat offender" and that some of the kids were "tired" of dealing with her. She was getting progressively smaller and smaller in her chair.

I asked the class if they would be willing to consider another approach to this problem that I might offer them as their consultant. They were eager to hear ideas. I don't think anyone liked the process of making someone else feel bad. I pointed out to them that even though they hadn't used names, they all knew, and even I already knew, who they were talking about. They nodded. I asked them if they could guess if Johanna was feeling better or worse after their suggestions. The class acknowledged that Johanna probably felt worse. I reminded the class that they had agreed to work to be helpful, not hurtful, in class meetings and suggested that instead of focusing on consequences they might focus on solutions. Solutions are a way to solve the problem that happened in a way that is helpful and when suggesting solutions the whole class can get ideas on how to prevent problems similar to this one. I asked Johanna and the class if they might be willing to try this. They agreed and started over with suggestions.

This time the suggestions included: "She could ask to borrow the pencil." "We could make a pencil store for the class." "She could trade something for the pencil and then trade back when she is done so Alex doesn't worry he won't get his pencil back." It was amazing to watch Johanna "grow" again in her chair. After the small penguin they were using as a talking object made its way around the circle and all who had wanted to contribute had, I supported the student leader in asking Johanna and Alex which solution they could both agree on. The scribe read the list of solutions and Alex and Johanna agreed that asking for the pencil would work well and that they would report back to the class on their solution in one week.

The solution seemed obvious, respectful, and encouraging. The issue felt resolved. The power for me in watching this was watching Johanna shrink and grow. I thought to myself afterward, "What did the class learn from this?" My sense was that this "repeat offender" felt supported and welcomed by the group, maybe for the first time. She seemed empowered by the simple suggestion to ask before borrowing.

Will she have trouble again? Probably. But now she and the class have tools for solving problems that give the message "you are one of us" instead of "you aren't one of us and you need to be excluded."

When children and adults first start brainstorming for solutions to a problem, you'll find that many suggestions are punitive. Sometimes it is helpful to interrupt the brainstorming process and suggest that they focus on solutions. Another option is to wait until they are finished brainstorming and then go over the list of suggestions and ask family members or students to eliminate all the suggestions that don't fit all of the Three R's and an H for Focusing on Solutions. Sometimes teachers and parents also ask children to eliminate anything that is hurtful or impractical. For example, a trip to Hawaii might be helpful, but it isn't practical. After hurtful and impractical suggestions are eliminated, the people with the problems can choose the solution they think would be the most helpful. The feeling of respect and accountability is greatly increased when people can choose a solution rather than having someone else tell them what they should choose—or having the class vote on the solution a student should experience.

It has often been said that, when given the opportunity, children are better problem solvers than adults. The following example is a case in point:

At another elementary school there were some problems on the playground used by first and second graders. The kids were cheating and being aggressive at tetherball. The teachers did not have any great ideas about how to solve the problem, and the playground supervisors were getting increasingly frustrated about how to "hold the kids accountable." It seemed like an impossible task.

During a class meeting where the problem was discussed, one group of second graders offered unusual insight. One of the reasons for the cheating and aggressive behavior was that winning at tetherball was a high-stakes deal. The longer you won, the longer you got to play. That made people want to win, and it took a long time for other kids to get a turn to play.

Katie had a great solution to the problem: Instead of allowing the winner to continue, she suggested that both players go to the end of the line. That way there was less incentive to win (or to cheat) and more kids could play during recess. The students agreed and proposed the rule to the other first- and second-grade classes. They all agreed to try the solution for several weeks. The teachers were skeptical. They figured that the kids would just find a way around this rule and that any success would be short-lived.

They were quite surprised. The kids liked the new rule. In fact they were empowered by the idea that one of them, a second grader, had come up with an idea that worked. The playground atmosphere changed dramatically and the young students felt empowered by the success of their problem solving. In subsequent class meetings, several different classes creatively looked for solutions to other problems, such as playing with the same kid all the time when there were an even number in the game, and exclusive "clubs" that had been forming all year. Also, the teachers became convinced of the value of class meetings, not only to solve problems but to teach valuable life skills.

When children decide (because you ask how they can solve this problem) to go get a sponge and towel when they spill their milk, that is RRR and H (related, respectful, reasonable, and helpful). You are teaching a life skill and providing an opportunity for them to develop the perception that they are capable.

When your teen has come home later than the agreed-upon time, and after you have both calmed down (the next day usually), and you invite your son or daughter to brainstorm solutions that are respectful to all involved, it is RRR and H, and you are teaching accountability and problem-solving skills as well as being clear about being respectful of your needs.

When your son or daughter bops the baseball through the garage window and together you decide that the solution is to fix the window (with the materials purchased from his or her allowance), you have been RRR and H. So long as you stay out of a blaming mode and see the mistake as an opportunity to learn, you have both practiced problem-solving skills and respect, and have had some quality time together.

One valuable life skill that is inherent in the process of focusing on solutions is teaching the value of a cooling-off period. It is important to understand and to teach children that, in most cases, a cooling-off period is necessary before trying to find a solution. Since it is difficult to focus on solutions when we are upset and coming from our primitive brains, where the only option is fight or flight, it is helpful to wait until we have calmed down and can access our rational brains. Positive Time-out can help.

POSITIVE TIME-OUT

How would you feel, what would you think, and what would you do if your spouse or colleague cornered you and said, "I don't like what you did. You can just go to time-out and think about what you did"? Would you feel grateful for the help, or would you feel indignant? Would you think, "Wow, this is so helpful and so encouraging"? Or would you think, "This is so insulting. Who do you think you are?" Would you decide to bring all your problems to this person because he or she is so helpful, or would you decide to emotionally withdraw or find another partner?

Since this kind of treatment would not be respectful or effective with adults, why do adults think it is effective with children? Adults do many ineffective things because they don't really think it through. They don't think of the long-term results. They don't think about how the child is feeling, what the child is thinking, and what the child is deciding about himself, others, and what to do in the future. They don't think about what they say.

I ask parents and teachers why it is silly to say, "And you think about what you did." It is silly because the assumption is that adults can control what children think about. They can't. It is unlikely that children who are sent to time-out are thinking about what they did. It is more likely that they are thinking about what you did and how disrespectful and unfair you are. Some children may be filled with anger and resentment and are thinking about how to get even or to avoid getting caught the next time. Saddest of all are those who are thinking they are "a bad person" or "not good enough."

Positive Time-out is very different. It is designed to help children feel better (so they can access their rational brains), not to make them feel worse (as a false motivator), not to make them "pay" for what they have done. It is not effective to focus on solutions until everyone has calmed down enough to have access to their rational brains. There are four guidelines to follow when getting children involved in creating a Positive Time-out area.

1. *Take time for training.* Talk about how helpful Positive Time-out can be before you use it. Teach children about the value of a cooling-off period and the importance of waiting until everyone feels better before trying to solve conflicts.

   A great way to teach children about the use of Positive Time-outs or "regathering times" is by using them yourself. Parents can keep a copy of a favorite humor book in the bathroom drawer and retreat to the bathroom for a few minutes to regather. In one classroom the regathering area is a corner decorated like a tropical island. The kids can go to "Hawaii" for a few minutes to regather. The teacher doesn't usually get up and go to the corner, but she has an inflatable palm tree in her drawer, and when she needs a break she "goes to Hawaii" by putting the palm tree on her desk. The students know that when the teacher is "in Hawaii," they need to leave her alone for the few moments it takes for her to regather and calm herself down again.

2. *Allow children to create their own time-out area—an area that will help them feel better so they can then do better.* It is important for children to create (or at least help create) their own Positive Time-out area. If they aren't old enough to help plan it and to choose it, they aren't old enough to use it. Explain that the purpose of Positive Time-out is not to punish or to cause suffering.

Brainstorm to come up with suggestions of things the child could do to feel better while in the Positive Time-out area such as reading, playing with toys, resting, or listening to music.

The idea that children can be allowed to do something enjoyable while in time-out is objectionable to many parents and teachers. They believe that allowing a child to play with toys, read, rest, or listen to music is rewarding the misbehavior. These adults are steeped in the belief that children will do better if they are punished (feel worse) and have not grasped the fact that children do better when they feel better.

Because time-out has such a punitive reputation, it is a good idea to let your children or students give it another name. A preschool teacher shared that she and her students created a place called Space. They hung some dark netting in a corner and hung planets from the ceiling. The corner was filled with two beanbags because sometimes they took a time-out buddy (or Space buddy) with them, some books, stuffed animals, and earphones for listening to music. Another preschool teacher created a time-out "grandma" by stuffing some old clothing with soft cloth. The children would be asked, "Would it help you to go sit on Grandma's lap for a while?"

Notice the words "Would it help you?" It is very respectful to give a child two choices. "What would help you the most right now, to go to our 'cool-off place' or to put this problem on the class meeting or family agenda?"

3. *Develop a plan with the children (or students) in advance.* Explain that either one of you or both of you may find it helpful to take some time-out until you feel better before trying to solve a problem. Parents and teachers often admit that they are the ones who need to take some time-out—even if that means taking some deep

breaths. Let children know that they can "choose" the Positive Time-out area if they think it will be helpful.

When a child is misbehaving, some parents say, "Would it help you to go to your 'happy place'?" If the child is too upset and says no, the parent can say, "Would you like me to go with you?" And why not? You probably need some time-out just as much as the child. If not, remember that the purpose is to help the child feel better, so the child will be able to do better. If the child still says no, you can say, "Okay, I think I'll go," so you can model for your child that time-out is not a bad thing.

4. *Finally, teach children that when they feel better, they can follow up by working on a solution or making amends if there is still a problem.* Adults who are offended by the idea of allowing children to do something enjoyable while in time-out usually don't even hear the last guideline.

Some schools that use Positive Discipline have a Positive Time-out bench on the playground. Students are taught that they can use it anytime they need a cooling-off period (to feel better) until they are ready to be respectful of others or the playground equipment. It is important for the teacher or playground supervisor to have an attitude of respect, kindness, and firmness when they ask a student, "Do you think it would be helpful for you to sit on the time-out bench until you feel better? Or would it be more helpful to you to work out a solution now, or to put the problem on the agenda?"

It isn't always necessary to follow up by finding a solution. Sometimes Positive Time-out is enough to interrupt the problem behavior. Just feeling better is enough to redirect the child to more socially acceptable behavior. When it does seem appropriate to follow up to find a solution, it can be very helpful to use curiosity questions (discussed on pages 20 and 134) to help children explore the consequences of their choices and to use what they learned to solve the problem. Sometimes the child may want more help to find a solution by putting the problem on the family or class meeting agenda.

Martha, a student in one of my child development classes, shared that she sent her child to his room because he was misbehaving. When he came out of his room a few minutes later, she sent him right back. When asked if her child was still misbehaving when he came out of his room, she admitted he wasn't. She grinned as she realized it would not have been necessary to send him back to his room if she had kept in mind her goal of helping him change his behavior rather than her power to ensure suffering. We then discussed that it would be even more effective if it was his choice to go to his "special place," a place that he had helped design, until he felt better.

Most parents and teachers have not been trained in effective alternatives to punishment. It helps when they know that waiting for a cooling-off period is not "letting the child get away with something" and it is not "permissiveness." Positive methods that are both kind and firm just make sense when adults understand human behavior and the long-term effects of discipline methods. It also helps when parents and teachers know that follow-up may be required after Positive Time-out. One of the best ways to follow up and focus on solutions is to help children explore the consequences of their choices through curiosity questions.

CURIOSITY QUESTIONS

Helping children *explore* the consequences of their choices is much different from *imposing* consequences on them. Exploring invites the participation of children to think for themselves and figure things out for themselves, and to decide what is important to them and what they want. The end result is focusing on solutions to the problem instead of consequences. Imposing consequences often invites rebellion and defensive thinking instead of explorative thinking. The key to helping children explore is to stop telling and to start asking curiosity questions.

Too often adults *tell* children what happened or what is wrong, what caused it to happen, how the child should feel about it, what the child should learn from it, and what the child should do about it. It is much more respectful, encouraging, and inviting of skill development when we ask what happened or what is wrong, what the child thinks caused it, how she feels about it, what she has learned, what ideas she has to solve the problem, or how she can use in the future what she has learned. This is the true meaning of *education,* which comes from the Latin word *ēducāre,* which means "to draw forth." Too often adult try to stuff in instead of draw forth, and then wonder why children don't learn.

Typical Curiosity Questions

What were you trying to accomplish?
How do you feel about what happened?
What do you think caused it to happen?
What did you learn from this?
How can you use in the future what you learned?
What ideas do you have for solutions now?

I call these typical curiosity questions because it is important not to have a script. The point is to get into the child's world. You'll notice that "Why?" isn't one of the suggested questions. The reason is that "Why?" usually sounds accusatory and invites defensiveness. In truth, all of the questions can be asked in an accusatory tone of voice. "Why?" actually works when children feel that you are truly interested in their point of view. The following guidelines will help when using curiosity questions:

1. Don't have an agenda. You aren't getting into the child's world if you have an agenda about how the child should answer these questions. That is why they are called *curiosity* questions.
2. Don't ask questions if either of you is upset. Wait until you are both feeling calm.
3. Ask curiosity questions from your heart. Use your wisdom to guide you as to how to get into the child's world and show empathy and acceptance.

One of my favorite examples is the time my daughter shared with me her intention to get drunk at a party. I gulped and said, "Tell me more. Why are you thinking of doing that?" She said, "Lots of kids do it and it looks like they are having fun." I stifled my temptation to lecture and asked, "What do your friends say about you now that you don't drink?" She thought about this and said, "They are always telling me how much they admire me and how proud they are of me." I continued, "What do you think they'll think or say after you get drunk?" Again, I could watch her think before she said, "I'll bet they'll be disappointed." I followed with, "How do you think you'll feel about yourself?" I could tell this question made her think a little more. She paused and said, "I'll probably feel like a loser." This was soon followed by, "I don't think I will."

If I hadn't known about curiosity questions and the value of helping her explore the consequences of her choices, I would have been tempted to impose a punitive consequence, such as grounding her. Chances are that this would have inspired her to get sneaky instead of trusting that she could discuss things with me. The biggest loss would have been that she would not have had the opportunity to explore for herself the consequences of her choices and what she really wanted in her life.

REVIEW

In summary, focusing on solutions teaches children:

What to do to learn from a mistake. How can we fix this? What is necessary? Some things can't be entirely fixed, but what is the best that can be done.

How children can develop their strengths. When the solutions come from children, or are brainstormed together and children choose what will be most helpful, they feel encouraged to use their personal power in constructive and contributing ways.

How mistakes are opportunities to learn. Children learn that mistakes aren't horrible if you don't beat yourself up about them and if you look at mistakes as ways to learn.

How to develop problem-solving skills. Can you imagine what the world would be like if everyone had these skills?

How to stop, calm down, and solve a problem instead of reacting. A great life skill!

How to be creative in the face of an unanticipated problem instead of feeling bad and giving up.

How to develop appropriate (socially useful) responses.
Children learn what to do instead of what not to do. The
most effective logical consequences are also solutions.
(They are helpful.)

Parents and teachers who are just beginning to use Positive
Discipline methods should work on only one thing at a time and
remember to have the courage to be imperfect. To end the discipline war (peace in the world can start with peace in homes and
schools), it is imperative to stay out of power struggles and create an atmosphere where the long-term effects for both children
and adults are mutual respect, accountability, a sense of capability, resourcefulness, and problem-solving skills. It is important
to see mistakes as opportunities to learn. Focusing on solutions
is one of the best ways to accomplish these goals.

Positive Discipline Tools

1. Focus on solutions.
2. The Three R's and an H to help focus on solutions.
3. Identify the problem and brainstorm for a solution.
4. Eliminate disrespectful solutions before asking children
   to choose the solution they think will be most helpful.
5. Cooling off before solving a problem.
6. Positive Time-out.
7. Asking children what would help them—and, when
   possible, giving at least two choices.
8. Using the family or class meeting to solve problems.
9. Curiosity questions to help children explore the
   consequences of their choices.

Questions

1. What are the Three R's and an H for focusing on solutions?
2. What is the theme of focusing on solutions?
3. What is the difference between brainstormed lists that focus on consequences and those that focus on solutions?
4. What questions can you ask to help children eliminate punitive suggestions?
5. Why is a cooling-off period important before looking for solutions?
6. How is Positive Time-out different from the conventional use of time-out?
7. As an adult, what would you feel, think, and decide if a partner banished you to punitive time-out?
8. What would you feel, think, and decide if you knew you could go to a Positive Time-out of your own creation whenever you needed to feel better?
9. Why is it silly to admonish a child to "think about what you did"?
10. What are the important guidelines for teaching children about Positive Time-out?
11. What is a good process to use to follow up with children after a Positive Time-out, or to help them explore the consequences of their choices?
12. What is the difference between imposing a consequence on children and helping children explore the consequences of their choices?
13. Why is it important to be kind and firm at the same time?
14. Why is it difficult for adults to be kind and firm at the same time?

15. Why is it a good idea to avoid dealing with a conflict when you are upset?
16. What are adults afraid will happen if they don't deal with a conflict immediately?
17. Why is it more effective to involve children in setting limits?

Chapter Seven

USING ENCOURAGEMENT EFFECTIVELY

Do your eyes light up when they walk into the room?
—Toni Morrison

If a child came up to you and innocently said, "I am a child, and I just want to belong," would you get angry and put that child down in any way? Of course not! What most adults don't realize is that any child who is misbehaving is subconsciously saying, "I just want to belong, and I have some mistaken ideas about how to accomplish belonging." Of course, this message is spoken in code. Adults can be more encouraging to children when they learn to understand the "misbehavior code."

As discussed in chapter four, misbehaving children are discouraged children. Their misbehavior is letting you know they do not feel a sense of belonging and significance, and they have a mistaken belief about how to find belonging and significance. You will be more effective in redirecting the misbehavior to positive behavior when you remember that there is a hidden, discouraging belief behind the behavior.

Dreikurs emphasized encouragement and felt it was the most important skill adults could learn in helping children. He said many times, "Children need encouragement, just as plants need water. They cannot survive without it." Accepting this premise, it is obvious that the best way to help a misbehaving child is through encouragement. When discouragement is removed, the motivation for misbehavior will be gone also. Even though this is true, it is not easy to act encouraging toward a child who is misbehaving, and many adults don't know what encouragement looks like.

Sometimes encouragement is not easy because it is normal for adults to get hooked into reacting to the misbehavior in negative ways instead of acting in ways that deal with the message behind the misbehavior and that motivate children to do better. Another reason encouragement is not easy is that so many adults are steeped in the notion that punishment motivates children to improve their behavior. Most parents and teachers who believe punishment works have not explored the long-term negative results. Even those who have explored the long-term results of punishment, and accepted that it isn't a good thing, still get hooked.

It may be encouraging to know that getting "hooked" is normal. We all have "buttons" and children know how to push them. When our buttons get pushed we seem to revert to our primitive reptilian brains. We may not "eat" our young, but we certainly do nibble away at their sense of belonging and significance when we are upset and react. During a time of conflict both adults and children are likely to react irrationally. No wonder no one is listening. This is not a good time to teach anything constructive, yet it is often the time adults think they have to deal with the conflict. If they don't, they are "letting the child get away with something." This is just one reason for Positive Time-out—so adults and children can calm down and feel better (and access their rational brains) before they try to resolve a problem.

Even when adults are calm, the idea of encouragement can sound so nice, but it seems vague in application when they don't know what it looks like. Encouragement is the focus of this book. Every method discussed is designed to help children and adults feel encouraged. Encouragement is providing opportunities for children to develop the perceptions "I'm capable, I can contribute, and I can influence what happens to me or how I respond." Encouragement is teaching children the life skills and social responsibility they need to be successful in life and relationships. Encouragement can be as simple as a hug to help children feel better and thus do better.

Many years ago I decided to test this theory. My two-year-old son had been whining and I was so annoyed I felt like spanking him. Instead, remembering the concept of encouragement, I knelt down, gave him a hug, and told him how much I loved him. Not only did he stop whining and crying, but my annoyance magically disappeared when I remembered the hidden message behind his behavior and took a few minutes to do something encouraging rather than punishing.

Unfortunately, encouragement is not always as simple as the previous example might indicate. There are three main reasons for this:

1. Adults have a difficult time remembering that a misbehaving child is really saying, "I just want to belong."
2. Although adults are usually very skilled at punishment, they are unskilled at encouragement.
3. Children aren't always ready for encouragement at the time of conflict.

TIMING

In the previous example, my son responded favorably to encouragement while he was whining. Sometimes encouragement is favorably received only after a cooling-off period. At the time of conflict, especially if the mistaken goal is power or revenge, both adults and children may be feeling too angry to be able to give or receive encouragement. For this reason, friendly withdrawal (Positive Time-out for you or your child—or both) is often the most effective thing to do at the time of conflict. If you simply can't ignore the conflict-causing behavior until you both have a chance to cool off, at least use "I" messages to express your feelings and intentions, rather than hurtful comments or blame.

Adults can withdraw from the conflict by stating, "I think we are both too upset to discuss this now, but I would like to get together with you when we have both had time to cool off." This is especially effective if you have discussed the concept of a Positive Time-out for a cooling-off period during a class meeting, and if your students have helped create a Positive Time-out area in your classroom. If you are having class meetings or family meetings you could also offer a choice: "Would you like to put this problem on the meeting agenda, or should I?" Another choice might be, "What would help you the most right now— to take some Positive Time-out or to put this problem on the agenda so we can get some help later?"

If you do not have success with encouragement, it could be that your timing is off. Recognizing the importance of a cooling-off period will increase your success.

MUTUAL RESPECT

Mutual respect incorporates attitudes of (a) faith in the abilities of yourself and others; (b) interest in the point of view of others as well as your own; and (c) willingness to take responsibility and ownership for your own contribution to the problem. The best way to teach these attitudes to children is by modeling them. You will see how the concepts of timing and winning cooperation can be merged with the concept of mutual respect.

Jason, a student in Mr. Bradshaw's fifth-grade class, often lost his temper and would loudly express his hostility to others, including Mr. Bradshaw, during class. Mr. Bradshaw had tried several forms of punishment, which only seemed to intensify Jason's outbursts. He had tried sending him to the principal's office. He had tried having Jason stay after school to write five hundred sentences about controlling his temper. He finally tried demanding that Jason leave the room to sit outside the classroom on a bench until he cooled down. Jason would slam the door on his way out. Sometimes he would pop up and down in front of the window, pulling faces. When he came back into the room, his demeanor was one of belligerence, and he would soon have another angry outburst.

Mr. Bradshaw decided to try encouragement, keeping in mind the concepts of timing, winning cooperation, and mutual respect. He began by asking Jason to stay after class, when they could be alone. When Jason came to Mr. Bradshaw after school, he found a much friendlier teacher. First, Mr. Bradshaw thanked Jason for using his valuable time to stay after school. Then he told Jason he would very much like to work out something so they would both feel good about the solution. He owned his part of the problem by sharing with Jason that no matter how much it upset him when the outbursts disrupted the class, he had been disrespectful to use punishment as a mistaken attempt to motivate Jason to do better. Mr. Bradshaw continued the conversation by telling Jason that he didn't want to use punishment anymore and that he needed Jason's help. He asked Jason if he would be willing to work on a solution with him.

Jason was not yet willing to cooperate and showed his hostility by claiming he couldn't help it that the kids made him so mad. (Remember, it may take a while for children to trust us when we change our behavior.) Mr. Bradshaw agreed he could understand that feeling, because sometimes other people made him very angry also. This got Jason's attention. He glanced up at Mr. Bradshaw with surprise and relief showing in his eyes. Mr. Bradshaw went on to share with Jason that he was aware of certain things happening in his body when he got angry, such as a knot in his stomach and stiffening in his shoulders. He asked Jason if he was aware of things happening to his body when he got angry. Jason couldn't think of any. Mr. Bradshaw then asked Jason if he would be willing to try an experiment and pay attention to what happened to his body the next time he lost his temper. Jason said he would. They agreed to get together after school the next time it happened so that Jason could share what he discovered.

It was five days before Jason had another angry outburst in class—a long time for Jason. It is possible that he felt belonging and significance just because Mr. Bradshaw had taken the time to work with him in a friendly, respectful manner. He didn't feel the need to find belonging through misbehavior for a while. However, it didn't last forever.

The next time Jason had a temper tantrum, Mr. Bradshaw gently put his hand on his shoulder and said, "Jason, did you notice what happened to your body just now?" That question interrupted Jason's tantrum by inviting him to think. Mr. Bradshaw sounded interested and excited as he added, "Come see me after school and let me know."

When Jason gave his report after school, he told Mr. Bradshaw he had noticed that he started clenching his fists and his teeth when he was getting angry. Mr. Bradshaw asked Jason if he would be willing to catch himself next time he started to get angry, and to take responsibility for himself by stepping outside the door for some Positive Time-out until he had cooled off. Mr. Bradshaw added that he wouldn't have to ask permission, because he would know what Jason was doing and had faith in him to handle it all by himself. Mr. Bradshaw then asked Jason what he could do while standing outside the door to help himself feel better.

Jason said, "I don't know."

Mr. Bradshaw said, "How about counting to ten or a hundred, or thinking happy thoughts, or simply appreciating the beautiful day?"

Jason said, "Okay."

Again, it was five or six days before Jason had another temper tantrum. Again, he had felt the encouragement of discussing the problem respectfully. Again, the encouragement didn't last forever. The next week Jason stepped outside the door three times, remaining outside for three to five minutes before coming back into the classroom, noticeably calmer. Each time Mr. Bradshaw gave him a thumbs-up sign and a wink in acknowledgment of his responsible behavior. Mr. Bradshaw was not sure what Jason did to help himself calm down, but he was grateful that Jason wasn't making faces through the window. Jason continued taking responsibility for his anger and would leave the classroom four or five times a week. It was three weeks before he lost his temper and shouted out at a classmate, forgetting to step outside.

Mr. Bradshaw talked with Jason during lunch recess and commented on how well he had been doing. He added that everyone makes mistakes while learning and asked if he would be willing to keep working for improvement. Jason agreed. Mr. Bradshaw reported that for the rest of the year Jason would occasionally step outside the door, but had very few outbursts. When Jason would come back in the room after cooling off, Mr. Bradshaw continued to wink at him and smile. Jason did not become perfect, but he improved significantly. Mr. Bradshaw gave the following report during a faculty meeting: "Jason used to lose his temper several times a day. Now he loses control once or twice a month. I'll take it." Mr. Bradshaw was especially pleased because rapport between them improved so that their relationship became more enjoyable.

IMPROVEMENT, NOT PERFECTION

The above example also illustrates the concept of working for improvement, instead of expecting perfection. Perfection is such an unrealistic expectation, and very discouraging to those who

feel they must live up to it. Children would rather not try at all than experience constant discouragement because they don't live up to an adult's expectation of perfection—or their own. Recognition of improvement is encouraging and inspires children to continue their efforts.

Mrs. Bradley was feeling discouraged because her son, Alberto, was getting into trouble at school. His teacher was punishing him by having him write fifty sentences every time he misbehaved. Alberto would refuse, so his teacher would double the number. Mrs. Bradley was worried that Alberto was becoming a delinquent, so she started lecturing and scolding him. Alberto was now getting punished at home and at school. He rebelled further by acting like he didn't care, and he hated school. Mrs. Bradley finally asked for a parent-teacher conference. During the conference she asked the teacher what percentage of Alberto's behavior was "bad." The teacher said, "About fifteen percent." Mrs. Bradley was amazed to realize the negative reputation Alberto was getting (and living up to) because more attention was being paid to the 15 percent misbehavior than to the 85 percent good behavior.

Mrs. Bradley was involved in a parent study group and shared some of the things she was learning. Alberto's teacher was very much interested in hearing about nonpunitive solutions. They agreed to develop a positive plan for working with Alberto. During another conference, with Alberto present, they all agreed that every time he was disruptive or disrespectful in class, he would make up for it by doing something to contribute, such as doing tasks for the teacher, tutoring another member of the class who needed help, or teaching a segment of a lesson. Alberto's misbehavior was redirected into contributing behavior. He had very few behavior problems after that. His teacher also started having class meetings, so problems that did occur were solved by the class as a whole.

Negative punishment encourages rebellion and is very discouraging to the child, the parent, and the teacher. When adults use mutual respect, problem solving, encouragement, and focusing on solutions, children feel belonging and develop responsible behavior.

BUILD ON STRENGTHS, NOT WEAKNESSES

As the following chart shows, your child or student may have 85 percent strengths and 15 percent weaknesses, yet what do most parents and teachers focus on?

WHAT YOU SEE IS WHAT YOU GET

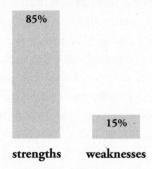

When you spend 85 percent of your time and energy focusing on the 15 percent that is negative, the negative will grow and the positive will soon disappear. What you see is what you get. On the other hand, if you focus 85 percent of your time and energy acknowledging and encouraging the positive, it won't be long before the negative disappears and the positive will grow to 100 percent because that is all you see. It is encouraging to yourself and others when you focus on the positive.

REDIRECTING MISBEHAVIOR

Look for the strengths in every child's behavior. Children who are disruptive often have good leadership skills. When you see that, it is not too difficult to work with a child and help redirect the behavior in a contributing direction. The peer counseling program described in Appendix II was based on this concept. Teachers recommended their students who had leadership skills but were using them in a disruptive direction. These students were trained to be peer counselors and used their leadership skills to help other students.

One preschool teacher mastered the concept of redirecting misbehavior and used it many times. Debbie didn't want to clean up her messes after art activities. The teacher put Debbie in charge and taught her how to teach the other children exactly what to do. Sean was always knocking other kids' blocks over. The teacher assigned Sean the job of block patrol leader. His job was to teach other children how to cooperate when they played with the blocks and help them when it was time to pick them up.

MAKING AMENDS

This is very close to redirecting misbehavior, but gets children more involved in the problem-solving process. When children do something irresponsible or disrespectful, give them the opportunity to make up for it by doing something that will make the person they offended feel better. When Alberto was disruptive in class, he made the teacher's job more difficult. He was given the opportunity to make amends by doing something to make the teacher's job easier. This does not work if the adult's attitude is punitive. It is very effective when the adult's attitude is friendly and respectful and when the child is involved in the decision about how to make amends.

Judy and Linda threw oranges at a neighbor's car. Their mother sat down with them and involved them in a discussion by asking curiosity questions in a friendly manner. First she acknowledged, "It must have seemed adventurous and fun to throw oranges at Mr. Siebert's car, but I'd like to make a guess about something. I'll bet you didn't think about how he would feel when he saw the mess it made on his car."

Both girls looked a little guilty.

Mom continued, "How do you think he felt? What would you feel if someone did that to your car?"

The girls admitted that they wouldn't like it.

Mom then asked, "What do you think you could do to make amends to Mr. Siebert?"

The girls shrugged and said they didn't know.

Mom persisted. "Girls, this isn't about getting you into trouble. We all make mistakes. This is about learning from mistakes and doing whatever you can to fix it. You are good problem-solvers. What would make you feel better if you had a car and someone threw oranges at it?"

Linda said, "I guess I would want them to say they were sorry."

Mom said, "Anything else?"

Judy said, "I would want them to wash my car."

Mom said, "Those sound like excellent ideas. Would you be willing to do that for Mr. Siebert?"

Both girls felt reluctant, but agreed it would be the right thing to do.

Mom said, "I know this is hard, and I also know you'll feel better about yourselves after you do it. Do you want me to go with you, or do you want to talk to Mr. Siebert yourselves?"

The girls agreed that they would talk to him by themselves.

Judy and Linda were lucky that Mr. Siebert was appreciative. He acknowledged that it took courage for them to admit their mistake and to do something about it. If he had been a grouch, Mom still would have supported them in making amends. Even when people aren't gracious about accepting amends, it is easy to imagine that Linda and Judy will think more about the consequences of their choices in the future.

Five boys in an elementary school were caught defacing classroom doors. The janitor let them make amends by helping him paint the doors. The janitor's attitude was so respectful that he inspired these boys to take pride in their work and to discourage other children from vandalizing.

Making amends is encouraging because it teaches social responsibility. Children feel better about themselves when they are helping others. Making amends is encouraging when used in a nonpunitive manner because children experience the opportunity to learn from their mistakes and correct any resulting problems. Making amends is encouraging because children learn that they can be responsible and accountable for their behavior without fear of blame, shame, and pain.

It is sad that some adults think it is more important for children to feel blame, shame, and pain for what they have done than to make amends and to experience the kind of encouragement that will motivate them to stop misbehaving. Actually, most of these adults mistakenly believe that helping a child feel better is rewarding the misbehavior and will encourage further misbehavior. It is important to notice that children do not "get away" with misbehavior when they are encouraged to make amends. They learn to be accountable with their dignity and respect intact.

AVOID SOCIAL PRESSURE

It can be difficult to use effective procedures with children when adults feel social pressure. When friends, neighbors, relatives, or other teachers are observing your interaction with misbehaving children, you may feel your effectiveness as a parent or teacher will be judged by how well you handle the situation. It is easy, under these circumstances, to feel that these observers expect immediate perfection—so the pressure is on. You may be tempted to use punishment to satisfy the observers, since it appears to achieve the quickest results.

It takes a great deal of courage to think clearly during a

time of social pressure and to do what will achieve the most effective results. One summer we went backpacking with several friends. Our ten-year-old son, Mark, was a very good sport and carried his pack the long six miles into the canyon. When we were getting ready for the long, steep trek back out, Mark complained about how uncomfortable his pack was. His dad jokingly remarked, "You can take it. You're the son of a marine."

Mark was in too much pain to think this was very funny, but he started the climb anyway. He hadn't gone very far ahead of us when we heard his pack come crashing down the hill toward us. I thought he had fallen and asked, with concern, what had happened. Mark angrily cried, "Nothing! It hurts!" He continued climbing without his pack. Everyone else observed this with interest. One adult offered to carry the pack for him. I was feeling very embarrassed—and had the additional social pressure of having written a book on Positive Discipline.

I quickly overcame my ego and remembered that the most important thing was to solve the problem in a way that would help Mark feel encouraged and responsible. I first asked the rest of the party to please hike on ahead so that we could handle the problem in private. We then used the Four Steps for Winning Cooperation, described in chapter two.

I said to Mark, "I'll bet you felt really angry that we wouldn't pay serious attention when you tried to tell us your pack hurt before we even started."

Mark said, "Yeah, and I'm not carrying it."

I told him I didn't blame him and would feel exactly the same way under the circumstances.

His dad said he was sorry and asked for another chance to solve the problem.

Mark visibly dropped his anger. He was now ready to cooperate. He and his dad figured out a way to stuff his coat over the sore part to cushion the pack. Mark carried the pack the rest of the way, with very few, minor complaints.

When under social pressure, get away from the audience. Leave the scene yourself or respectfully request that others leave so that you can solve the problem privately.

SCHEDULE SPECIAL TIME

One of the most encouraging things parents can do for their children is to spend regular, scheduled special time with them. You may already spend lots of time with your children. However, there is a difference between "have-to time," "casual time," and "scheduled special time."

Children under two require lots of time and are not really old enough to comprehend "special time." As long as they feel your enjoyment, scheduled special time is not necessary. Between the ages of two and six, children need at least ten minutes a day of special time that they can count on. Even more time is better, but you'll be surprised how magical it can be even if ten minutes is all you can manage in your busy schedule.

From ages six to twelve, children may not require special time every day (you be the judge), but they like to count on at least half an hour a week. The particular time and amount would be individual for each family. It could be cookies and milk while sharing after school, or an hour every Saturday. The important part is that children know exactly when they can count on time that has been set aside especially for them.

There are several reasons why special time is so encouraging:

1. Children feel a sense of belonging and significance when they can count on special time with you. They feel that they are important to you.
2. Scheduled special time is a reminder to you about why you had children in the first place—to enjoy them.
3. When you are busy and your children want your attention, it is easier for them to accept that you don't

have time when you say, "Honey, I can't right now, but I
sure am looking forward to our special time at four-
thirty."

Plan the special time with your children. Brainstorm to come
up with a list of things you would like to do together during
your special time. When first brainstorming to develop your list,
don't evaluate or eliminate. Later you can look at your list together and categorize. If some things cost too much money, put
them on a list of things to save money for. If the list contains
things that take longer than the ten to thirty minutes you have
scheduled for the special time, put these items on a list that can
be put on a calendar for longer family fun times.

I often suggest that parents take the phone off the hook for
special emphasis that this is special, uninterrupted time. However, one mother would leave the phone on the hook during her
special time with her three-year-old daughter. If the phone
would ring, she would answer and say, "I'm sorry I can't talk with
you now. This is my special time with Lori." Lori would grin as
she heard her mother tell other people how important it was to
spend time with her.

Teachers may be surprised at how effective it can be to spend
two or three minutes after school with a child and *not* talk about
the child's problems. Instead teachers can ask questions such as,
"What is your favorite thing to do for fun?" Then share what
you like to do for fun. Students feel very special when a teacher
also shares things that reveal who they are as a person. Many
teachers have reported that simply spending a few minutes after
school with a child for special time has helped the child feel encouraged enough to stop misbehaving, even though the misbehavior is not mentioned during this time.

Mrs. Petersen was concerned about a child in her room whose
mistaken goal was power. Debbie often refused to do her work
and openly displayed hostility with sneers and sullen looks. Mrs.

Petersen asked Debbie to stay after school one day. Debbie stayed, looking as if she were ready for a battle. Mrs. Petersen did not mention any problem behavior; she instead asked Debbie if she would tell her about the most fun thing she had done the night before. Debbie would not answer. Mrs. Petersen thought, "This isn't working," but continued, "Well, I would like to tell you what I did for fun last night." She then went on to share something she had done with her family the night before. Debbie still refused to respond. Mrs. Petersen told Debbie she could leave, but she would love to hear from her anytime she felt like sharing what she liked to do for fun.

Mrs. Petersen felt discouraged, thinking the exchange had not been very helpful. However, the next day she noticed Debbie no longer had a chip on her shoulder and did not display any hostility. After school Debbie showed Mrs. Petersen a picture she had drawn of herself and a friend riding bikes. She explained this was the most fun thing she had done the night before. Mrs. Petersen then shared another fun thing she had done.

If you analyze it, you will understand why such a brief exchange can have such dramatic results. First, the child feels singled out for special attention. The child may reject this special attention at first because of the suspicion that it will probably be another session for blaming and lecturing. Second, the child experiences the unexpected when the teacher ignores behavior problems. Third, adults often show interest in having children share, but they don't demonstrate mutual respect by sharing themselves. A child may feel extra belonging and significance when you share something about yourself.

It is suggested that teachers spend a few minutes of special time with each student in their class during the year. Start with the children who seem the most discouraged, but keep track to make sure you don't miss anyone. Many teachers complain that they don't have time for special time. It is true that teachers are feeling a lot of pressure to help students pass academic tests. However, teachers who understand that encouragement is just as important as academics, if not more important, find a few minutes for special time while children are doing seat work, during recess, or after school.

Parents can apply the concept of special time as part of the bedtime routine (although the bedtime routine should not replace daytime special time). When Mrs. Bruner tucked her children into bed at night, she asked them first to share the saddest thing that happened to them during the day and then the happiest thing. She then shared her saddest and happiest events. At first her children went overboard on this opportunity to complain about sad things and would sometimes end up crying. She would patiently wait for them to calm down and then say, "I'm glad you can share your feelings with me. Tomorrow, when you don't feel so upset, we'll talk about it some more to see if we can figure out some solutions. Now tell me your happiest thing." If the child couldn't think of a happy thing, Mrs. Bruner would share her happy event. After the children got used to this routine, the sad events were reported in a matter-of-fact way, followed by ideas for solving or avoiding a similar problem in the future. The children soon enjoyed sharing their happy events more than their sad events.

ENCOURAGEMENT VERSUS PRAISE

For many years there has been a great campaign for the virtues of praise in helping children gain a positive self-concept and improve their behavior. This is another time when we must "beware of what works." Praise may inspire some children to improve their behavior. The problem is that they may become pleasers and approval junkies. These children (and later these adults) may develop self-concepts that are totally dependent on the opinions of others. Other children resent and rebel against praise, either because they don't want to live up to the expectations of others or because they fear they can't compete with those who seem to get praise so easily. Even though praise may seem to work, we must consider the long-term effects. The long-term effect of encouragement is that it invites self-confidence. The long-term effect of praise invites dependence on others.

As discussed earlier, another mistake adults have made regarding praise is the notion that they can "give" a child self-esteem. Self-esteem can't be given or received, it is developed through a sense of capability and the self-confidence gained from dealing with disappointments, solving problems, and having lots of opportunities to learn from mistakes. The successful use of encouragement requires adult attitudes of respect, interest in the child's point of view, and a desire to provide opportunities for children to develop life skills that will lead to self-confident independence from the negative opinions of others. Some characteristics of both praise and encouragement are outlined below.

The differences between encouragement and praise can be difficult to grasp for those who believe in praise and have seen immediate results. They have seen children respond to praise with beaming faces. However, they don't think about the long-term effects of dependence on the opinions of others. Even those who want to change from praise to encouragement find it awkward to stop and think before making statements that have become habitual.

It may help to keep the following questions in mind when wondering whether the statements you make to children are praise or encouragement:

- Am I inspiring self-evaluation or dependence on the evaluation of others?
- Am I being respectful or patronizing?
- Am I seeing the child's point of view or only my own?
- Would I make this comment to a friend?

I have found the last question especially helpful. The comments we make to friends usually fit the criteria for encouragement.

DIFFERENCES BETWEEN PRAISE AND ENCOURAGEMENT[1]

	PRAISE	ENCOURAGEMENT
Dictionary definition	1. To express favorable judgment of 2. To glorify, especially by attribution of perfection 3. An expression of approval	1. To inspire with courage 2. To spur on: stimulate
Addresses	The doer: "Good girl."	The deed: "Good job."
Recognizes	Only complete, perfect product: "You did it right."	Effort and improvement: "You gave it your best." Or, "How do you feel about what you accomplished?"
Attitude	Patronizing, manipulative: "I like the way Suzie is sitting."	Respectful, appreciative: "Who can show me how we should be sitting now?"
"I" message	Judgmental: "I like the way you did that."	Self-directing: "I appreciate your cooperation."
Used most often with	Children: "You're such a good girl."	Adults: "Thanks for helping."
Examples	Robs person of ownership of own achievement: "I'm proud of you for getting an A."	Recognizes ownership and responsibility for effort: "That A reflects your hard work."
Invites	Children to change for others: Approval junkies.	Children to change for themselves: "Inner direction"
Locus of control	External: "What do others think?"	Internal: "What do I think?"

	PRAISE	ENCOURAGEMENT
Teaches	What to think. Dependence on the evaluation of others	How to think. Self-evaluation.
Goal	Conformity: "You did it right."	Understanding: "What do you think/learn/feel?"
Effect on sense of self-worth	Feel worthwhile when others approve.	Feel worthwhile without the approval of others.
Long-term effect	Dependence on others.	Self-confidence, self-reliance.

ENCOURAGEMENT VERSUS CRITICISM

It is a mistake to think the best way to help children do better is to criticize what they do wrong. Many argue that constructive criticism is helpful. Sid Simon had an excellent definition for constructive criticism: constrictive crudicism. When you think about it, constructive criticism is a contradiction in terms. *Constructive* means to build up. *Criticism* means to tear down. This does not mean you shouldn't let children know when there is room for improvement. It does mean that you don't have to make them feel worse in order to get them to do better. An effective way to discuss areas that need improvement is to ask the child, "In which areas do you think you are doing well? In which areas do you think you need improvement?" Children usually know without being told, and it is better when the acknowledgment for the need to improve comes from them. Ask the child, "How would you like to improve? What do you need to do to accomplish your goals?" You can then join them in brainstorming to come up with ways that would help them improve. This teaches children the value of goal setting and self-evaluation.

ENCOURAGING SELF-EVALUATION

Cory brought her writing assignment on the letter *g* to her third-grade teacher, Mrs. Tuttle, who looked at the paper and asked Cory to point out her favorite one. After Cory pointed to her favorite *g*, Mrs. Tuttle said, "May I point out my favorite one?" Cory happily agreed. Mrs. Tuttle pointed to another nicely executed *g*. Next Mrs. Tuttle pointed to a *g* with a double tail and asked Cory to tell her about that one.

Cory showed her surprise by covering her mouth with her hand as she said, "Oh." Mrs. Tuttle asked Cory if she could fix it by herself, or did she need help? Cory said she could and went back to her desk to fix it.

Mrs. Tuttle did not point out only the error. She focused on strengths first and then asked Cory to evaluate the error herself. If we ask children what areas they need to work on for improvement, they can usually tell us without being told. This example incorporates the concept of building on strengths, not weaknesses. When you point out what has been done well, children usually want to continue doing as well or better.

As parents and teachers, we are responsible for helping children learn and improve academic and social skills. However, encouragement is usually the best way to inspire a child to want to do better. If other methods are used, such as those that follow, they will be most effective if the child has first been won over through encouragement so that he or she will be receptive.

TAKE TIME FOR TRAINING

This is not as obvious as it may sound. Adults often expect children to accomplish tasks for which there has not been adequate training. This is more typical in homes than in schools. Parents may expect children to clean their rooms, but never teach them how. Children go into their messy rooms and feel overwhelmed. It would help if a parent said, "Put your clean clothes in your drawers and your dirty clothes in the hamper and then I'll let you know what is next." Next they could put their toys on the shelves or in toy boxes. To make it more fun, suggest all toys with wheels first, then toys with body parts, then toys that are animals.

H. Stephen Glenn pointed out in his lectures that parents often tell children what expectations they have without ever bothering to specify exactly how these expectations should be met. There is often a great communication gap. Taking time for specific training can eliminate the misunderstanding.

Glenn demonstrated the communication gap by the following conversation:

Mom: Jill, clean up your room!
Jill: I did. (Meaning: I can walk through it.)
Mom: No you didn't. (Meaning: I can't eat off the floor.)

Taking time for training means being very specific about your terms and expectations. One mother spent several years helping her children make their beds. She gave them pointers such as, "What would happen if you pulled here?" (It would straighten a wrinkle.) She bought bedspreads with plaids or stripes so that her children could learn to have straight lines along the edges. By the time they were six, they had enough training to know how to make their beds almost well enough to pass an army inspection.

When you ask children to clean the kitchen, make sure they know what that means to you. To them it may mean simply putting the dishes in the sink. Many parents get upset when their children do a terrible job with chores, even though they have never taken time for training. Taking time for training does not mean children will do things as well as you would like. Improvement is a lifelong process. And, remember, the things you want them to do may not be a high priority for them until they become adults with children of their own. We all do better at things that have a high priority in our lives. Even though cleanliness and manners may not be a high priority for children, they still need to learn these qualities. Adults, however, need to remember that kids are kids.

Once you feel there has been adequate training, check it out by asking the child, "What is your understanding of what needs to be done for the kitchen to be clean?" If the child says, "Put the dishes in the dishwasher," ask, "What about the floors and the counters? What do you need to do to make sure they are clean?" You may experience rolled eyes as the child sarcastically replies, "Sweep the floor, wipe the counters." Let it go and acknowledge, "Great. I'm glad we have the same understanding."

Time for training can be fun. Choose one night a week to practice table manners. Invite everyone to exaggerate saying, "Pleeeeese pass the butter," etc. Make a game of getting points for catching others with their elbows on the table, talking with their mouths full, interrupting others, complaining, or reaching across the table. The one with the most points gets to choose the after-dinner game.[2]

Taking time for training also includes telling your children when you are going to change your methods. Mrs. Roberts heard me talk about how important it is to allow children to dress themselves. Her daughter, Connie, was in the third grade. Mrs. Roberts had stopped dressing Connie, but she was laying her clothes out for her every night. She decided she would stop doing this and have faith in Connie to handle it. However, she didn't tell Connie about her new decision. The next morning she heard Connie yell in an irritated voice, "Mother, where are my clothes?"

Mrs. Roberts replied very respectfully, "They are in the closet, dear. I'm sure you can find them yourself."

Connie retorted, "Mother, when you decide to do these things, will you please let me know?"

Connie was right. It is a good idea to respectfully discuss changes with those involved before implementing them.

ROUTINE CHARTS

The more children do for themselves, the more capable and encouraged they feel. One of the best ways to avoid bedtime hassles and morning hassles is to get children involved in creating routine charts and then letting them follow their charts instead of telling them what to do. Start by having your child make a list of all the things she needs to do before going to bed. The list might include: pick up toys, snack, bath, jammies, brush teeth, choose clothes for the next morning, bedtime story, hugs. Copy (or when children are old enough, let them copy) all the items on a chart. Children love it when you take pictures of them doing each task so they can paste the picture after each item. Then hang the chart where she can see it. Let the routine chart be the boss. Instead of telling your child what to do, ask, "What is next on your routine chart?" Often, you don't have to ask. Your child will tell you.

Choosing clothes the night before is one task that eliminates some morning hassles when children follow their morning routine (for which you may have another chart). If they have laid out what they want to wear the night before, they don't get upset trying to find something at the last minute. Other bedtime routine tasks that make morning routines go more smoothly is for children to make their school lunch the night before.

Remember that the goal is to help children feel capable and encouraged. A nice fringe benefit is that you will be able to stop nagging and will experience more peaceful bedtimes and mornings.

TEACH THAT MISTAKES ARE WONDERFUL
OPPORTUNITIES FOR LEARNING

Even when children don't live with blame, shame, and pain, they seem to pick up self-criticism from somewhere. Often, they decide all on their own that they "should" be more perfect. We need to teach over and over again that mistakes are wonderful opportunities for learning. Kathy Schinski attended a Positive Discipline workshop and shared the following words to a song she had written. You may want to make up your own tune and teach this to your children or students.

A Little Imperfection
by Kathy Schinski

A little imperfection is not so bad.
A little imperfection shouldn't make you feel sad.
It keeps you in touch with reality
And with all the not-so-perfect people
Just like me.

A little imperfection is not so tough.
You need a little of it to be perfect enough.
It puts your feet back on the earth
And lets the other people keep
Their own self-worth.

A little imperfection in just the perfect place
Can make this not-so-perfect world easier to face.
More of us could go in the right direction
If we could learn to put up with a little imperfection.

A little imperfection is not so bad.
A little imperfection shouldn't make you feel sad.

It keeps you in touch with reality
And with all the not-so-perfect people
Just like me.

CURIOSITY QUESTIONS

Curiosity questions were discussed in the last chapter to help children explore the consequences of their choices. They can also be used as part of the "taking time for training" process. You will achieve greater participation and understanding, and will create a more encouraging and respectful atmosphere, if you ask curiosity questions of children rather than making statements (usually in the form of demands or lectures). Curiosity questions are effective only when you are really interested in the answers—not when you are hoping they will give the answer you want.

When children answer your questions, they are actively involved. When you make statements, they are passively involved. When they answer questions, you have an opportunity to hear whether or not their understanding is the same as yours. For example, instead of telling your child to clean up the kitchen, ask, "What can you see that needs to be done before the kitchen is clean?"

Your child may say, "Wash the dishes."

You can then ask, "What about the things on the table?"

Your child may admit, "Oh, well, I guess they need to be put away."

You can reply, "Right, and what about the things on the stove? And what do you need to do about the table, counters, and stove surfaces after everything is put away?"

By using this method, you are also taking time for training, inviting children to think, and actively involving them in problem-solving skills—all very encouraging. Sometimes the best way to be encouraging is a simple hug.

TRY A HUG

In many cases adults can help children change their behavior when they stop dealing with the misbehavior and deal with the underlying cause: discouragement. A young father was frustrated and perplexed about the continuous temper tantrums displayed by his four-year-old son. Scolding or punishing only increased the tantrums. The father learned in his parenting class that a misbehaving child is a discouraged child and that encouragement is the best way to deal with the misbehavior. The idea seemed backward to the father—sort of like rewarding misbehavior. Still, he was intrigued with the idea that children do better when they feel better. He decided to test the theory.

The next time his small son started having a temper tantrum, the father got down on one knee and shouted above the tantrum, "I need a hug."

His son paused and asked through his sobs, "What?"

The father shouted again, "I need a hug."

His son stopped sobbing long enough to ask incredulously, "Now?"

The father said, "Yes, now."

The son seemed totally bewildered, but he stopped his temper tantrum and said somewhat begrudgingly, "Okay." Then he stiffly gave his father a hug. Soon the stiffness disappeared and they melted into each other's arms.

After a few moments the father said, "Thanks, I needed that."

His son said, with a small tremor on his lips, "So did I."

Remember timing. Sometimes hugs don't work because the child is too upset to give or receive a hug or any kind of encouragement. You can still try. If the child is unwilling, you can say, "I sure would like a hug whenever you are ready," and then leave the area. Parents report that when they try this, the child usually comes after them right away, wanting a hug.

Some people ask, "After the hug, then what? What about the misbehavior?" Often, encouragement is enough to interrupt the misbehavior and nothing more needs to be done. Other times hugs can create an atmosphere of encouragement in which children are willing and able to learn. This may be the perfect opportunity to take time for training, ask curiosity questions, give a limited choice, use distraction, or engage in joint problem-solving.

Another excellent way to encourage children is to help them feel useful by making a contribution. What a wonderful way to let them contribute—by making *you* feel better when they give you a hug. Of course, the fringe benefit is that they also feel better.

Remember, a misbehaving child is a discouraged child. Too many people think children must pay for what they have done in the form of blame, shame, or pain (in other words, punishment). Try a hug instead.

If none of the above methods is effective, you may be in a power struggle or a revenge cycle that increases discouragement. Share your mistakes with your child and ask for help to start over. Admitting your mistakes is one of the most encouraging things you can do.

A CHILD'S POINT OF VIEW

An excellent way to help you remember a child's point of view is to remember your own childhood. Close your eyes and think back to your childhood. Remember an incident between you and an adult at home or school when you felt discouraged, misunderstood, humiliated, or treated unfairly, or any combination of the above. Relive the experience. Remember exactly what happened and how you felt. Relive those feelings.

With your eyes still closed, remember another incident between an adult and you as a child when you felt encouraged, understood, appreciated, special, inspired to do better, or any combination of the above. Relive this experience. Remember exactly what happened and how you felt. Relive those feelings.

When you felt discouraged as a child, you may have felt misunderstood, humiliated, or treated unfairly. You may have felt some form of blame, shame, or pain. You may have felt worthless or rebellious. It is likely that you did not feel inspired to improve as a result of these discouraging experiences, even though that was usually the adult's goal. You perhaps gave up trying to improve a skill such as piano, reading, penmanship, or sports because of the discouraging criticism you received from an adult.

When you felt encouraged as a child, you felt understood, appreciated, and special. These experiences perhaps inspired you to do better and to pursue worthwhile skills or goals. Most of the encouraging experiences you had as a child most likely involved very little time on the part of an adult when he or she offered a few words of recognition and appreciation.

In the next two chapters you will see how important it is to get children actively involved in the encouragement process through class and family meetings.

REVIEW

Positive Discipline Tools

1. Pay attention to timing. Wait for "no conflict" time (possibly after some Positive Time-out for you and your child), when you are ready to give encouragement and your child is ready to receive it.
2. Use an "I" message, where you take responsibility for your feelings.
3. Withdraw from the conflict. (Take some Positive Time-out if possible.)

4. Make an appointment to get together when you have both had time to calm down and feel better.

5. Invite the child to put the problem on the family or class meeting agenda (or do so yourself).

6. Listen. Remember that children will listen to you after they feel listened to.

7. Use the Four Steps for Winning Cooperation.

8. Build on strengths, not weaknesses. Acknowledge and encourage the percentage that is going well and that percentage will increase.

9. Engage in joint problem-solving to find mutually respectful solutions in areas that need improvement.

10. Focus on and acknowledge improvement, not perfection.

11. Redirect misbehavior. Look for the talent or skill in the misbehavior and redirect the child to use that talent or skill in useful, contributing ways.

12. Support children in making amends for their mistakes. Use curiosity questions to help children decide for themselves what they can do to make amends.

13. Avoid social pressure. Sometimes it is appropriate to wait until you have "private time" to engage a child in a friendly problem-solving discussion so you can avoid the social pressure of worrying about the judgments of others.

14. Plan regularly scheduled "special time" with each of your children.

15. When tucking children into bed, allow time for them to share their saddest and happiest times of the day. Then share yours.

16. Use encouragement instead of praise.

17. Avoid criticism. Ask the child, "How would you like to improve? What do you need to do to accomplish your goals?"

18. Encourage self-evaluation.
19. Take time for training so expectations are clear.
20. Ask, "What is your understanding of what we decided?"
21. Let your child know in advance when you decide what you are going to do.
22. Involve children in the creation of routine charts.
23. Teach that mistakes are wonderful opportunities to learn.
24. Stop telling, lecturing, and demanding and ask curiosity questions.
25. Try a hug.

QUESTIONS

1. What is a misbehaving child?
2. What is the hidden message behind the misbehavior?
3. What did Dreikurs think was the most important skill adults could learn to help children?
4. What is the importance of timing?
5. What are the Four Steps for Winning Cooperation?
6. What are the necessary adult attitudes for the Four Steps for Winning Cooperation to be effective?
7. What are the necessary adult attitudes for mutual respect?
8. Why is a "special time" so powerful for encouraging children and motivating them to improve their behavior?
9. What are the dangers of praise?
10. What are the long-range effects of encouragement?
11. What are some of the differences between praise and encouragement?
12. What are the questions you should ask as a self-check to determine whether your statements are encouragement or praise?

13. What are the benefits of getting children involved in creating routine charts?
14. What is the purpose of mistakes?
15. What other ways can you think of to encourage children?

Chapter Eight

CLASS MEETINGS

The effectiveness of the positive approach depends on adult attitudes of mutual respect and concern for the long-term effects
on children. It has been promised that children who experience
the respectful interaction outlined in this book will learn self-
discipline, cooperation, responsibility, resilience, resourcefulness,
problem-solving skills, and other social and life skills for good
character.

The culmination of all these promises and attitudes is most
fully realized and experienced in regularly scheduled family and
class meetings. Such meetings provide the best possible circumstances for adults and children to learn and practice the demo-
cratic procedures of cooperation, mutual respect, and focusing
on solutions. Class meetings and family meetings are two of the
best ways to give children an opportunity to develop strength in
all of the Significant Seven Perceptions and Skills mentioned in
chapter one. These are the most beneficial long-term goals that
parents, teachers, and children will achieve when they implement family and class meetings. However, some parents and
teachers are motivated by the fringe benefit of eliminating discipline problems. This is fine, so long as they understand that
eliminating or reducing discipline problems is a fringe benefit,

and not the primary goal of family and class meetings—but what a great fringe benefit it is. As one teacher said, "I did not get into teaching to become a policeman, judge, jury, and executioner. Since we started class meetings, my students became respectful and helpful. They solve their own problems and I have more time for teaching."

Learning and practicing to be "good finders" (a term used by Thomas J. Peters in his book, *In Search of Excellence*) through compliments, as well as developing problem-solving skills through brainstorming for respectful solutions, are benefits for students that will serve them in every important life endeavor. These skills are as important as academics and need to be practiced on a daily basis. I often ask teachers if they would consider exposing their students to reading or math just once a week. They always say no. When I ask why not, they reply that students need daily exposure to math and reading in order to practice and retain the skills. I then ask if they think students can learn and retain the social and life skills they need for good character if they practice them only once a week (and just hear lectures about them the rest of the time). Of course, they get the point.

Whenever students have problems, teachers can suggest, "Would you be willing to put that problem on our class meeting agenda?" This alone is enough of an immediate solution to give satisfaction, while providing for a cooling-off period before trying to solve the problem. One teacher objected that her special education students needed immediate help when they were upset. I suggested that she try having them put their problems on the agenda to see what would happen. She reported that they would walk over to the agenda sheet, obviously upset, write their problem on it, and walk away calmly. It was enough for them to know that their problem would be addressed soon.

A cooling-off period of at least one day is recommended before discussing a problem. It is discouraging to have to wait much longer than three days. This is a reason why once-a-week meetings may be ineffective. (A shorter cooling-off period works for younger children. In kindergarten, one hour is often long enough.) Putting a problem on the agenda can serve as a short cooling-off period.

Students are often able to solve problems much better than the teacher simply because there are more of them and the brainstorming process generates unique ideas. They have many excellent ideas when they are allowed and encouraged to express them. Eventually, many discipline problems are eliminated because students feel encouraged when they are listened to and taken seriously, and when their thoughts and ideas are validated. They also have ownership in the process, and are motivated to follow rules or solutions they have helped create. Teachers find that children are much more willing to cooperate when they have been involved in the decisions, even when the final solution is one that has been suggested by the teacher many times in the past to no avail.

There are many more benefits derived from meetings that involve children. Teachers are frequently amazed at the academic and social skills children learn in class meetings. Because they are intensely involved in solving problems that are relevant for them, they learn listening skills, language development, extended thinking, logical consequences of their choices, memory skills, and objective thinking skills. They solve problems related to health and safety. They learn and practice conflict resolution—both preventative and immediate. The enhanced value of the conflict-resolution piece is that it involves every student, not just a select few. They also gain an appreciation for the value and mechanics of learning. During one class meeting, cheating was on the agenda. The kids discussed all the reasons why they should not cheat (including "you don't learn") that seem to go in one ear and out the other when adults lecture about these reasons.

ATTITUDE AND GUIDELINES FOR
SUCCESSFUL CLASS MEETINGS

Some attitudes and actions to avoid in class meetings are:

1. Do not use the class meeting as another platform for lecturing and moralizing. It is essential for teachers to be as objective and nonjudgmental as possible. This does not mean you cannot have input into the meetings. You can still put items on the agenda and give your opinion.
2. Do not use the class meeting as a guise to continue excessive control. Children see through this approach and will not cooperate.

Class meetings should be held every day (or at least three times a week) in elementary schools. If class meetings are not held often enough, students will be discouraged from putting items on the agenda because it will take too long to get to them, in addition to not retaining the skills through daily practice.

Middle school and high school students can learn the class meeting process more quickly and retain it longer, so once a week may be enough. However, upper-grade students still cooperate better when they are listened to and respected for their abilities on a regular basis. For this reason, some middle schools and high schools have a homeroom period for class meetings. Others have teachers of different subjects hold class meetings once a week. Thus, English teachers have class meetings on Mondays, math teachers on Tuesdays, history teachers on Wednesdays, and so on. Teachers of special classes such as music can hold a quick class meeting when problems occur, if students are familiar with the process.

In the first edition of *Positive Discipline,* it was suggested that decisions be made by a majority vote. A majority vote is appropriate when the topic being discussed concerns everyone in the class. When this is the case, a majority vote does not cause feelings of division among students. It provides a great opportunity for students to learn that everyone doesn't think and feel the same way. However, some teachers still like to continue the problem-solving process until consensus is reached.

When the topic being discussed focuses on one or two students (even though the whole class may be concerned and wants to help), the students involved should be allowed to choose the suggestion they think would be most helpful to them. This encourages students to feel good about being accountable for their mistakes, and to appreciate the many ideas they can receive from other students who are focused on solutions instead of blame, shame, or pain. Students soon learn that their suggestions are most helpful when they are respectful and practical, not punitive.

It is important to note that class meetings usually are not successful at the beginning. It takes time for students (and teachers) to learn the skills. I used to tell teachers to prepare for a month of hell when starting class meetings, but that it was worth it if they understood the long-term benefits. The reason for the month of hell was that students are not used to helping one another; they are more used to punishment. They are not used to seeing mistakes as opportunities to learn and solve problems; they are used to avoiding accountability because of their fear of blame, shame, and pain.

I have since found that the month of hell can be eliminated when teachers take time during the first four class meetings (or longer) to teach students the skills of the Eight Building Blocks for Effective Class Meetings, outlined in the book *Positive Discipline in the Classroom* by Jane Nelsen, Lynn Lott, and H. Stephen Glenn.[1]

The Eight Building Blocks for Effective Class Meetings

1. Forming a circle
2. Practicing compliments and appreciation
3. Creating an agenda
4. Developing communication skills
5. Learning about separate realities
6. Role-playing and brainstorming
7. Recognizing the four reasons people do what they do
8. Focusing on nonpunitive solutions

We have developed *Positive Discipline in the Classroom Teacher's Guide,*[2] which contains activities for teachers and activities for students to help them learn and practice skills in each of the Eight Building Blocks. Class meetings are more effective when students develop skills and a positive attitude about nonpunitive solutions before they try to help one another solve "real problems." The purposes of class meetings must be explained, discussed, and experienced through experiential activities before actual agenda items are dealt with.

Purposes of Class Meetings

1. To give compliments
2. To help one another
3. To solve problems
4. To plan events

Some teachers (especially in the primary grades) start every meeting by asking their students, "What are the two main purposes of class meetings?" after establishing that the two main purposes are to help one another and to solve problems.

SOME OF THE GOALS OF CLASS MEETINGS

Teaching Mutual Respect

One way to teach the meaning of mutual respect is by having a discussion of the following questions with students:

1. Why is it disrespectful when more than one person talks at the same time? (We can't hear what everyone is saying. The person who is supposed to be talking feels that others don't care, and so on.)
2. Why is it disrespectful to disturb others? (They can't concentrate and learn from what is going on.)
3. Why is it important to listen when others are speaking? (So that we can learn from one another, to show respect for one another, and because we like to have others listen to us.)

Giving Compliments, Acknowledgment, and Appreciation

Middle and high school students usually prefer using the words *acknowledgment* and *appreciation*. Elementary school students usually do better using the word *compliment*. Despite the difference in terminology, the concept is the same.

Spend some time with students exploring the meaning of *compliment* or *acknowledgment* and *appreciation* using language appropriate to the age of your students. This can be done informally during the first meeting. Help your students understand that compliments, acknowledgment, and appreciation should focus on what others do in the following areas:

- Accomplishments
- Helpfulness to others
- Anything someone might feel good about

Have the students brainstorm to come up with specific examples in each of these areas. Then teach them to use the words, "I would like to compliment or acknowledge (a person's name) for (something specific that person did)." Using these words helps students stay on the task of recognizing what others do, rather than what they wear or how they look. I have visited hundreds of classrooms to observe class meetings in schools that have adopted this program. In every classroom where they did not use the suggested phrasing, the compliments or acknowledgments were less specific and more superficial, and the discussion seemed to wander into other subjects.

At first many children might say, "I would like to compliment Jill for being my friend." Let this go for a while during the learning process, but eventually the group could again brainstorm on how to be specific about what a friend does that we would like to recognize and appreciate.

The teacher may start by giving several compliments (from notes taken during the day when noticing things children did that would merit recognition). Many teachers model giving compliments every day, making sure they eventually cover every child in their classroom, a few each day.

During the first meeting, have everyone give at least one compliment to make sure they know how to do it. If someone has difficulty, have the class help by asking if anyone has any ideas on something that happened to this student during the day that he or she could compliment someone for, like playing together during recess, helping with homework, loaning a pencil, or listening to a problem. As soon as you know that students have the skill, pass a talking stick (or some other item) around the circle. When students have the item in their hands, they can give a compliment or pass. An important part of the compliment process is to teach students to say thank you after receiving a compliment.

You may have several class meetings just for compliments

while the students learn this process. Many teachers have shared that compliments alone have been significant in creating a more positive atmosphere in their classrooms. After the initial awkwardness, children love looking for, giving, and receiving positive recognition.

Focusing on Solutions

Teach your students to focus on solutions before trying to solve any problems. Start by having them brainstorm about natural consequences by asking what happens in the following circumstances if no one interferes:

- If you stand in the rain? (You get wet.)
- If you play on the freeway? (You might get killed.)
- If you don't sleep? (You get tired.)
- If you don't eat? (You get hungry.)

Usually the best way to help children learn is to allow them to experience the natural consequences without brainstorming for solutions. If adults interfere at all, it could be to show empathy or to use curiosity questions to help children explore the consequences of their choices.

When it is time to brainstorm for solutions, students seem to get just as mixed up about logical consequences as adults do—and often try to disguise a punishment by calling it a logical consequence. However, they catch on quickly when they are asked to focus on solutions that are related, respectful, reasonable, and helpful. Explain that brainstorming for solutions means making suggestions that others can use to help them to be responsible for their behavior and learn from their mistakes. Explain the Three R's and an H for Focusing on Solutions (Related, Respectful, Reasonable, and Helpful), as explained in chapter six. It is a good idea to make a poster of the Three R's and an H for the stu-

dents to refer to. Then have them brainstorm solutions for the
following problems:

- Someone who writes on a desk
- Someone who rides the tetherball
- Someone who doesn't do his or her work during class time
- Someone who is late for school

In the beginning, it is best to give the students practice by
working on hypothetical situations, so that there is a lack of
emotional involvement and blame. After receiving as many suggestions as possible, and writing them down, go over each one
and have the children see how well they fit the criteria for the
Three R's and an H for Focusing on Solutions. Have them discuss the reasons why they think each suggestion is or isn't related, respectful, reasonable, or helpful. Have them discuss how
each suggestion will be helpful to the person, or whether it will
be hurtful. Have the class decide which suggestions should be
eliminated because they do not meet the guidelines of the Three
R's and an H or because they are in some other way hurtful or
impractical.

Going Beyond Logical Consequences

Although logical consequences can be effective to help students
learn from their mistakes and encourage them to do better, as
discussed in chapter five, I am concerned about how often I see
logical consequences misused. When teachers try to disguise
punishment by calling it a logical consequence, students learn to
do the same thing. Many class meetings have started to feel like
a kangaroo court because teachers and students focus on logical
consequences that feel more hurtful than helpful to the students
involved. Students need to be taught that too often logical consequences focus on the past instead of the future. Learning from

the past so we can do better in the future is a good idea. However, it is counterproductive to focus on the past in order to inflict blame, shame, and pain.

It is a mistake to think that finding a logical consequence is the answer to every behavior problem. Even though an understanding of logical consequences can be helpful to teachers and students, it is more effective to focus on solutions. When given the opportunity, students can come up with a wealth of solutions that don't have anything to do with consequences. Let them practice brainstorming solutions to several hypothetical problems.

THE HOW-TOS OF CLASS MEETINGS

Using the Agenda

Introduce the agenda to the group. Some teachers reserve space on a bulletin board. Others keep a notebook where it is easily accessible. The advantage of a notebook is that everyone can look back and see how past problems were solved. Explain to the students that you are going to teach them to solve problems rather than trying to solve all of them by yourself. From now on, instead of coming to you with problems, they can put their name on the agenda, followed by a few words to help them remember what the problem is about. In the beginning do not include the names of other children involved in the problem. Let them know that they can add other people's names when they have learned to be respectful and helpful. In this way, others can feel excited about having their name on the agenda because they know they will soon be receiving valuable help from their classmates. Warn students that at first they may forget and still come to you for solutions, but you will remind them to put it on the agenda. These problems will then be solved during the class meetings.

When I was an elementary school counselor, anytime teachers or parents asked me for solutions to problems they were having with children, my consistent answer was to put it on the agenda. I always suggested solving the problems during class meetings because children would come up with the best solutions and were most willing to cooperate when they were involved in the decisions.

When solutions do not seem to work, simply put the problem back on the agenda for more discussion and problem solving. When you yourself put items on the agenda, be sure to own the problem rather than trying to place blame. Children feel good about helping you with your problem. The items on the agenda are to be covered in chronological order in the amount of time you have allotted for class meetings. Any problem that is not finished before the end of the meeting will be continued the next day. It really doesn't matter if all problems are solved immediately. It is the problem-solving process that is important. Quite often, by the time an agenda item comes up for discussion, the person who put it on the agenda will say that it has already been taken care of. Some adults say, "Fine," and go on to the next item. Others ask the child if he or she would like to share the solution.

Using the Cooling-Off Period

Explain why problems can't be solved when people are upset. Students love hearing the reptilian brain analogy used in chapter seven (when people are upset, they are irrational and unwilling to listen to other points of view). With older children you can stimulate discussion by asking them why it is difficult to solve problems when we are upset. With younger children, explain that the purpose of waiting a few hours or a few days before solving problems on the agenda is to give people a chance to cool off and calm down so that problems can be solved respectfully.

Meeting in a Circle

It is important that students sit in a circle for class meetings. Remaining at their desks not only creates physical barriers that interfere with the process, but I have yet to see a class meeting where students could keep from fidgeting with items in or on their desk while remaining at their desks.

Take time to train students to move their desks with as little noise and confusion as possible. Some classes spend several days practicing. I have seen every kind of desk moved from all kinds of arrangements so that students could sit in a circle facing one another. The shortest time was fifteen seconds. Most can do it in thirty to sixty seconds.

Training can involve several steps. First you might ask the students what they think they need to do to move with as little noise and confusion as possible. They will usually come up with all the ideas necessary for a smooth transition. Then ask them how many times they think they will need to practice before they can implement their good ideas effectively.

Some teachers like to assign seats. On the first day they have one student at a time move his or her desk and chair into the assigned space. Other teachers have a few at a time move their desks and chairs by row or by team. If they are noisy and disruptive, have them practice until they solve the problem. Once they have learned to do it quietly, they can all move at once.

Class-Meeting Structure

Before I learned the format for structuring class meetings, some of the class meetings I conducted failed. When students were not immediately impressed with what I was trying to accomplish and became disruptive, I would give up, commenting to the students, "Well, obviously you don't want a class meeting now.

We'll try again later when you are ready." In other words, not only did I not take responsibility for my own lack of readiness, but I also gave in to anarchy. Success is increased when students first learn the building blocks for effective class meetings and then use the following format:

1. Begin with compliments. Pass an item (such as a beanbag or talking stick) around the circle. Students who want to give someone a compliment can take the opportunity when they have the item in their hand. Go around the circle once so every student has an opportunity to give a compliment or to pass. When going around the circle it is important to start and stop at the same place. This avoids the accusations of "unfair" when a teacher calls on students at random and arbitrarily chooses when to stop. There is always one who claims he or she didn't get called on.

2. Read the first item on the agenda. Ask the person who wrote the item if it is still a problem. If the student says no, go on to the next item. If you have time, you might ask if the student would like to share how the problem was solved.

3. If the problem hasn't been solved, pass an item around the circle for comments and suggestions. Start with the person who wrote the item on the agenda and end just before this person. I suggest going around the circle twice because students often think of more to say or more suggestions after listening to others. The second time never takes very long.

4. Write down every suggestion exactly as it is given. This can be a student's job if old enough. (You will find suggestions on what to do if children are being hurtful rather than helpful under "Common Questions" at the end of this chapter.)

5. Read (or have a student read) all the suggestions before asking the student involved which one he or she thinks will be the most helpful. When more than one student is involved, each can choose a solution. It is okay if they choose different ones when they are all helpful ideas. If two students choose solutions that seem conflicting, invite them to have a private discussion to decide what will work for both of them without conflict.

6. Ask the student when he or she would like to do whatever was chosen. You may want to give a limited choice such as today or tomorrow, or during recess or after school. There is some psychological benefit in giving students a choice of when they would like to try the suggestion. It gives them a sense of accountability and commitment.

This format provides a process that can be followed step by step. However, it is not so rigid as to eliminate room for teacher individuality and creativity.

Hand signals are a great way for all the children to let their opinions be known during a class meeting without being disrespectful or disruptive. One teacher taught his students to move their hands crossing back and forth over their lap when they wanted to express disagreement. When they agreed with what was being said, they moved their fist up and down above their shoulder.

I invited a group of people to observe a class meeting where a child chose the suggestion to apologize in front of the class for a misbehavior that was put on the agenda. This was a concern to one of the observers. During question time she commented that she thought it was humiliating for the child to apologize in front of everyone. I invited her to ask the child and other members of the class if it bothered them to apologize in front of everyone. The class unanimously agreed that it did not bother them. The point is that it helps to get into the children's world, rather than projecting our own world onto them.

TEACHER ATTITUDES AND SKILLS

1. Let Go of Control to Invite Cooperation

The *Positive Discipline in the Classroom Teacher's Guide*[3] includes activities that help teachers experience the rationale for using Positive Discipline. During the activity called "Please Be Seated" participants form triads. In each triad one person role-plays a student sitting in a chair. The other two role-play adults who stand behind the chair with their hands on the student's shoulders. The object is for the student to try to get out of the chair, while the adults keep him or her in the chair. While processing this activity, by asking each person what they were thinking, feeling, or deciding to do in the future, all the issues and short- and long-term results of control are discussed. Those playing students share their feelings of anger, resentment, or complete discouragement. They also share their decisions to spend all their time figuring out how to defeat the controlling adult, get even, or (even worse) give up and conform, with great loss to their personal sense of value. Those playing adults share how they feel out of control even though they are acting controlling. Some discuss how easy it is to get into the power struggle without considering the long-term results. All they can think about is winning or not being defeated. No one considers that even if they could win, the price would be for the student to be the loser.

2. Model What You Want to Teach

There are several teacher skills that greatly enhance class meetings. It is most important to model what you are hoping the children will learn—social and life skills for good character. It helps when teachers model courtesy statements, such as please, thank you, you are welcome, and so on.

3. Ask Curiosity Questions (the Socratic Method)

Curiosity questions, as described in chapter six, are a little different when used during class meetings. One of the most important skills that both models mutual respect and allows children to develop their perceptions of personal capability is open-ended questioning. Any statement you might like to make can be put in the form of a question. If you want to let children know that you think they are being too noisy, ask, "How many think it is getting too noisy in here?" It is especially effective if you ask the question both ways. If you ask how many think it is okay, also ask how many think it is not okay. The less you let your own biases show, the more you invite children to think for themselves. It is amazing how often children come up with the same kind of lecturing and moralizing statements they reject when they are spoken by an adult.

Open-ended questions can change an atmosphere from negative to positive, as in the following example: A teacher requested a counselor's help with Stephen, a student who was causing a great deal of trouble on the playground. The counselor felt the best way to handle the problem was through a class meeting. This teacher had never held a class meeting, so the counselor used this opportunity to demonstrate.

The counselor asked Stephen to leave the classroom and go to the library. The general rule is that you do not discuss a child who is not there, but in this case she knew that a positive atmosphere had not been created and she did not want to take the chance that Stephen would be hurt by the comments. The class meeting was started by asking who was the biggest troublemaker in the class. The students all chorused, "Stephen." They were then asked what kind of things Stephen did to cause trouble.

They mentioned fighting, stealing balls, swearing, calling names, and so on. These first questions allowed the children to express what they have been thinking and feeling.

The next questions allowed the children an opportunity to think and feel in a positive direction. "Why do you think Stephen does these things?" The answers included such things as "Because he is mean." "He is a bully." Finally one student said, "Maybe it is because he doesn't have any friends." Another student chimed in with the information that Stephen was a foster child. When the children were asked to discuss what it means to be a foster child, they offered such ideas as how hard it must be to leave your family, move so much, and so forth. They were now expressing understanding for Stephen instead of hostility.

When asked, "How many of you would be willing to help Stephen?" every student in the class raised his or her hand. A list was made on the board of all their suggestions of what they could do to help. These included walking to and from school with Stephen, playing with him during recess, walking to school with him, eating lunch with him, and about ten other ideas. Specific volunteers were then listed after each suggestion.

Later, the counselor told Stephen that the class had discussed the problems he had been having on the playground. When he was asked if he had any idea how many of the students wanted to help him, he looked at the ground and replied, "Probably none of them." When he was told that every one of the students wanted to help him, he looked up with wide eyes and asked as though he couldn't believe it, "Everyone?" It was obvious that Stephen felt very encouraged by this turn of events.

When the whole class decided to help Stephen, and followed through on their commitments, he felt such a sense of belonging that his behavior improved dramatically.

4. Be Accountable for Your Part in the Relationship (and the Problem)

Another skill is to be willing to take ownership for some problems and ask for help. A seventh-grade teacher shared her experience with toothpick chewing. It drove her crazy because not only did she think it looked disgusting, but she found toothpicks lying all over the classroom and school grounds. It was a problem for her, but not for her students. She had lectured and implored the students many times to please stop chewing toothpicks. Nothing happened.

Finally she put it on the agenda and admitted she could understand that it was not a problem for them, but she would appreciate it if they would help her with a solution to her problem. Because they had only fifty minutes for class, they could not spend more than ten minutes a day for a class meeting, so quite often they didn't come up with a final solution to a problem for several days. On the third day of discussing toothpicks, she started by saying, "We still haven't solved the problem of toothpick chewing."

One of the students asked her if she had seen anyone chewing toothpicks lately. She admitted that she hadn't. This student said, "Maybe the problem has been solved."

The teacher said with surprise, "Maybe it has."

This is an excellent example of how many times just discussing a problem is enough to make everyone aware of it and to continue working toward solutions outside the class meeting setting.

5. Be Objective and Nonjudgmental

Be as nonjudgmental as possible. When students feel they can discuss anything without being judged, they will bring many things out in the open for discussion and learning. One teacher expressed concern that if she talked about some things, such as spitting in the bathroom, it might give other students ideas they hadn't thought of before. As we talked, she realized that the students knew what was going on and that not talking about it openly would not make it go away.

Do not censor agenda items. Some adults want to censor items on the agenda that they consider "tattletale" items. What may seem like a tattletale item to you is a real concern to the child. Other adults want to eliminate items if a similar problem has been discussed before. Again, it may be similar to you, but unique to the child. Remember that the process is even more important than the solution. Even if the item seems the same to you, the children may solve it differently or more quickly because of their past experience with the process.

6. Look for the Positive Intent Behind Every Behavior

Finally, it is important to be able to find the positive intent behind every behavior. This enables children to feel validated and valued, essential prerequisites to changing behavior. During one class meeting, the students were discussing a problem of cheating. The girl whose problem it was explained that she had looked at the words before her spelling test because she wanted to pass the test. Mr. Meder asked, "How many think it is really great that people want to pass their tests?" Most of the class raised their hands. Another boy admitted that he had been caught cheating and had had to take a test over again. Mr. Meder asked, "Did it help you out?" The boy said yes. These are two examples of finding the positive in what could be seen only as negative. The class went on to make suggestions for improving the behavior.

COMMON QUESTIONS

During a seminar on Positive Discipline in the Classroom for a school in North Carolina, the following questions and answers were recorded and transcribed. They represent the concerns of many teachers.

Q: Don't children need immediate solutions to their problems? I don't think my students could wait three days for their problems to come up on the agenda.

A: I worked with another teacher who felt the same way. She had been having class meetings right after lunch to handle all problems that occurred during lunch recess. I encouraged her to try having her students put their problems on an agenda and wait at least one day to solve them in a class meeting. She later reported that she was surprised at how much satisfaction the students demonstrated just from the simple act of writing their problem on the agenda. That was their immediate solution. Their body language indicated relief as they walked away from the agenda. She also reported that one to three days later the discussion of the problems was much more rational and helpful because tempers had cooled considerably.

Q: What if a solution that has been decided on doesn't work effectively?

A: The decision should stay in effect until someone puts the problem back on the agenda. In one class they were having the problem of students leaning back in their chairs. The class decided that anyone who leaned back would have to stand up behind his or her chair. This did not work effectively, because too many children enjoyed standing up behind their chairs and it was disruptive to the class meeting. The teacher put this problem back on the agenda. The students agreed that it was disruptive and decided that anyone who leaned back would have to leave the class meeting as a reminder, but that they could come back when they were ready to sit correctly.

Q: What if someone feels that a consequence is unfair?

A: This is usually not a problem if the student chooses the solution he or she feels will be most helpful. This problem is also avoided when you focus on solutions instead of consequences.

Q: What do you do if students suggest punishment instead of solutions?

A: Write all suggestions down. When students are first learning, it is helpful to ask them to go over each suggestion made after the brainstorming time and to eliminate the ones they think are not respectful or helpful. This provides more time for students to think about the long-term results of the suggestions. Another option is to ask volunteers to role-play punitive suggestions. After the role-play, proceed by asking the person who experienced the punishment what he or she was feeling, what he or she was learning, and what he or she was deciding to do in the future. This is another great way to teach the long-term results of punishment.

Q: What if students start to gang up on another child?

A: This does happen sometimes, even after the students have learned to be positive and helpful most of the time. During one class-meeting demonstration being led by Frank Meder, they were discussing the problem of a new student who had used "bad" language on the playground. The students seemed to be ganging up on her in hurtful ways. Frank redirected them through effective questioning. He asked, "How many know what it feels like to be a new kid in school?" Several students commented on their experience with this. Then Frank asked how many of them had taken the time to be her friend and tell her about school rules. No hands were raised. Frank turned to the new girl and asked her if students used bad language at her old school. She acknowledged that they did. Frank then asked how many would be willing to make friends with her and tell her about our rules. Many raised their hands. They then went back to the regular format, but the atmosphere was now very positive and helpful. The students decided a discussion was enough this time, because she didn't know about their rules.

In one eighth-grade class meeting it seemed obvious that the student being discussed felt he was being ganged up on. I asked the students, "How many of you would feel you were being helped if you were in Bill's position right now?" No one raised a hand. I then asked, "How many of you would feel you were being ganged up on if you were in Bill's position?" Most of them raised their hands. I then asked, "How many of you would be willing to imagine yourself in the other person's position when making comments and suggestions?" They all agreed they would and admitted it was funny they hadn't thought of that before.

Q: What if a problem involves a student from another class-room?

A: Many schools have class meetings at the same time so other students can be invited from one classroom to the next. Before inviting another student into your classroom, have the students discuss what it might feel like to be called into another room. Have them discuss what they can do to make sure the invited student feels the purpose is to help and not to hurt. In some classrooms, students brainstorm on positive things about the in-vited student so that they can start with compliments.

Stuart was invited into Mrs. Petersen's classroom because some students complained that he had stomped on their sand castle. They started by complimenting him for his achievements in sports and his leadership abilities. Mrs. Petersen then asked Stuart if he knew why he destroyed the sand castles. He explained that one time it was an accident and another time it was because the bell had rung anyway. Stuart was asked if he had any suggestions for solving the problem. He didn't. Someone suggested he be the sand castle patrol to make sure no one destroyed sand castles. Stuart and the class agreed unanimously with his suggestion.

Starting with compliments reduces defensiveness and inspires cooperation. Some classes start all problem solving by complimenting both parties involved on the positive things others appreciate about them.

Q: How do you stop tattletales from being on the agenda?

A: You don't. It is more helpful to change your perception. These are so often the kinds of problems that are real to students. Be grateful for every opportunity students have to practice their skills. If teachers censor agenda items, students will lose faith in the process. Also, when students use the class-meeting process, these problems lose their tattletale connotation because students are trying to solve them in helpful, rather than hurtful, ways.

Q: What do you do when a few students monopolize the agenda?

A: Put it on the agenda and let the students solve the problem. One teacher shared that she had this problem. Tommy was putting as many as ten items a day on the agenda. I suggested she put the problem on the agenda, but she discovered that another student already had. The class decided that each person could put one thing on the agenda each day. This teacher admitted that if she had tried to solve the problem herself, she would have allowed three to five items a day, but she liked the kids' solution much better.

Q: Can students put the teacher on the agenda if they have a complaint?

A: If teachers have captured the spirit of the class-meeting process, they will feel comfortable discussing their own mistakes as an opportunity to learn. This is excellent modeling for the students.

Frank Meder brought his students in to demonstrate a class meeting for a Positive Discipline in the Classroom workshop. An item on the agenda for discussion was that Frank had taken a bag of potato chips from a student during recess because of the school rule against eating on the playground. On the way back to the teachers' room, Frank had eaten some of the potato chips. The solution suggested (and the one he chose) was for Mr. Meder to buy the student another bag of potato chips—but he could eat half of them first, because the bag was only half full when he got it.

Another time, a student put Mr. Meder on the agenda for making a student run around the track for misbehaving during physical education. The students decided that this was punishment rather than a solution. They decided that Mr. Meder should run the track four times. Frank accepted their decision, but after running the track, he put it on the agenda and discussed that it was unfair for him to be required to run four times when the student had only had to run once. He used this as an opportunity to discuss how easy it is to get into revenge when punishment is involved.

Q: What do you do when children won't admit they did whatever they have been accused of?

A: Once an atmosphere of trust and helpfulness has been established, it is rare that students don't feel free to take responsibility for their actions. Before this atmosphere has been established, you might ask if anyone else in the class saw what happened. Some teachers have the students role-play what happened. The role-playing usually gets so humorous that everyone is laughing. This sometimes inspires the reluctant student to tell how it really happened.

You could take this opportunity to ask some questions about why students might feel reluctant to admit they did something, such as, "How many of you would want to admit you had done something if you thought other people might want to hurt you instead of help you?" "How many of you have had other people accuse you of doing something when you did not think you had done anything?" Many teachers have found it effective to ask the students if they would be willing to take the person's word that they didn't do it this time and put it on the agenda if it happens again.

Q: What do you do if students use the agenda as revenge? My students go to the agenda and if their name is on it, they put the person on the agenda who put them on.

A: This happens quite often before students learn and believe that the purpose of the agenda is to help one another rather than to "get" one another. Many teachers solve this problem by using a shoe box for the agenda. They have students write their problem on different-colored paper for different days of the week, so that they can tell which problems are the oldest. Meanwhile the teacher invites discussion about what can be done to increase trust. Another option is to have students put the problem on the agenda without any names. Then the students focus on solutions for a typical problem—no matter who is involved. This process helps students get used to the idea of focusing on solutions. Most teachers who use the shoe box at first start using the open agenda as soon as they feel their students are ready for it. Some teachers also have students put written compliments in the box. These written compliments are read before the oral compliments are given.

Q: What should I do about students gathering at the agenda on their way into the classroom after recess?

A: If students are gathering at the agenda when coming into the classroom, making it difficult to start lessons, have a rule that the agenda can be used only when leaving the classroom. Sometimes just waiting until the next recess is enough of a cooling-off period for the student to decide that something wasn't serious enough to put on the agenda. Some teachers start out with this rule and then later, when the students can handle this without being disruptive, they allow them to use the agenda anytime.

Q: Is it really necessary to have class meetings every day? I'm not having that many problems and hate to take so much time.

A: The main reason for having class meetings every day is to teach a process that allows students to practice social and life skills for good character. Many students do not really learn the process if there is a time span of a week between meetings. Several teachers have learned that having them every day can make the difference between success and failure. One teacher with a particularly difficult class was about to give up on class meetings until he started having them every day. He found that his students learned and trusted the process when it was done daily.

The atmosphere of his class changed because the students learned positive skills, which they continued to use throughout the day.

Another teacher said she hadn't been having class meetings because she had a very cooperative class and wasn't having problems. She tried to have a class meeting when a big problem came up and found that the class could not handle it because they had not learned the process. This teacher had not understood the importance of class meetings as a process to teach children skills that enable them to solve problems when they occur—and even more important, teaches them skills they can use every day of their lives.

Another elementary school teacher discovered that the reason his students weren't putting items on the agenda was that it took too long for items to come up when they had class meetings only once a week.

It is better to have class meetings every day at the elementary school level. If there are not any problems on the agenda, use the time after compliments for planning or discussing other issues.

Q: What if an item on the agenda involves a student who is absent?

A: If the absent student is the one who put the item on the agenda, cross it out and go on to the next item. If the absent student is involved in the problem, skip it, but leave it on the agenda as the first item to be discussed when the student returns. This reduces the possibility that absences are because of the agenda. However, if you suspect that students want to be absent because their name is on the agenda, this should be discussed in a class meeting so that the class can decide what they need to do to make sure people know they want to help one another, rather than hurt one another.

Q: What if parents object?

A: Invite them to come and observe. Very few parents object after they have seen the class meeting in action. Some students may feel they can get special attention from their parents by complaining about being picked on in class meetings. Even when students try to describe class meetings accurately, it can sound like a kangaroo court to parents. Express to parents that you can understand their concern and would probably feel the same way if you hadn't seen the process and the positive results in action. Some parents may come. Others will be reassured by your understanding and invitation. (I have included a letter to parents in Appendix III.)

If parents still object after visiting, or if they refuse to visit but still insist that their child cannot participate, arrange for their child to visit another classroom or the library during class meetings. One student complained to his mother who rushed to the school to "overprotect" her child. She insisted that he not participate. Her son later complained that he felt left out because he had to go to the library during class meetings.

Q: What if students don't want to participate?

A: Students should not have a choice in this matter, just as they do not have a choice regarding their participation in math. You might have a discussion about why people might not want to participate and how to improve the class meetings so everyone will want to participate.

Q: How do you enforce decisions?

A: It is not necessary for the teacher to enforce the decisions decided upon by individuals or the group. The students will be very aware of what happens, and if another student should "forget," he or she will be reminded, or it will go back on the agenda.

Q: Does the teacher or the students run the class meetings?

A: As soon as students are old enough, it is a good idea to have them take as much responsibility as possible. Many teachers rotate chairperson and secretarial duties. One student will be the chairperson for a week and will be in charge of the agenda and facilitate the class meeting. The secretary is the person responsible for writing down all suggestions and final decisions.

Q: How does this process work with kindergarten and first-grade children?

A: Great! I have visited many primary grades where the children were doing so well that I had to pinch myself to remember they were not really miniature sixth graders. They were using the same vocabulary and the same problem-solving skills.

Many preschools are now involving two-, three-, four-, and five-year-old children in class meetings. In *Positive Discipline for Preschoolers*[4] we share a story about a class trying to solve the problem of wood chips being thrown on the playground. The older children were making some excellent suggestions. When the beanbag came to two-and-a-half-year-old Cristina, she shared, "I had bananas on my cereal this morning." The teacher thanked her for sharing and the beanbag was passed to the next person. Even though Cristina did not yet understand the full purpose of class meetings, her participation was validated and she could feel significant. Meanwhile she was absorbing and learning from older children.

Younger children may need help putting their problems on

the agenda. Some primary teachers have the children come to them or an aide and dictate what they would like to put on the agenda. Others have the children write their name and draw a picture to remind them of their problem. In these early grades, half the problems are often solved because the child can't remember what happened by the time their name comes up on the agenda. A cooling-off period was all that was needed. Young children are quick to forget and forgive.

Also, younger children may need a little more direction and guidance, so the teacher may need to be more actively involved than with older children. At the beginning of each meeting, Mrs. Ater has her first-grade students recite the purposes:

1. To help one another
2. To solve problems

They then recite the three rules:

1. Don't bring any objects to the circle
2. Only one person can speak at a time
3. All six legs must be on the floor (two human and four chair).

OTHER SUGGESTIONS

Secret Pals

Some teachers like to use the Monday class meeting to have each student draw the name of a secret pal for the week. The Friday class meeting is then used for each student to guess who his or her secret pal was by sharing what nice things that secret pal did.

Some preliminary teaching is important for this to be effective. First, have the students brainstorm on things they could do for a secret pal, such as leaving nice notes, sharing something, helping, playing together, smiling and saying hello every day, or leaving a piece of candy in his desk. After several ideas have been listed on the board, have each student write down at least five that they would like to do. They can tape this list onto their desk and cross off an item after they have done it. This reduces the possibility that some students will be overlooked. This exercise has significantly increased positive feelings of friendship in many classrooms.

It could also be the job of each student to find something to compliment or acknowledge about his or her secret pal during class meetings. This can ensure that each student receives a compliment.

Classroom Rules

There are certain decisions students cannot be involved in, such as curriculum (unless you want to encourage them to talk to the adults who make those decisions). However, there are many areas where students could participate in decisions. When students are invited to participate and help make the decisions, they are more highly motivated to cooperate in the fulfillment of those decisions.

I am delighted to see how many teachers carry out this suggestion. Most classrooms have rules posted somewhere in the room. In classrooms where students brainstorm about what the rules should be, the rules have the heading "We Decided." The rules are almost identical to those posted by teachers without the input of children. Teachers who have tried both ways have noticed that cooperation and mutual respect improved when the students were involved in the rule discussion.

Many teachers have found that field trips are more successful if they are discussed first in a class meeting. Have the students discuss all the things that could go wrong on the field trip to make it a bad experience and decide on solutions to these potential problems. They can then discuss what they need to do to make it a pleasant trip.

Class meetings have also been helpful in making the substitute teacher's job easier. I often used this subject when first introducing students to class meetings. I would ask, "What kind of things do students do to 'bug a sub'?" They would give me a long list of things they did, such as switching names and seats and planning a timed book drop. Then I would ask them how a substitute might feel when being bugged. It is amazing how many students never consider the substitute's feelings. Their list would include feeling hurt, sad, or angry. I would then ask for ideas on how to make things pleasant for the substitute. It was always so gratifying to hear how thoughtful students could be when given the opportunity. Then I would ask how many would be willing to help instead of hurt. They would all agree. Many substitutes had commented on how pleasant it was to work in a classroom where students participated in regular class meetings.

How to End Class Meetings

When class meetings are effective, students often get so involved that they would like to continue beyond a reasonable time. This problem is eliminated if meetings are held just before lunch or recess. It is rare that students want to continue into lunchtime or recess time.

Things Often Get Worse Before They Get Better

Students quite often don't trust that adults are really willing to listen to them and take them seriously. It may take some time for them to get used to this. At first they may try to use this new power to be hurtful and punishing because this is the model they have been used to.

Keep your long-term goals in mind and maintain the courage

to be imperfect. Are there any students, no matter what their circumstances, who will not respond to being listened to and validated for their thoughts and ideas? Are there any students who will not benefit from learning to find nonpunitive solutions for problems? Are there any students who will not learn responsibility, accountability, and social responsibility when they know it is safe to be accountable for mistakes because they provide opportunities for learning instead of certain blame, shame, and pain through punishment? I don't think so.

Many teachers have been tempted to quit before they make it through the rough part. Some probably do. Those who "hang in there" express their delight with all the benefits for themselves and their students as things get smoother.

REVIEW

Class-Meeting Guidelines

1. Students sit in a circle, and the teacher sits in the circle at the same level. (In other words, if the students are on the floor, so is the teacher. If the students are sitting in chairs, so is the teacher—as opposed to standing and teaching.)
2. As soon as possible, students lead the meeting.
3. The student in charge will start the compliments by passing an item (such as a talking stick or beanbag) around the circle so every student has an opportunity to give a compliment, pass, or ask for a compliment.
4. The receiver of a compliment will say thank you.
5. The teacher or student in charge will handle the agenda and read off the next item to be discussed.
6. After the agenda item is read, the student who placed the item on the agenda can choose (a) sharing feelings while others listen, (b) discussion without fixing, or (c) asking for problem-solving help.

7. If the student asks for discussion without fixing or for problem-solving help, the item will be passed around the circle again for students to discuss without fixing, or to brainstorm for solutions. (Short comments are also encouraged.)

8. The teacher refrains from commenting on the students' suggestions (except to make sure students are giving suggestions—it may be necessary to say, "How could you turn that into a suggestion?"). When the item reaches the teacher, he or she can make a comment or suggestion—but only then.

9. Each suggestion is written in a notebook or on a flip chart by the teacher or, when possible, by students.

10. In most cases, the item will go around the circle twice to give children an opportunity to make a suggestion they didn't think of before listening to others. (This doesn't take as long as some fear.)

11. The student who put the problem on the agenda can choose the suggestion he or she thinks will be most helpful. When another student is involved, that student can also choose a solution. If the solutions conflict, the two students will be asked to get together in private to work out something that works for both of them. A vote will be taken only if the problem involves the whole class.

Six Reasons Class Meetings Fail

1. Not forming a circle
2. Not having class meetings on a regular basis (three to five times per week for elementary school)
3. Teacher censorship (judging concerns as tattling)
4. Not allowing time for students to learn nonpunitive problem-solving skills

5. Talking down to (patronizing) students instead of having faith in their abilities
6. Not passing an item (such as a talking stick) around the circle and allowing every student a chance to speak or pass.

Chapter Nine

FAMILY MEETINGS

When Jim and Betty married, they each brought three children to their newly blended family. The six children ranged in age from six to fourteen. Obviously, there were many adjustments to be made. Betty was employed outside the home. She really enjoyed her new family and was eager to get home to them after work—except for one problem. The first thing she would notice when she returned home was the mess. The children would come home from school and leave their books, sweaters, and shoes all over the house. To this they would add cookie crumbs, empty milk glasses, and toys. Betty would start nagging and cajoling. "Why can't you pick up your things? You know it upsets me. I enjoy being with you, but I get so angry when I see all this mess that I forget about the joy." The children would pick up their things, but by then Betty was upset and displeased with them and with herself.

Betty finally put the problem on the agenda for their weekly Monday-night family meeting. She admitted that it was her problem. It obviously didn't bother the children to have the house cluttered, but she asked if they would be willing to help her with her problem. The children felt the absence of blame and accusation and came up with a plan for a "safe-deposit box."

This was to be a big cardboard box they would put in the garage. The rule was that anything that was left in the common rooms, such as the living room, family room, and kitchen, could be picked up by anyone who saw it and put in the safe-deposit box. They also decided the item would have to stay there for a week before the owner could claim it. The plan worked beautifully. The clutter problem was taken care of, and the safe-deposit box was jammed with things. However, it caused some other problems, which tested the plan. If they hadn't stuck to the rules, the whole thing would have been ineffective. For instance, twelve-year-old David lost his school shoes. He looked everywhere and then remembered the safe-deposit box. Sure enough, that is where they were.

David wore his smelly old tennis shoes to school, but the next day he lost those. He didn't have any other shoes, but the children insisted he couldn't take them out for a week. David turned to his mother, who wisely said, "I'm sorry. I don't know what you are going to do, but I have to stick by the rules, too." His helpful siblings finally came up with the solution of his bedroom slippers. David didn't have a better idea, so he wore his slippers to school for three days. After that week, he never left his shoes out again.

Then David's sister, eight-year-old Susan, lost her coat. It was very difficult for her mom and dad to stay out of these situations. After all, what kind of parents let their children go to school in their slippers and outside without a coat when the weather was cold? They decided to forget about what other people might think and let Susan handle the problem by herself, as David had. Susan wore two sweaters to school for a week.

Jim also "lost" some ties, a sport coat, and magazines. The enlightening thing to Betty was how many of her own things disappeared into the safe-deposit box. She realized how much easier it was to see the clutter of others than to see her own.

This plan worked because of the following concepts.

- The problem was shared in a family meeting. The children created the solution.
- Mom and Dad did not take over responsibility when problems arose in carrying out the family's decision.
- The children enforced the rules because Mom and Dad stayed out of it.
- The rules applied to everyone in the family, including Mom and Dad.

Another family solved the same problem in almost the same way. In a family meeting, they decided on different rules for what they called the "disappear box." Anyone who lost an item could retrieve it any time they wanted it, but they had to put a dime in the "party jar." When the jar filled up with dimes, which it did frequently, they would use the money for a family party of ice cream or pizza. Another family called the box the "black hole" and people could claim their items at the end of the weekly family meeting.

Parents can avoid many hassles with their children by suggesting that problems be put on the family-meeting agenda so that they can be solved—after a cooling-off period. As with class meetings, the fact that involving children in meetings eliminates so many discipline hassles is a fringe benefit. The primary benefit is that children have opportunities to develop strength in the Significant Seven Perceptions and Skills (see page 6). They have the opportunity to learn and practice their problem-solving skills as a family on a weekly basis, and most families find that the weekly practice carries on during the week.

Family meetings can also be a successful method for enhancing family cooperation and closeness. They provide an opportunity to enhance family values and traditions. Their success, of course, depends on the same adult attitudes and skills that have been explained in previous chapters.

Chapter eight on class meetings should be read by parents: many of the concepts important for successful class meetings work for family meetings, and the format for family meetings is essentially the same as class meetings, except for six important differences.

HOW FAMILY MEETINGS DIFFER FROM CLASS MEETINGS

1. Family meetings should be held once a week rather than once a day. After a time has been decided upon for family meetings, nothing should interfere. If friends call, tell them you will call back later. (We unplug the phone.) Do not skip a family meeting because you are busy or have something else to do. Your children will follow your lead in determining the importance of family meetings. Once the tradition has been effectively established, everyone will look forward to this opportunity for family togetherness—until they become teenagers. (More about this later.)

2. Decisions should be made by consensus. If the family cannot come to a decision by consensus on an agenda item, it should be tabled until the next meeting, when it is likely that a consensus will be reached because of the additional cooling-off period and time to think of new ideas. A majority vote in a family meeting would accentuate a family division. Convey an attitude of faith in your family that you can work together to find solutions that are respectful to everyone.

3. Family meetings should include a review of the next week's activities. This is especially important as the children grow older and become involved in many activities, such as babysitting, sports, dates, lessons, and so on. Coordinating the calendar for car use and mutual convenience can be essential.

4. Family meetings should not end without planning a family fun activity during the coming week.
5. End the meeting by doing something together as a family. You might want to play a game together, pop corn, take turns making and serving desserts. Do not watch TV unless there is a program that the whole family looks forward to. If you do watch a TV program, be sure to end by turning off the TV and having a family discussion about what values (or lack thereof) were portrayed, and how this might apply in your lives.
6. Sitting at a cleared table is conducive to staying on task for problem solving. The table does not seem to be the barrier for families that desks are in a classroom. Sitting informally in a living room can also work, but it seems difficult to stay on task if a family meeting is part of dinnertime.

COMPONENTS OF THE FAMILY MEETING

Chairperson

This job should rotate. Children love to be the chairperson and can do a very good job after they reach the age of four or five. It is the chairperson's responsibility to call the meeting to order, start the compliments, begin the problem-solving sessions, and start the "talking stick" around the circle so everyone has a turn to voice an opinion or make a suggestion.

Secretary

This job should also rotate among members of the family who are able to write. The secretary keeps notes of problems discussed and decisions made. (Reading old family-meeting journals can be as much fun as looking at picture albums.)

Compliments

Begin every family meeting by having each person give every other member of the family a compliment. This may be awkward at first if the children have the habit of putting one another down. If this is the case, spend some time discussing the kinds of things they could look for to compliment one another about. Parents can model this behavior by beginning with compliments for each member of the family. Also, if you see something nice going on between the children, remind them to remember it for a compliment. You might even suggest that they write it on the agenda so they will remember.

Mrs. Stover shared the following incident that occurred when her family began giving compliments in their family meetings. Six-year-old Tammy volunteered to go first. She complimented her mom and her dad with joy and ease. When she came to her nine-year-old brother, Marcus, she paused and said, "This is really hard." Mr. and Mrs. Stover encouraged her to do it anyway. She finally thought of something she could compliment Marcus for, then added, "But he is also mean to me."

Her parents reminded her, "No buts." When it was Marcus's turn, he was not any more enthusiastic about complimenting Tammy, but he did it. Mrs. Stover said that now they compliment each other with ease and added, "It is wonderful to hear siblings saying nice things about each other when their pattern had been nothing but put-downs."

One summer our family got so busy that we did not follow my advice to not let anything interfere with regular family meetings. We stopped having them. It was a wonderful lesson for us because we felt the difference and learned again the importance of family meetings. Bickering and discipline hassles increased tremendously. The kids started insulting one another more often. Finally, I "got it" and called for a family meeting. The kids had been so mean to one another that I thought they would have difficulty giving one another compliments. However, their years of training came back to them and they gave one another very nice compliments. As we continued regular family meetings the insults decreased significantly, as did bickering and discipline hassles.

Gratitude

We alternate between compliments and sharing what we are grateful for. Having each family member share one thing he or she is grateful for helps us remember and appreciate so much that we usually take for granted.

The Agenda

The refrigerator seems to be the most popular place for family meeting agendas; it is so simple to use a magnet to hang a piece of paper on the front or side. I wish we had kept all those sheets of paper, so I now suggest you use three-hole punched paper and keep them in a family meeting album.[1]

Discuss agenda items in chronological order, so that a decision does not need to be made about which item is the most important.

Problem Solving

Discuss focusing on solutions with the children as outlined in chapter six. The Three R's and an H of Focusing on Solutions can be used to solve many problems in family meetings, just as in class meetings. In family meetings, however, solutions must be agreed upon by consensus. It is important to go beyond consequences in family meetings too. Many families have shared that power struggles were decreased significantly when they stopped trying to think of a consequence for every problem, and instead focused on solutions.

Planning Activities

Family members are more willing to cooperate when they have participated equally in planning events they will all enjoy. Weekly activities and vacations are more successful when the whole family participates in a discussion of possible conflicts and how to avoid them. The following article written by my husband, Barry Nelsen, provides an excellent example.

"Let's take the kids to Hawaii," my wife said.

"Are you kidding? They will make life miserable for all of us," I replied.

Little did I know that six weeks later I would return from one of my most enjoyable family outings in many years. The reason for the success of this trip was family meetings.

We have family meetings every Sunday night. Each member of the family is treated with respect, and every opinion is heard and discussed.

During a family meeting several weeks before our trip to Hawaii, I told the kids that Mom and I were going to Hawaii soon, and asked if they would like to go with us. Pandemonium broke loose. After we convinced them to calm down, Mom said, "If we take you to Hawaii, it needs to be fun for Dad and me, too. If you fight with each other, or argue about every little thing we ask you to do, it won't be fun for us."

The kids promised to be angels! I had heard that before, and knew we needed more than promises. We decided to brainstorm and list the things that make life miserable for parents on vacation with kids.

"What about things that make life miserable for kids?"

Mark interrupted. I squelched my "Don't be a smart aleck" response, and we all agreed that was a fair question. Mom listed the potential problems in two columns: hassles for parents, and hassles for kids.

The parent hassle list included begging for money, eating nothing but junk food, fighting with each other, arguing with us, not picking up their stuff, not carrying their own bags, running off without telling us where they are going, staying up too late, and not wanting to go to some of the places we want to go. The kid hassle list included eating at fancy restaurants, wearing fancy clothes, both sleeping in the same bed, not enough money, being told what they can or can't buy, and not getting a window seat on the airplane. The agreed-upon solutions were that the kids would save as much money as they could; we would add a specific amount (and no more); they would divide the total amount by seven days and have us give them that amount every day; we would not tell them how to spend their money and would not give them any more when it was gone; they agreed to be responsible for their own luggage and wouldn't pack more than they wanted to carry; Mark would take a sleeping bag and sleep on the floor if the only other choice was one bed for the two of them; they would eat at McDonald's when we ate at nicer restaurants; they would take turns at a window seat during takeoff and landing; they agreed not to fight and to always let us know where they were going.

"What happens if you forget and start to fight?" I asked.

"How about giving us a secret signal?" Mark suggested.

"Good idea," Mom said. "If we hear you fighting, we'll pull our earlobes to give you a silent reminder that you agreed not to fight."

"That goes for you, too, Dad," Mark chimed in.

"What do you mean by that?" I asked indignantly.

"When you start to lose your temper with me or Mary, is it okay if I pull on my ear to signal you?"

That little wise guy, I thought. But then I reflected and agreed. "Good idea, Son."

A week before we left, and three meetings later, our lists had grown. There was an atmosphere of excitement and cooperation throughout the family. The kids were getting ahead in their schoolwork, and money was being saved diligently.

One of the first conflicts came when Mark wanted to take his skateboard along. I explained all the problems it might cause on crowded Waikiki streets, the difficulty he would have carrying it along with his baggage. Since a feeling of cooperation had been established, he agreed to leave it home without arguing.

The two-hour drive to San Francisco to catch the plane turned out to be three hours. Mary started to whine about being thirsty while we were in a traffic jam on the Bay Bridge. When Mark reminded her that we had already talked about this sort of hassle, she quickly decided she could wait until we got to the airport. Another victory for family meetings!

The hotel room in Honolulu had two double beds. We were glad we had taken Mark's sleeping bag to avoid arguments.

Thanks to family meetings, we had a great time! There were a few hassles, but they were solved quickly with reminders of our agreements. The kids got lost once. We had a family meeting to decide how to avoid that possibility in the future. We decided we would go back to the last place we had seen each other together, and wait for the others to come back and find us. The kids also memorized our hotel's name and address so they would have that information for a police officer if they got lost again.

The closeness we felt as a family was an even greater experience than the trip to Hawaii. Two weeks after we got home, our oldest son called from Florida to say he was getting married in two months. "Let's take the kids," I said.

Planning for Family Fun

Planning weekly family fun activities is an important part of family meetings, but it is an area neglected by many families. It is so easy to think about how nice it would be to have a happy family that does fun and exciting things together. The catch is that so many families hope it will "just happen" without any effort on their part. It doesn't happen unless you do something to make it happen. To make it happen you must "plan and do."

Our family used the "Fun Things to Do" sheets (described on page 228) for planning and doing a family activity as follows: We decided that every Saturday night would be date night. The first Saturday, Mom and Mark did something together, while Dad and Mary were together. The first Saturday of the next month, we switched so that Mom and Mary spent special time together, while Dad and Mark had their special time. The second and fourth Saturdays of the month were date nights for Mom and Dad alone. The third Saturday we all did something together as a family.

Discussion of Chores

Discuss chores at a family meeting so that children can help solve the problems of getting them done. They are more cooperative when they can voice their feelings and be part of the planning and choosing.

At one family meeting, we listed all the chores done by Mom and Dad (including full-time employment) in an effort to eliminate "How come I have to do everything?" whenever we asked one of our children to do something. We then asked them to brainstorm to come up with a list of all the chores that could be done by children. We chimed in with all the things we could think of that they forgot. Still, their list wasn't nearly as long as ours. When they saw the comparison between what we ask of them and what we do, they were impressed. We then put the chores they could do on slips of paper that could be drawn from a jar each week. Each child drew four chores each week. There was a new drawing every week so that one child was never stuck with the same chore, such as the garbage, all the time.

This is not a magic solution. We find that the problem of getting chores done is put on our agenda at least once a month. I call it the "three-week syndrome." The first week, the kids usually enthusiastically follow the chore plan they helped create. The second week, they do their chores, but with less enthusiasm. By the third week they start complaining. That is our clue that chores should go on the family-meeting agenda again.

After one of my lectures, a woman came up to me and said, "We tried a family meeting once, and the kids did their chores for about a week. But then they stopped, so I didn't think it worked very well."

I asked, "Have you found anything else that motivates your kids to do their chores for a whole week?"

She said, "Well, no."

I said, "Sounds like a success to me. I suggest you keep doing it." I then told her about our three-week syndrome. Even though we need to keep working on it, we feel we get much greater cooperation by handling the problem through family meetings than any other way we have tried. We achieve great responsibility for a while. When it starts to slack off, we put it on the agenda.

The kids often come up with a new plan. For a while they enjoyed using a chore wheel that they made from a paper plate with pictures of chores around the edge and a brad in the middle to fasten a spinner. They would spin for a few chores each week. Later they each enjoyed making a chore chart with pockets across the top for "undone" chores, and pockets across the bottom for "done" chores. They seemed to get a sense of accomplishment when they could move a chore card to the "done" row.

Dealing with the problem of chores every three or four weeks is far preferable to hassling over them every day. My last two (of seven) children came up with a chore plan that worked for over six months instead of just three weeks. When they started to complain after the six-month period, they found a solution that worked for more than a year.

They decided that I should put two major chores for each of them on the white board near our phone. During the negotiation time, I wanted a rule that they should do these chores right after school. They wanted the freedom to choose the time of completion so long as the chores were done before they went to bed. I asked, "What happens if you don't do them before you go to bed?" They agreed that it would be a reasonable consequence for me to circle their name on the white board and then they would have to do all four chores the next day right after school. For six months this worked very well. Once in a while I would have to circle a name, and they would then do all four chores the next day right after school.

After six months, however, they both started to complain, asking, "How come he (or she) gets all the easy chores?" I had spent a lot of time trying to be fair by rotating the chores, but not from their point of view. I was so proud of myself that instead of lecturing about my fairness, I simply put the problem on the agenda. Their solution was so simple and so profound, I don't know why I didn't think of it sooner. It would have saved me a lot of work. Mark said, "Why don't you just put four chores on the board and first come first served." Once again I was reminded of what great solutions they can come up with when we give them a chance.

The first week they set their alarms to try beating each other to choose what they thought to be the easiest chores. However, that didn't last long. Soon they decided sleep was more important than easier chores, so the one who got to the board later accepted his or her fate with grace.

SOME SPECIAL CHALLENGES

Small Children

Some families find that children under four years of age are disruptive during the problem-solving part of family meetings. In my own family, we used to wait until babies and toddlers were in bed to have family meetings.

As soon as the children were old enough, we included them for some parts of the family meeting. Three-year-old children love to participate in a game of Hide the Button or Hide-and-Seek followed by dessert. They can even learn to give compliments. By the age of four, children are wonderfully creative at problem solving and are ready for full participation.

Teenagers

Power struggles and revenge cycles have often become well established in many homes by the time children become teenagers. Family meetings can change these patterns dramatically, but it takes special groundwork to get them established. The first requirement is enough humility from parents to admit that what they have been doing (being too controlling or too permissive) has not been working. The second step is to admit this to the teenagers.

Mr. Lyon shared how he won his teenagers over. He told them, "I have really been going down the wrong path with you guys. I have yelled at you about cooperating when what I really meant was 'Do it my way.' No wonder you didn't want to. I admire your perceptiveness in not falling for that. I would really like to start over, and I need your help. I've heard about the effectiveness of family meetings, where families sit down together and solve problems with mutual respect for the validity of everyone's opinions. I'll need your help to remind me when I start my old, controlling habits."

Mr. Lyon's teenagers were stunned speechless by this new behavior on the part of their father. Mr. Lyon was wise enough to add quickly, "I know this is really new to you. Why don't you think about it and let me know tomorrow if you would be willing to work with me on this."

Mr. Lyon charmingly shared with his parent study group, "How could they resist?" They couldn't. Mr. Lyon continued to share many wonderful experiences he had in his family meetings and how much he was now enjoying his teenagers—hassles and all.

It is interesting how often kids seem to want the opposite of what they have. Mr. Lyon's kids were happy to start family meetings as something new. When my kids became teenagers they started to complain about family meetings. Family meetings were old news to them. We put their complaints on the agenda, such as the meetings lasting too long. We agreed to take no longer than fifteen minutes.

One day Mary, the most frequent complainer, came home from an overnight visit with a friend and announced, "Wow, that family has problems. They should have family meetings." When Mary went to college, she had family meetings with her roommates.

Even though I had taught child development at a community college for ten years, I forgot about the individuation (rebellion) process that is normal and healthy for teenagers. How else are they going to discover who they want to be than to test all the values of their parents? I forgot about this normal testing period because my last two children (who were raised on Positive

Discipline) were so wonderful before they became teenagers. They had developed self-discipline, responsibility, and problem-solving skills. They weren't perfect (neither was I) but they were so willing to cooperate as we learned from our mistakes.

When my youngest children started their teenage individuation process I panicked. (I should mention that children who have learned confidence and self-reliance often feel free to flaunt their rebellion instead of being sneaky about it.) I have to admit that I worried about what people would think about me. I was ready to throw Positive Discipline out the window and go back to control and punishment. Actually, I tried that for a short time and created a real mess of power struggles and hurt feelings. Fortunately, I came to my senses and realized that my children were more important than my ego. I teamed up with Lynn Lott and went to work on the book *Positive Discipline for Teenagers.*[2] This got me back on track to find ways to work kindly, firmly, and respectfully with my teenagers, and to find ways to empower them—and myself—in the process.

Single Parents

It is a myth that children are deprived if they don't have two parents. Many great people have been raised by a single parent. Single-parent families simply provide different opportunities. In our book *Positive Discipline for Single Parents*[3] we make a plea for people to stop referring to single-parent homes as "broken homes." They are not broken, they are just different.

A parent's attitude is very important. If you feel guilty about your children having only a single full-time parent, they will sense that a tragedy is taking place and will act accordingly. If you accept the fact that you are doing the best you can under the circumstances and are moving toward success rather than failure, children will sense this and act accordingly.

The family-meeting process is equally effective for single-parent families. A family can consist of one parent and one child or one parent and several children. Family meetings are a good way to convey positive feelings to children and to get them involved in solutions rather than manipulation.

Mrs. Doherty and Mrs. Latimer are single parents of one child each, who all live together. They shared that they could not have survived without their weekly family meetings. Once a week they were able to talk about and solve all the problems that are typical between roommates, as well as those between parents and children and siblings.

SPICING UP FAMILY MEETINGS[4]

For many families, weekly meetings are a family tradition, providing children with a sense of well-being, self-confidence, significance, and belonging. They also provide family fun, mutual respect, problem-solving experiences, and happy memories.

Your family may enjoy some of the following activities to add variety and spice to your family meetings. Create a family-meeting album using a three-ring binder with a clear plastic cover where you can insert a family photo. This album is a place where you can place family-meeting agendas, lists of brainstormed suggestions and the chosen solutions, and the sheets from the following activities.

Family Mottos

Your family can create closeness and have a great time discussing family mottos. You might want to choose a different motto every month and make them more meaningful through the suggested activities. Several examples are included. You may want to use some of these and/or create your own.

Sample Mottos

1. One for all and all for one.
2. We love and support one another.
3. Anything worth doing is worth doing for the fun of it.
4. If it helps just one person, it is worth doing.
5. Mistakes are wonderful opportunities to learn.
6. We are good finders.
7. We are problem solvers.
8. We look for solutions rather than blame.
9. We have an attitude of gratitude.
10. We count our blessings every day.

Family-Meeting Motto Activities

1. Have the whole family choose a motto for the month.
2. Week One: Give each family member a blank family motto sheet. Ask all family members to think about the motto during the week and to write down their thoughts about what it means to them. (Set up special times to take dictation from children who are too young to write.)
3. Week Two: Plan time during the family meeting for all family members to share what they wrote. Place all these sheets in a family-meeting binder. Pass out another blank motto sheet and invite everyone to find some time during the week to draw a picture that represents what the motto means to them. You might want to plan a special time when everyone does this together.
4. Week Three: Plan time during the family meeting for all family members to share their picture and talk about it. Place the pictures on the refrigerator or some other place where everyone can enjoy them. Ask everyone to notice

how they apply the family motto in action during the
following week.

5. Week Four: Plan time during the family meeting for all
   family members to share an example of how they used
   the family motto in action. Invite family members to be
   thinking about another motto to begin the next month.

6. Week One of the Next Month: Put all the drawings of
   the last motto in the binder. Choose another motto, and
   repeat the process described above.

Gratitude Pages

An attitude of gratitude does not come naturally. It must be
learned. Regular practice and sharing will help all family members develop an attitude of gratitude.

Family-Meeting Gratitude Activity

1. At the end of each family meeting, pass out a blank
   "gratitude page." Encourage family members to put the
   page in a place where they can access it easily and write
   down the things for which they are grateful.

2. Allow time during family meetings (or meals) for people
   to share the things for which they are grateful.

3. During each family meeting, collect the gratitude pages
   and place them in the family-meeting binder.

Compliments Pages

You can create a positive atmosphere in your family when everyone learns to look for the good in one another and to verbalize
positive comments. Please don't expect perfection. Some sibling
squabbling is normal. However, when children (and parents)
learn to give and receive compliments, negative tension is re-

duced considerably. Of course, a positive atmosphere is increased even more when families have regular family meetings to find solutions to problems.

Family-Meeting Compliment Activity

1. Place blank compliment sheets on the refrigerator (or another spot) where everyone can write down compliments for others each day. (Young children can dictate their compliments to older members of the family.)
2. When you see that someone deserves a compliment, write it down, or ask a child who also observed something someone else did, "Would you like to write that on our compliment sheet?" Once children develop the habit of noticing compliments, they won't need reminders.
3. At the beginning of each family meeting, family members can read their compliments.
4. Ask for any verbal compliments that were not written down.
5. Make sure every family member receives at least one compliment.
6. Place the compliment sheet in the family-meeting binder, and place another blank sheet on the refrigerator to be filled out during the week.

Family Fun Pages

Many families do not spend enough time together doing fun things. Often, we have good intentions, but we don't take the time to plan and schedule events on a calendar.

The first step in planning is to give each member of the family a sheet of paper with the following headings:

FUN THINGS TO DO

	Together as a Family	Husband and Wife	Alone
free	_____	_____	_____
	_____	_____	_____
	_____	_____	_____
	_____	_____	_____
	_____	_____	_____
for $	_____	_____	_____
	_____	_____	_____
	_____	_____	_____
	_____	_____	_____

Family-Meeting Fun-Things-to-Do Activity

1. During a family meeting use a "fun things to do" sheet for a brainstorming session with the whole family under the "Together as a Family Column." See how many ideas you can come up with that the family can do together—free things to do and things that cost money.
2. Give a sheet to all family members so they can continue to list things they think of during the week, not only for the whole family, but things to do alone. Husband and wife can also work on their list. Have all family members work on their sheets for at least a week so that they have plenty of time to add everything they can think of.
3. If you have a bunch of magazines, let family members cut out pictures to paste onto their fun-things-to-do pages.
4. During family meetings, use your lists to let the family choose something to place on the calendar. Decide which days or nights of the week or month you can set aside for family fun. Decide when you can spend money and how much, and when you should plan free things.

Then work for a consensus as to which of the fun things you want to do on each of the designated days or nights for the next three months. Plot each decision on the calendar.

5. Follow your planned calendar.

Family-Meeting Mistakes-and-What-I-Learned Activity

Teach children that mistakes are wonderful opportunities for learning. Periodically, give each family member a "mistakes and what I learned" sheet. Ask each person to use the sheet to record a mistake and what they learned from it and be ready to read it at the next family meeting. (You can take dictation from children four and over who can't write yet. Under four is too young for this activity.) Set up the mistakes-and-what-I-learned sheet as follows:

MISTAKES AND WHAT I LEARNED

Mistake	What I Learned	What I'll Do in the Future
_____	_____	_____
_____	_____	_____
_____	_____	_____
_____	_____	_____
_____	_____	_____

Be sure to save these sheets in your family meeting album. Can you imagine what fun your children will have reading these when they are adults?

FAMILY MEAL PLANNING

The family meal provides an excellent opportunity to teach co-operation and contribution. Even small children can take a turn cooking a simple meal such as soup and toasted cheese sandwiches, a vegetable, lettuce salad, and Jell-O.

Family-Meeting Meal-Planning Activity

1. Bring magazines that contain recipes to the family
   meeting. Let children (and parents) choose new recipes
   they might want to try. (It can be fun to make a family
   cookbook by cutting out the recipes and pictures and
   putting them in a binder. Family members might first
   want to rate the recipes for taste and save only the ones
   that receive a high rating.)
2. Use 3 × 5 cards for recipes. On the back of the recipe,
   write all the ingredients needed from the store. (Save
   these cards in a special index-card box so they can be
   used over and over.)
3. During the family meeting, use a "family meal
   planning" page to get every family member involved in
   planning the meals for a week with the following
   headings:

FAMILY MEAL PLANNING

	Cook	Main dish	Vegetable	Salad	Dessert
Mon.					
Tues.					
Wed.					
Thurs.					
Fri.					
Sat.					
Sun.					

Under the "cook" column, write the name of the
person who will cook each day of the week. That person
will choose a main dish, vegetable, salad, and dessert.
(Of course you can change this form in any way that
suits your family.)

4. On shopping day, take the whole family to the grocery store. Children who are old enough can take a basket and find all the ingredients listed on the back of one or two recipe cards. Younger children can help an older sibling or parent find the ingredients from other recipe cards.

REVIEW

Holding regular family meetings is one of the most valuable things you can do as a family. Why? Family meetings provide an opportunity to teach children valuable social and life skills for good character. They will learn:

- Listening skills
- Brainstorming skills
- Problem-solving skills
- Mutual respect
- The value of cooling off before solving a problem
- Concern for others
- Cooperation
- Accountability in a safe environment
- How to choose solutions that are respectful to everyone concerned
- A sense of belonging and significance
- Social responsibility
- That mistakes are wonderful opportunities for learning.

Family meetings provide an opportunity for parents to:

- Avoid power struggles by respectfully sharing control
- Avoid micromanaging children, so children learn self-discipline
- Listen in ways that invite children to listen

• Respectfully share responsibility
• Create good memories through a family tradition
• Model all of the skills they want their children to learn.

If parents really understood the value of family meetings, it would be their most valuable parenting tool—and they would make every effort to schedule fifteen to thirty minutes a week for family meetings.

Positive Discipline Tools

1. Family meetings.
2. Focus on solutions.
3. The "safe-deposit box" for clutter.
4. Involving children in creating solutions and family rules.
5. Stick to the rules. Avoid rescuing.
6. Show faith in your children to deal with problems.
7. Use consensus for family solutions.
8. Schedule family fun time on the calendar.
9. Find solutions, with children, to typical problems in advance.
10. When solutions don't work, put the problem back on the agenda.
11. Use a variety of chore plans to motivate kids.
12. Have faith in teens while they go through their individuation process.
13. Tools for spicing up family meetings.
14. Regular family sharing of mistakes and what family members learned from them.
15. Plan and share cooking and cleanup responsibilities.

Questions

1. What are some of the basic concepts and adult attitudes that are important for family meetings to be successful?
2. What are some of the skills children will learn by participating in family meetings?
3. What are six differences between family meetings and class meetings, and why should they be different?
4. What is the value of having every person compliment every other member of the family?
5. What is the value of having children share what they are grateful for?
6. What are the four concepts that contributed to the success of the safe-deposit-box plan?
7. How can your family achieve a hassle-free vacation?
8. What is the best way to teach children cooperation and responsibility regarding chores?
9. Why is it just as important for single-parent families to have family meetings?
10. What are some of the benefits you might realize from trying the "Fun Things to Do" activity? Discuss.
11. What are the spicing-up-family-meetings activities? Which do you find most interesting? What benefits for your family do you see in each activity?
12. How do family meetings help children and adults achieve each of the items in the lists on pages 231 and 232?

Chapter Ten

PERSONALITY: HOW YOURS
AFFECTS THEIRS

In chapter four, you learned about the mistaken goals of children. Adults also have mistaken goals. They are called lifestyle priorities. Just as children are not consciously aware of their mistaken goals, adults may not be aware of their lifestyle priorities. These hidden priorities can lead to adult misbehavior that has an impact on children. Before we go into more details about adult lifestyle priorities, let's take a look at some homes to see what they look like in real life, and how they affect children.

It is bedtime at the Jasper home. Bedtime routines are too much bother for Mrs. Jasper, who has a comfort lifestyle priority; she would rather wait until the children fall asleep on the floor and carry them to bed than create stress for herself by arguing. She prefers avoiding emotional pain and stress in life, and thinks that avoiding bedtime conflict is one way to keep things comfortable.

Mr. Jasper, however, does not agree. He has a control lifestyle priority; he believes it is important for the children to have a schedule and he is willing to take responsibility for it. When he is in charge, he walks the children through every step of their routine, making sure they are in their pajamas, have their teeth thoroughly brushed, and are in bed by 7:30 P.M. He believes that being in control of himself, of situations, or of others is a way to avoid humiliation and criticism.

The Jaspers act differently in situations that appear potentially challenging to them. Their differing syles are confusing to their children and often motivate testing and misbehavior. Parents with a comfort lifestyle priority want to avoid pain and stress. While avoiding their perceptions of pain and stress, these parents may not help their children learn limits and organization. Their children may develop the belief that they can always do their own thing and don't have to abide by any rules of social responsibility. Parents with a control lifestyle priority believe they can avoid criticism and humiliation by being in control (sometimes of situations, sometimes of themselves, and sometimes of others). They may be too strict and don't take time to involve their children in creating limits. Some children feel thwarted and decide to rebel. Other children may give in and decide they always need to please others to get love.

What is a lifestyle priority? Where does it come from? How does it relate to parenting styles and what impact do they have on children? Before answering these questions, let's peek into the Sanchez home and look at two more lifestyle priorities.

It's bedtime in the Sanchez home, too. Mrs. Sanchez believes it is good for children to be in bed on time and tries to convince her children by lecturing them about their responsibility to do what is "right." She is constantly frustrated that her children don't take her wisdom (lectures) seriously. They hardly listen while she talks. What an insult! Mrs. Sanchez has a superiority lifestyle priority. Meaninglessness is the one thing in life she wants to avoid, and she believes doing things "right" is one way to make life meaningful.

Mr. Sanchez has a very different approach. He just wants his children to be happy and bedtime to be easy. He has a pleasing lifestyle priority, and to make things pleasant, he tries "loving" his children into bed. He plays games with them to get them

into their pajamas and to brush their teeth. He reads them stories; he fetches glass after glass of water and returns for endless
"last" hugs. He feels he can win their love and avoid rejection by
making bedtime fun and by doing what he thinks will please the
children.

Mr. and Mrs. Sanchez, too, are very different and invite lots
of testing from their children. Parents with a superiority lifestyle
priority don't realize that their need to be right, in order to avoid
meaninglessness and unimportance, invites their children to feel
inadequate. How can they ever live up to their parents' high ex-
pections? These children may become depressed and give up, or
they may decide to excel at great cost to their sense of being
loved unconditionally. Parents with a pleasing lifestyle want to
avoid rejection. However, their efforts to please may invite their
children to take advantage and decide, "I belong only when others are taking care of me and giving me whatever I want."

These are extreme examples. However, most parents can recognize a few of their tendencies, which illustrate the concept of
lifestyle priorities. What a challenge it can be to unravel all the
actions and interactions of family members with very different
personalities, beliefs, and private logic. Knowledge and awareness can help.

In previous chapters we've spent a great deal of time looking
at the decisions that shape children's behavior. In this chapter we
will focus on how children are affected by adult decisions and
behaviors, originally defined by a theory called lifestyle priorities, developed by Israeli Adlerian psychologist Nira Kefir. It is
important for parents and teachers to know how their lifestyle
choices influence their parenting and teaching styles, and thus,
the lifestyle choices of their children.

There are assets and liabilities to each style that affect how we
interact with our children. With understanding, we can learn to
build on the assets and avoid getting hooked into the liabilities

of our style (at least some of the time). But the first step is to understand.

WHAT ARE LIFESTYLE PRIORITIES?

You have accumulated a wealth of subconscious decisions from childhood that combine to form your lifestyle priority. Right now your children are developing theirs. Lifestyle priorities do not describe who you are. They do represent the decisions you have made throughout your life that affect the way you attempt to find a sense of belonging and significance.

Adults actually form both a primary and a secondary lifestyle priority. The information in this chapter will help you identify your primary priority (what you may do when feeling insecure or threatened about your sense of belonging and significance in the world) and your secondary priority (your usual behaviors when you are feeling secure).

Most people want to claim the assets of each priority and reject the liabilities. For example, most people like to have some control of their lives and dislike criticism and humiliation. However, criticism and humiliation are more difficult for a person with the control lifestyle priority to endure than they are for people with the other priorities. It is a matter of degree. A person with a control lifestyle priority believes that the best way to avoid humiliation is to maintain control. Remember, this is a personal belief, not reality. Another person may laugh at a situation that would seem humiliating to someone with a control lifestyle priority. It is a matter of perception. It is important to note that controlling others is usually not the focus of people with a control lifestyle priority. They want to have control of themselves and the situation to feel secure. However, it is easy for children to interpret this as control over them—and may invite rebellion. During one Positive Discipline workshop a parent slapped her

TABLE 10.1 THE FOUR LIFESTYLE PRIORITIES: COMFORT, CONTROL, PLEASING, AND SUPERIORITY

Priority	Worst fear	Believes the way to avoid the worst fear is to:	Assets	Liabilities	Unknowingly invites from others	Creates then complains about
COMFORT	Emotional and physical pain and stress; expectations from others; being cornered by others	Seek comfort; ask for special service; make others comfortable; choose the easiest way	Easygoing; few demands; minds own business; peacemaker; mellow; empathetic; predictable	Doesn't develop talents; limits productivity; avoids personal growth	Annoyance; irritation; boredom; impatience	Diminished productivity; impatience; lack of personal growth
CONTROL	Humiliation; criticism; the unexpected	Control self and/or others and/or situation	Leadership; organized; productive; persistent; assertive; follows rules	Rigid; doesn't develop creativity, spontaneity, or social closeness	Rebellion; resistance; challenge; frustration	Lack of friends and closeness; feeling uptight
PLEASING	Rejection; abandonment; hassles	Please others; active—demand approval passive—evoke pity	Friendly; considerate; compromises; nonaggressive; volunteers	Doesn't check with others about what pleases them; doesn't take care of self	Pleasure at first and then demands for approval and reciprocation	Lack of respect for self and others; resentment
SUPERIORITY	Meaninglessness; unimportance	Do more; be better than others; be right; be more useful; be more competent	Knowledgeable; idealistic; persistent; social interest; gets things done	Workaholic; overburdened; overresponsible; overinvolved	Feelings of inadequacy and guilt; "How can I measure up?"; lying to avoid judgments	Being overwhelmed; lack of time; "I have to do everything"

hand to her forehead and said, "Now I see what my children have been trying to tell me and why they are so 'defiant.' "

Many people want superiority (in the form of excellence) and would be uncomfortable with meaninglessness and unimportance. However, meaninglessness and unimportance are to be avoided at all costs for a person with the superiority lifestyle priority. Another important note: people with a superiority top card seldom want to be superior to others. They simply have the mistaken belief that they aren't good enough unless they are superior, which often invites children to feel inadequate. Another parent had a great insight during a workshop and said, "Oh my goodness. I could never understand why my son felt so inadequate. I kept telling him he could do better if he would just try. All that did was make him feel more inadequate. I want to learn everything I can to get out of his way and be encouraging instead of discouraging."

Just about everyone wants comfort in his or her life and wants to avoid emotional and physical pain and stress. However, trying to avoid pain and stress can be the primary concern that motivates the behavior of a person with the comfort lifestyle priority. People with other priorities aren't thrilled with pain and stress, but they don't base their life on trying to avoid them. This style may invite children to be spoiled and demanding. As one mother put it, "Good grief. Now I can see why I'm always stressed out. I haven't taught my children how to take care of themselves and to contribute in helpful ways. I sure had things upside down."

Few people enjoy rejection and feeling left out. However, trying to avoid rejection is a primary theme and the basis for behavior when the person with the pleasing lifestyle priority feels insecure. This can invite others to take advantage, or to feel annoyed by the energy of insecurity. As one father said, "No wonder my children didn't appreciate all I did for them. I didn't bother to ask their opinion. I just thought they were ungrateful and inconsiderate. I can see that I was the one who was being inconsiderate by not checking with them and finding out who they are and what they want."

An interesting twist is that the behavior motivated by each priority often creates the opposite of what the individual intends. For example, an adult who tries to please children may fail because he forgot to check out if pleasing children is in their best interests. The adult who wants comfort may create more stress by avoiding steps that seem uncomfortable at the time but could create greater discomfort and stress in the future when children make demands instead of learning cooperation. Adults who think they have to have control often invite criticism and humiliation when their children rebel, and adults who try to avoid feeling meaningless by striving for superiority may create the worst kind of meaninglessness when they discover that their children have developed feelings of inadequacy, or follow their parents' footsteps and spend their lives trying too hard to prove themselves.

The main point for all of the lifestyle priorities is that the primary motivation is to find belonging and significance. However, just like children who choose a mistaken goal in their "mistaken" attempts to achieve belonging and significance, adults choose "mistaken" ways—and achieve just the opposite. We "misbehave" and create distance in our relationships instead of belonging and significance. Awareness and humor can help all of us get beyond our self-defeating beliefs and behaviors. We can then be more effective with our children—and in our lives.

DISCOVERING YOUR PRIMARY PRIORITY

Personality priorities are developed when children perceive their world, make decisions about it, and come to some basic conclusions that include a "therefore, I must . . ." belief. The following examples illustrate the different decisions children might make based on the same circumstances.

- "I'm little; others are big. Therefore, I must get others to take care of me." (Comfort)
- "I'm little; others are big. Therefore, I must maintain control of myself and situations so I don't feel humiliated." (Control)
- "I'm little; others are big. Therefore, I must please others so I will be loved." (Pleasing)
- "I'm little; others are big. Therefore, I must try harder to catch up, and do even better." (Superiority)

The results of these early decisions lie in the future. Do you find it daunting to think that the blueprint for your behavior in life was created by a three-year-old?

YOUR BLUEPRINT FOR LIVING

Would you hire a three-year-old to create a blueprint for your dream house? You may be laughing at how ridiculous that sounds. Yet your life is based on a blueprint for living created by you as a small child. Actually, you began creating your blueprint the moment you were born but, like most people, you don't remember the decisions you made as an infant or toddler. However, those early decisions were confirmed by you (still subconsciously) at three, four, and five years of age. Then you, as a six- to ten-year-old, subconsciously added some advice, continuing the creation of your blueprint for living. And, just for fun, as a teenager—raging hormones and all—you threw in some decisions, thoughts, feelings, and attitudes to complete the picture. Is it any wonder that your blueprint for living has some flaws? What else could you expect from a small child, or even a teenager, with no training in creating blueprints for living and not enough life experience to interpret life with the objectivity that sometimes comes with age.

Understanding your blueprint for life (your lifestyle priority) provides you with the opportunity to make some revisions. It will also help you recognize which blueprints your children are beginning to use and will enable you to better understand their reactions when they are feeling insecure. If you are still having trouble deciding which lifestyle priority is yours, choose the statement that fits you best:

- "I feel best about myself when I and those around me are comfortable. I feel worst about myself when there is tension, pain, and stress." (Comfort)
- "I feel best about myself when things are orderly and organized and I am in control of myself and the situation. I feel worst about myself when I feel embarrassed and humiliated or criticized about something I think I should have known or done." (Control)
- "I feel best about myself when I can please other people and avoid conflicts so that life is fun, not difficult. I feel worst about myself when I feel rejected, left out, or unappreciated." (Pleasing)
- "I feel best about myself when I am achieving success and am making a meaningful contribution. I feel worst about myself when I feel worthless, meaningless, and stupid." (Superiority)

The statement that is truest of you in times of stress (or insecurity) is your primary priority. "In times of stress" is an important factor in understanding lifestyle priorities. When not under stress, we are not worried about humiliation, rejection, meaninglessness, or pain. During peaceful times in our lives, we are usually not hooked into old childhood decisions, patterns of behavior, and beliefs. It is only when we perceive stress or feel insecure that we are catapulted into the negative aspects of our priority lifestyle behaviors. These behaviors are often at the root of our power struggles with children.

I say "perceived" stress because that is what stress is. What is stressful to one person may not be stressful to another—only our thinking makes it so. Adler said, "Your thoughts have no meaning except the meaning you give them." (You can find more information on this important concept in *Serenity: Eliminating Stress and Finding Joy and Peace in Life and Relationships.*[1])

DISCOVERING YOUR SECONDARY PRIORITY

You may say, "Well, I certainly want to avoid humiliation and embarrassment, but I don't think I try to control others or situations. In fact, I usually try very hard to please others." If that is the case, you have just identified your secondary priority. Your usual method of operation, or "style," is pleasing. This is your secondary priority because it is what you usually do when you are feeling secure. It is only when you feel insecure or pressured that you may fall back into your "must have" beliefs. Then you may give up pleasing and use your control methods to avoid perceived humiliation.

We choose one priority as our method of operation (or secondary priority) that we use on a daily basis when we feel secure. When we feel stressed, insecure, or threatened we tend to fall back on our primary priority. In other words, under different conditions and in different situations we will choose behaviors from different priorities, but it is always for the purpose of maintaining our "must have" priority. For example, a control lifestyle priority person may please others to obtain control, strive for excellence to obtain control, or make people or situations comfortable to obtain a sense of control.

LIFESTYLE PRIORITIES AND PARENTING
AND TEACHING STYLES

The many assets and liabilities of each priority affect how you behave as a parent. The purpose of understanding lifestyle priorities is *not* to create stereotypes, but to increase awareness that will help you make informed choices instead of being blind victims to perceptions you had and decisions you made as a child, then subsequently "forgot." When you understand the possible liabilities of your lifestyle priorities, you can develop strategies to overcome them. You can take more responsibility for what you create with your choices and behavior instead of acting like a victim—including the challenges you experience with children

Comfort

On the asset side, adults with a comfort lifestyle priority may model for children the benefits of being easygoing, diplomatic, and predictable. Their children or students may learn to enjoy simple pleasures in life and take time to "smell the roses." Positive Discipline skills can help these adults understand their tendency to be too permissive with children because it seems easier at the time. Comfort-seeking adults often choose a laissez-faire, permissive style, which may create a tendency toward "spoiled brattiness," or chaos in the classroom. Comfort-priority adults can become more effective when they get their children involved in setting limits, creating routines, setting goals, and solving problems together during family or class meetings.

Mrs. Carter's priority is comfort. She often left too many decisions to her children and was too quick to give in to their demands because it seemed "easier." But oddly enough, taking the easy way out didn't always make life easier. She began to suffer a great deal of stress and discomfort (as did her children) because the only way they knew to get along was through emotional

TABLE 10.2: HOW LIFESTYLE PRIORITIES MAY INFLUENCE PARENTING AND TEACHING

Priority	Possible parenting assets	Possible parenting liabilities	May need to practice
Comfort	Models for children the benefits of being easygoing, diplomatic, predictable, and enjoying simple pleasures	Permissiveness, which may invite children to be spoiled and demanding. More interest in comfort than in the "needs of the situation"	Creating routines; setting goals; solving problems together; teaching life skills; allowing children to experience the natural consequences of their choices; family meetings
Control	May teach children organizational skills, leadership skills, productive persistence, assertiveness, respect for law and order, time management skills	Rigid; controlling. May invite rebellion and resistance or unhealthy pleasing	Letting go; offering choices; asking curiosity questions; involving children in decisions; family meetings
Pleasing	May help children learn to be friendly, considerate, and nonaggressive, peacemakers, compromisers, volunteers, and champions of the underdog	Doormats, keep score (now you owe me.) May invite resentment, depression, or revenge	Having faith in children to solve their own problems; joint problem-solving; emotional honesty; learn to give and take; family meetings
Superiority	Models success and achievement, teaches children to assess quality and motivates to excellence	Lecture, preach, expect too much; invite feelings of inadequacy and failure to "measure up"; see things in terms of right and wrong instead of possibilities	Letting go of the need to be right; getting into the child's world and supporting needs and goals; unconditional love; enjoying the process and developing a sense of humor; holding family meetings where all ideas are valued

Adapted from *Positive Discipline for Preschoolers Facilitator's Guide* by Jane Nelsen, Cheryl Erwin, and Roslyn Duffy (available from Empowering People Books, Tapes, and Videos: 1-800-456-7770; www.empoweringpeople.com).

tyranny (whining or throwing tantrums until their mom gave in). Instead of making them comfortable, Mrs. Carter had unwittingly created a family atmosphere of great tension. Mrs. Carter was excited to learn how understanding priorities could help her emphasize her assets instead of her liabilities. She started taking time to teach her children mutual respect and life skills and provided opportunities for them to practice what they were learning. She gave them allowances, discussed saving and spending, and then allowed them to experience the consequences of their choices.

When her children made demands, she put their requests on the family meeting agenda to be discussed at a later time. During the family meetings, she invited discussion and brainstorming on various ways the children could get what they wanted through their own efforts. They created morning and bedtime routines, decided on plans to accomplish chores, and planned simple family outings. Mrs. Carter learned that she needed to make many decisions, such as choosing a suitable preschool, determining safety issues, and setting clear and consistent boundaries and expectations for behavior. It was not appropriate to ask her children whether it was okay with them if she took the freeway instead of the slower route home, whether they wanted baths at night, or whether she could offer to baby-sit their cousin over the weekend. Such decisions were her responsibility. Once she quit burdening them with such choices, the children felt more secure. Clear expectations give children a feeling of safety, whereas Mrs. Carter's previous behavior invited anxiety, the opposite of the comfort she sought. Mrs. Carter was grateful to realize that she was more comfortable, there was less tension in the home, and the children were more comfortable, having learned skills to get their needs met.

Control

On the asset side, parents and teachers with a control priority may be very good at helping their children learn organization skills, leadership skills, productive persistence, assertiveness, and respect for law and order. Positive Discipline parenting skills can help parents with a control priority curb their tendency to be too rigid and controlling of their children. Excessive control invites rebellion or resistance, instead of encouraging children to learn the skills these parents want to teach. Control-priority adults may be more effective if they make an effort to recognize their need for excessive control and practice the skills of letting go, offering choices, asking curiosity questions, and of getting their children more involved in decision making.

Mrs. Jones's lifestyle priority is control. She used to tell her children what to do, how to do it, and when to do it, and she certainly didn't allow any back talk from them. She truly believed that this was what responsible parents were supposed to do. Her controlling behavior was actually counterproductive to the goal of helping her children learn self-discipline, responsibility, cooperation, and problem-solving skills. Two of her three children were in constant rebellion, doing as little as they could get away with and always testing the limits until they were punished. This made Mrs. Jones feel out of control, the very thing she was trying to avoid. She was in a perpetual power struggle with these two children.

Her other child was becoming a "pleaser." He tried to live up to his mother's expectations and to gain her approval by pleasing her. However, instead of developing the life skills he needed to be a happy, successful citizen of the world, he was losing a sense of what pleased him and lived with the fear that he would never be able to make people happy enough. He was becoming an approval junkie.

Learning about priorities helped Mrs. Jones emphasize her assets instead of her liabilities. She started using family meetings with her children to involve them in solving problems. She learned to risk asking curiosity questions to help herself and her children discover the consequences of their decisions and to learn from their mistakes in an atmosphere of unconditional love. She stopped needing to be in charge of everything and invited suggestions and discussions about solving problems. She was grateful when she realized that as she let go of her need to be in control, she and the children all felt more in control.

Pleasing

On the asset side, parents and teachers with a pleasing priority may be very good at helping their children learn friendly, considerate, nonaggressive behavior. They are often peacemakers because of their desire to make everyone happy. They are good at compromising and often volunteer to help others. They are champions of the underdog. Unfortunately, excessive pleasing may invite resentment and depression when pleasing adults work too hard to please children or partners at their own expense (and when others don't return the courtesy). And recipients of the pleasing may feel resentful because of the expectations placed on them that they should appreciate what is done and are now expected to return the courtesy. Positive Discipline skills can help these adults curb their tendency to go overboard in trying to make everyone happy.

Pleasing-priority parents and teachers can be more effective when they stop focusing exclusively on others' needs and take care of their own needs so they have more to give. They need to have faith in their children's ability to please themselves and teach them the skills of emotional honesty and joint problem-solving. Both adult and child will benefit from learning to express what they think, feel, and want without expecting anyone else to think the same, to feel the same, or to give them what they want—easily said, but not so easily done! Learning to value everyone's needs—including their own—is crucial to fostering mutual respect.

Mr. Smith's lifestyle priority is pleasing. He expended huge amounts of energy and effort trying to make his children be nice to each other, the neighbors, their grandparents, the members of their church, and their teachers. He was more concerned with how they treated others than with helping them with their own feelings. At other times he would give them too much special service when they whined or cried. For example, he would try to please them when they demanded snacks or more stories before bedtime. Then he would get angry when the snacks and stories didn't satisfy them enough to make them go to bed cheerfully. All too often, everyone went to bed upset. No one was pleased!

It was also important to Mr. Smith that his children like him and approve of him as their father. It seemed only logical to him that his children would also want to please him. He couldn't understand it when his children complained that he didn't care about their feelings. It was a vicious circle; he was sure they didn't care about his feelings, even after "all he did for them."

Mr. Smith wasn't sure whether or not he believed the information about lifestyle priorities. But when he started using family meetings with his children to involve them in joint problem-solving, he couldn't help but notice the changed atmosphere in his family. Mr. Smith and his children learned to use emotional honesty to express their feelings. They discussed the idea of "separate realities" and the fact that people perceive situations in different ways (none of which are necessarily wrong), that different things please different people, and that it is respectful to ask instead of to assume.

He discovered that it was important to take his own needs into consideration, as well as the needs of the situation. He learned to respond to his children's bedtime demands by kindly and firmly saying, "It is bedtime now. What is next on your bedtime routine chart?" At first he had to repeat that simple statement several times. However, once his children learned he meant what he said, they gave up trying to manipulate him.

Mr. Smith eventually realized that when he tried to please his children without first discovering what pleased them, he wasn't really pleasing anyone. This family began listening to one another, asking for what they wanted, and being honest about whether or not they would grant one another's wishes. When Mr. Smith learned about priorities and Positive Discipline parenting skills, his children began to enjoy being his children and Mr. Smith began to truly enjoy being a parent. Everyone was pleased—at least, most of the time.

Superiority

Parents and teachers with a superiority lifestyle priority may be very good at modeling success and achievement. They often are able to judge and encourage quality and seem to have a knack for "motivating to excellence." Their children, however, sometimes see this as "badgering to perfection" and feel inadequate to meet the high expectations of their parents or teachers.

Positive Discipline skills can help these adults curb their tendency to expect too much from children. Excessive superiority often invites feelings of inadequacy instead of the desire for achievement these adults want to inspire. Superiority-priority adults will be more effective if they make an effort to let go of their need for things to be "right" and "best" (according to their own standards, of course) and practice the skills of getting into their children's worlds to discover what is important to them, remembering that there is more than one "right" way to do things, and always making sure the message of unconditional love gets through.

They can also learn to model and teach that mistakes are wonderful opportunities for learning, and listen to and accept their children's ideas for solving problems. Sometimes superiority adults are so focused on the final goal that they completely miss the joy of the process.

Mr. Lyndol's lifestyle priority is superiority. He used to tell his children about all his wonderful accomplishments, as well as what he expected from them. He believed this would inspire and motivate them to follow in his footsteps, and he invested much of his self-worth in the expectation that they would surpass him. Also, he was a workaholic and often neglected his family so he could "provide the best for them." He didn't know that spending time with him (without demands) was what they longed for.

This dad's superiority personality was actually counterproductive to the goal of helping his children achieve excellence. One of his children became a troublemaker at school. (If he couldn't be the best of the best and live up to his dad's expectations, he could at least be the best of the worst.) This child also had developed a superiority lifestyle, but was exercising it in opposition to his dad. His other child became a perfectionist who couldn't stand to lose, and he couldn't relax and enjoy his accomplishments even when he won because he was constantly afraid of the embarrassment and humiliation of failure.

Mr. Lyndol was motivated to emphasize the assets of his superiority lifestyle instead of his liabilities and to be the sort of father he'd always intended. He and his family worked to cultivate a sense of humor when discussing mistakes and began projects they could work on together. Sometimes they would even risk making mistakes together, just to reassure themselves that it was okay. Mr. Lyndol learned to use family meetings to improve communication with his children. They worked at enjoying and cooperating on the process and not just emphasizing the excellence of the finished product.

Mr. Lyndol stopped lecturing and invited discussions about differences of opinions. He and his children decided to work on a community service project, which they planned together. Mr.

Lyndol discovered that he was better able to communicate with his children and felt encouraged by what he was learning from and with them. The children began to exhibit signs that they, too, were encouraged: they were enthusiastic and willingly cooperated both at home and at school.

Mr. Lyndol also volunteered as a coach for a children's soccer team. At first, he had wanted only children who had strong skills and who wanted to practice hard; he especially wanted children who wanted to win. Mr. Lyndol's new insights helped him to see that all of the children had potential if he would only encourage them. He began to work with these children, to hone their kicking and running and passing. He taught them that it was more important to do their best than to win a game—a lesson he was learning, too.

They won many games (and lost a few), but Mr. Lyndol found his greatest pleasure in the attitude his team displayed. They worked together and enjoyed the work.

CONFLICTING LIFESTYLE PRIORITIES

We have discussed what happens when parents and teachers learn about lifestyle priority styles and Positive Discipline parenting skills. An understanding of priority styles coupled with Positive Discipline skills can also help adults and children live and work together with fewer conflicts. Remember the two couples we introduced in the beginning of this chapter? As Alfred Adler often said, "Opposites attract, but they have difficulty living together." Each is attracted to the other for possessing the assets he or she lacks. But sometimes what seemed cute and adorable at first becomes downright irritating after marriage. Take the case of Mr. and Mrs. Johnson.

David and Suzanne Johnson met on the ski slopes. There was an immediate attraction between the two, and a relationship quickly developed. Suzanne was attracted to David because he was relaxed, easygoing, and really comfortable to be around. Even when he skied, he seemed to glide easily down the mountain.

For his part, David was attracted to Suzanne because she was bright, attractive, articulate, creative—one of the most successful and talented women he had ever met. They had a lot in common. And they both loved to ski. Little did they realize how the ups and downs of the ski slope would become a metaphor for their relationship and for their parenting styles when their first child arrived.

David's priority was comfort, while Suzanne's priority was superiority. We are often attracted to someone who seems to have what we believe we lack. David never stood in the way of Suzanne's many activities; in fact, he encouraged her accomplishments. After all, her ambition and drive made life easy for him. David's easy charm and relaxed manner were a perfect foil for Suzanne's lofty goals and excessive energy.

Then their first baby arrived. Before long (and with absolutely no knowledge of lifestyle priorities), the baby seemed to have an uncanny ability to cause David discomfort and to make Suzanne feel less than the best. The baby also had an ability to get them arguing about parenting skills and styles. Dad was too easy, Mom too hard. Or at least, that's what David and Suzanne had to say about each other.

When a kind soul eventually explained lifestyle priorities to them, things began to turn around for David and Suzanne. They attended a parenting class together and made an effort to parent their youngster as a team. They focused on appreciating the assets of their priorities (which had brought them together in the first place). They agreed that each of them would work on his or her own liabilities and that each would offer support and understanding rather than criticism. They were especially delighted to find that their new Positive Discipline parenting skills fit both their styles and helped them achieve what they most wanted to create: a happy family.

Growth happens when we learn to turn our liabilities into assets. As we gain insight and awareness, growth can be exciting and rewarding. Understanding our own lifestyle priority and how it influences our relationships with our children can help us learn, with time and patience, to be the best parents—and the best people—we can be.

REVIEW

In lieu of tools or questions for this chapter, use the following activity to help you understand your lifestyle priority. It is more educational to do this in a group. You can then break up into smaller groups that represent each lifestyle and brainstorm together to fill in the blanks left for:

1. Creating a bumper sticker
2. Your assets (what most members of the group see they have in common)
3. Your liabilities (what most members of the group see they have in common)
4. What this style may invite from children
5. Specific steps for improvement that would enhance your life and your relationships with children.

LIFESTYLE PRIORITY ACTIVITY

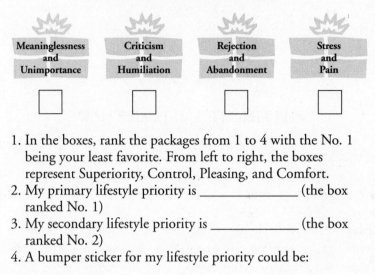

Meaninglessness and Unimportance	Criticism and Humiliation	Rejection and Abandonment	Stress and Pain
☐	☐	☐	☐

1. In the boxes, rank the packages from 1 to 4 with the No. 1 being your least favorite. From left to right, the boxes represent Superiority, Control, Pleasing, and Comfort.
2. My primary lifestyle priority is _____ (the box ranked No. 1)
3. My secondary lifestyle priority is _____ (the box ranked No. 2)
4. A bumper sticker for my lifestyle priority could be:

_____

5. My best assets are:

_____

_____

6. My biggest liabilities are:

_____

_____

7. What my lifestyle priority may invite from children:

_____

_____

8. Specific steps for improvement:

_____

_____

Chapter Eleven

PUTTING IT ALL TOGETHER

Most of the principles described in this book require the understanding and application of basic concepts and adult attitudes. When we put them all together, we have an excellent toolbox to help children develop the characteristics that will serve them well throughout their lives. There isn't one tool that works for every child and situation so it is comforting to have many options. Many of the tools presented in this chapter have been discussed in previous chapters. In this chapter you will find new examples of adult/child interactions regarding discipline challenges and the value of using several tools together.

THE BATHROOM TECHNIQUE

The value of Positive Time-out for a cooling-off period has been mentioned several times. Remember that the purpose of "cooling off" is to wait until you can access your "rational brain" instead of trying to solve a conflict while you are accessing your "reptilian" brain, so some form of withdrawal is helpful. Instead of thinking in terms of children taking some time-out, it can be helpful for parents to be the ones to withdraw.

Before you withdraw, explain to your children what you plan

to do and why. (Younger children will learn from your actions, not your words.) The explanation can take place during a family meeting or on an individual basis. You might tell them, "When I'm upset, I'll go somewhere to calm down until I can feel better and we can work together to find a respectful solution." This is a great model for your children.

A good place for parents to withdraw to is the bathroom. Dreikurs is well known for "the bathroom technique." He suggested the bathroom because it is the only room in many houses with a lock on the door. If you find the need to spend a lot of time cooling off in the bathroom, you might like to make it as comfortable for yourself as possible, with books, magazines, and a stereo. Just joking, but you get the point.

Some parents prefer to get into the shower, take a walk, or go shopping if they have a friend or spouse with whom they can leave your children. Sometimes a prearranged signal between you and the children can help—an exaggerated pulling of the hair, flapping of the arms to signify going batty, or flashing the peace sign.

A respectful attitude is important in using any type of cooling-off period. You might say, "I need some time-out to take care of myself. I know I'll do better when I feel better." Reassure children that you are not leaving to get away from them, but to take care of yourself because you know that when everyone feels better, the problem can be solved with respect and cooperation.

THE NOVEL TECHNIQUE

Since teachers cannot leave children alone in the classroom, one way they can withdraw is to sit down and read a novel during times of conflict. (Teachers who have tried this find it is very effective, but many teachers do not feel comfortable with it. Try it if it fits your style.)

The first step is to tell the children your plan. Let them know that your job is to teach—theirs is to learn. If they are not willing to do their job, you cannot do yours; so from now on, whenever they are being disruptive and you are unable to teach, you will sit down and read your novel and they can let you know when they are ready to do their job so that you can do yours.

The reason some teachers do not like this method is that they can't stand the testing period, when things get worse before they get better. The children will often be very disruptive as they test their new freedom. However, before too long, the children will settle down and let the teacher know they are ready to learn. In many classes the students do not test their freedom. They simply are not aware that they are being disrespectful until they notice the teacher reading his or her novel. As soon as they see this nonverbal clue, they quiet down immediately.

This method is effective only for teachers who have earned the admiration and respect of the children because they are well prepared and effective. It is also most effective with children in elementary grades. It could be disastrous with teenagers, who are more concerned with peer approval than adult approval.

Mr. Rasmussen, a special education teacher of fourth-, fifth-, and sixth-grade students, received permission from his principal to leave the room when his students were being disruptive. He first explained to the students that he would leave when they were not ready to learn. They were instructed to come get him from the teachers' lounge when they were ready. That same day the students got so noisy they could not hear him unless he raised his voice. He and his aide took their coffee cups and left the room.

Mr. Rasmussen got very nervous while he was sitting in the teachers' lounge. He was not at all sure this would work. His imagination went wild as he considered the things the children could be doing in the room. When they had not come to get him after thirty minutes, he began to wonder if he would lose his teaching contract.

After forty-five minutes, one of the students came to the teachers' lounge to tell Mr. Rasmussen they were ready for him to come back and teach. He was amazed at how cooperative the children were for the next few days.

The next time the students became disruptive, Mr. Rasmussen and his aide took their coffee cups off the shelf. Immediately the children settled down and said they were ready. It is important to note that these students really liked Mr. Rasmussen. He had earned their respect and was now demonstrating how he would respect himself.

After hearing this story, another special education teacher tried it. She reported that her students came to her in twenty minutes with a signed petition stating they were ready to cooperate.

Another teacher forgot to tell her students where they could find her. They went to the office and had her paged over the intercom when they were ready.

I'm not advocating you try this if there are strict rules in your school against it. Some principals will give permission for this kind of risk-taking.

POSITIVE TIME-OUT

A cooling-off period can be effective for discouraged children if the rationale is explained in advance, if the children help design a place that will help them feel better, and when parents or teachers ask, "Would it help you to go to the Positive Time-out area?" (or whatever they have decided to call it).

The bathroom and novel techniques are sometimes better, because you are deciding what you will do instead of what you are asking the child to do. But many parents and teachers like to use Positive Time-out instead of the bathroom technique because they feel it is too inconvenient for them to withdraw to the bathroom if they are busy with a task, such as fixing dinner or teaching a class. (However, sometimes a short period of inconvenience is a small price to pay in order to encourage and empower children to learn responsibility and cooperation.)

An important concept to review *again* is: Where did we ever get the crazy idea that in order to make children do better, first we have to make them feel worse? Most adults have the mistaken idea that the whole point of sending children to their rooms is to make them suffer. "You go to your room and think about what you did." The tone of voice usually implies, "And you suffer." One parent even complained, "It doesn't do any good to send my child to his room. He enjoys it."

I said, "Great. That will produce better results." In fact, I suggest to parents that they teach their children about Positive Time-out (as discussed in chapter six) during a calm, happy time. "When you feel upset or angry, it might be helpful to you to go into your room and do something to make yourself feel better. You can read a book, play with your toys, listen to music, or take a nap. Then, when you feel better, come on out and we will work on a solution." For parents who are concerned that this is rewarding misbehavior, this could be true if they don't follow through with problem solving when everyone is feeling better. Please refer to *Positive Time-Out and Over 50 Ways to Avoid Power Struggles in Homes and Classrooms*[1] for more details about how to get children involved in creating personal time-out areas that they can "choose" instead of being "sent to."

Children under the age of three are usually too young to be sent to (or to choose) time-out—even Positive Time-out. However, you could go to time-out with them. You probably both need it. Mrs. James started taking Ann to her bedroom for misbehavior when she was fourteen months old. She would hold Ann on her lap and read to her for a few minutes before bringing her back out. If Ann was having a temper tantrum, Mom would just quietly sit on Ann's bed and "let her" have her feelings. When Ann finally calmed down, Mrs. James would say, "Are you ready for a hug yet?"

Remember that this is not rewarding the misbehavior. It is modeling a respectful way for Ann to deal with her feelings when she is upset—that it is okay to feel whatever she feels, but not to do whatever she wants. This method is based on the basic concept of encouragement as the most powerful motivator to improve behavior. It is also based on sound child development principles—that a fourteen-month-old child doesn't really understand cause and effect at the sophisticated level where she can control her behavior without supervision, so why punish?

When Ann engaged in "discouraged behavior," such as whining, or "testing behavior," such as jumping on the furniture, Mrs. James would kindly and firmly take her to her room and sit with her. Sometimes Mrs. James would get Ann involved by asking her to find the timer and set it to the number of minutes she guessed it might take her to feel better (distraction). Sometimes she would give her the choice, "Would you like to go to your room by yourself, or would you like me to keep you company until you feel better?"

By the time Ann was four, she was very familiar with this routine. When she needed time to calm down and feel better, she would either go to her room by herself or would ask her mother to come with her. Sometimes she would cry or pout for a while (because she had learned that feelings are always okay) before indicating she had calmed down and felt better. Other times she would simply play in her room for a while or fall asleep. When she came out she was ready to change her behavior—or to work on a respectful solution. Ann was able to practice self-control using Positive Time-out because she didn't feel she had to "rebel" about being "sent" to time-out.

Mrs. James learned the effectiveness of the bathroom technique (taking some time-out herself) when she had surgery and did not have the strength to go with Ann to her bedroom when she misbehaved. One day Ann was whining, so Mrs. James hobbled down the hall to the bathroom. Ann followed her and started pounding on the door crying, "I want you to come out." After a few minutes Mrs. James heard Ann try to control some involuntary sobs before she said in a happy voice, "I'm ready for you to come out."

When Mrs. James came out she said, "I'm so glad you are ready. I love spending time with you. Why don't we put whining on the family meeting agenda so we can use our good ideas to figure out some solutions."

DECIDE WHAT YOU WILL DO, NOT WHAT YOU WILL MAKE CHILDREN DO

The potential danger in telling children to go to their rooms (or any other request) is that you may be inviting a power struggle if they refuse, or a revenge cycle if they perceive it as punishment and feel hurt. This is especially true with older children. The possibility is eliminated when you allow children to learn from the natural or logical consequences of what you decide to do, rather than what you try to make them do.

Bonnie married a widower with six children. The oldest was eight years old and the youngest were two-year-old twins. The mother of these children had died in childbirth when the twins were born. You can imagine how difficult it was to find a babysitter for six children, including baby twins. Even those who were desperate for a job did not stay long, so the children had not had the stability of consistent discipline before Bonnie became their new mother. This was especially evident during mealtime, which was a terrible ordeal because the children would fight, argue, and throw food at one another.

Bonnie had taught Positive Discipline principles before she had a chance to practice them. Now she had her chance. The first thing Bonnie did was hold a family meeting. She did not even discuss their mealtime behavior. She simply asked them to decide how much time they needed to eat their food after it was on the table. They talked it over and decided fifteen minutes was plenty of time. (They forgot to consider how much time it takes to fight, argue, and throw food.) They all willingly agreed to a family rule that dinner would be served at six o'clock and the table cleared at six-fifteen.

The next evening Bonnie and her husband ignored the fighting while they ate their food. At six-fifteen Bonnie cleared the table. The children protested that they were still hungry and were not through eating. Bonnie kindly and firmly replied, "I am just following the rule we agreed on. I am sure you can make it until breakfast." She then sat in front of the refrigerator with a novel and earplugs for the rest of the evening.

The next night was a repeat of the previous night as the children tested to see if their new mother was "for real." By the third night they knew she was, and they were so busy eating that they did not have time to fight, argue, or throw food.

There is a lovely sequel to this story. Six years later I had the opportunity to stay with these children while their parents took a weekend vacation. They were so responsible and capable that I did not lift a finger the whole weekend.

The children prepared all the meals and did their chores without any interference from me. They showed me their meal and chore plan. They planned all their menus for a month during the first family meeting of the month. They all had a night to cook, except Bonnie (who did all the shopping) and the oldest boy (who had football practice).

I asked them if things always ran so smoothly. They assured me, "Not always." One of the girls told me that they used to have a rule that whoever cooked did not clean the kitchen. This caused problems because those who had the cleanup chore always complained about the messy cooks. They decided to change the rule so that the cook also cleaned the kitchen. This ended the complaints and gave everyone a longer break before it was their turn to work again.

This example illustrates several points that are important in making the method successful:

- Let the children know, in advance, what you are going to do. If possible, get their agreement as to what will be done under certain circumstances.
- Use kind and firm actions, not words. When children test your new plan, the fewer words you use, the better. Keep your mouth shut and act.
- The few words you do use should be stated in a kind and friendly manner.
- Ignore the temptation to become involved in a power struggle or revenge cycle. Children will do their best to test you and get you sucked into your usual response.
- When following through with your plan, it may seem that you are letting the children "get away with something" while you ignore their misbehavior. It is true that punishment would get more immediate results, but this method helps children develop responsibility and other life skills for the future (long-term results).
- Things may get worse before they get better. Be consistent with your new plan of action and children will learn a new response-ability. (The play on words is intended.)

Following are some other examples of deciding what you will do instead of what you will make children do:

- Don't try to make children put their dirty clothes in the hamper. Simply decide that you will wash only the clothes that are in the hamper. Children will soon learn from the natural consequence of not having clean clothes when they want them.

• Don't nag at children to clean up the kitchen. Simply refuse to cook until the kitchen is clean. Think how much fun you can have reading a good novel while you wait. At first the children might think it is just great to fix their own peanut butter sandwiches whenever they are hungry. This gets old after a while, and children soon see that cooperation is a two-way street, if they want to enjoy the finer meals of life.

• Do not distort this method into a power struggle or revenge cycle. Some parents misunderstand this concept and try to use it to bully or shame children into doing what they want them to do or to "get even" with them for not doing what they "should" do. The idea is to become unconcerned with what children do in these situations. In other words, don't be concerned if your child chooses to wear dirty clothes instead of taking responsibility for putting them in the hamper. Don't be concerned if your children would prefer to eat peanut butter sandwiches instead of cleaning up the kitchen so that you will cook. Enjoy the vacation from the kitchen.

Being unconcerned is extremely effective for those parents and teachers who feel comfortable using it. They follow up with other methods, such as family or class meetings to work on solutions for the problem, taking time for training, curiosity questions, and encouragement. Those who cannot stand to become unconcerned can use other methods. There is never just one way to deal with a problem. The more tools we have in our parenting toolbox, the more effective we can be. In our book *Positive Discipline A–Z*[2], we have over one thousand nonpunitive solutions and methods to prevent problems in the future for specific behavior challenges. *Positive Discipline: A Teacher's A–Z Guide*[3] does the same thing for a long list of behaviors that are challenging for teachers. Parents and teachers can choose the suggestions they feel most comfortable with, or the ones they think would work best with their children or students. Some parents and teachers call for a time-out and read the suggestions regarding a particular behavior challenge with their children so they can choose, together, which one they think would work best.

EMOTIONAL WITHDRAWAL

The purpose of a cooling-off period is to withdraw from the situation until the emotional conflict is over, instead of getting into power struggles or revenge cycles. You can then solve problems rationally. The bathroom technique or Positive Time-out is suggested because most adults and children have difficulty cooling off until they leave the area of conflict. It would not be necessary to leave the area if we could withdraw emotionally and avoid becoming involved in a power struggle.

Bonnie and her husband (mentioned earlier) had to withdraw emotionally in order to be able to ignore the children's misbehavior at the dinner table while they followed their new plan of action.

Mrs. Valdez, a third-grade teacher, invited me to observe her class meeting. I arrived early and had the opportunity to witness how effectively she used emotional withdrawal. It was time to change from a math activity to reading. The children were becoming noisy and disruptive. I saw Mrs. Valdez stare at the back wall as though she had gone into a trance. The children noticed also and started whispering, "She's counting." The word was passed, and soon the children were sitting quietly at attention.

Later, in the teachers' room, I asked Mrs. Valdez, "How high do you count, and what do you do after you get there?"

She said, "I'm not really counting. I have just decided I can't teach until the children are quiet, so I might as well take a break. Since I stare at the back wall while I'm waiting, the children assume I'm looking at the clock and counting. They never seemed to hear me when I nagged at them to settle down, but they get quiet very quickly since I have decided not to teach until they are ready."

Emotional withdrawal does not mean withdrawing love from the child. It does mean withdrawing from a conflict-producing situation. All withdrawal methods should be followed with encouragement, training, redirecting, or problem-solving activities after the cooling-off period.

AVOIDING MORNING HASSLES

The following story illustrates several concepts, attitudes, and methods previously discussed, as well as the importance of establishing routines.

Mornings at DaniRie's house are usually very hectic. She finds this an excellent time to keep her mother busy with her. The scene usually goes something like this: "DaniRie, will you please get up! . . . This is the last time I'm going to call you! . . . How should I know where your books are? Where did you leave them? . . . You're still not dressed and the bus will be here in five minutes! . . . DaniRie, I mean it, this is absolutely the last time I'm going to drive you when you miss the bus. You have got to learn to be more responsible."

If this sounds familiar and you believe the old adage, "Misery loves company," you may find some consolation in knowing that this scene is repeated in millions of homes every morning. This is not the last time her mother will drive DaniRie to school when she misses the bus, a fact DaniRie is well aware of. She has heard this threat many times and knows it is meaningless.

Her mother is right: DaniRie should learn to be more respon-

sible. But through morning scenes like this, her mother is actually training DaniRie to be more and more irresponsible. Instead
of giving her practice in responsibility, she is giving her practice
in calculated manipulation. Her mother is the one who is responsible when she is constantly reminding DaniRie of everything she needs to do. DaniRie will learn responsible behavior
when her mother stays out of the way and allows her to experience the consequences of being late. She may have to walk to
school if she misses her bus, or her teacher may have her make
up the time she misses. Also, DaniRie is more likely to be more
responsible if she creates her own morning routine chart.

ROUTINE CHARTS

Morning hassles can be avoided through taking time for training, involving children in establishing routines, problem solving,
and following through with kindness and firmness, as described
in chapter seven.

Classrooms with established routines run much more smoothly
than classrooms without routines. Routines are especially effective when children have helped plan them. Students can make
posters listing the routines and hang them up in the classroom.
The routines then become the boss. When students get off track,
the teacher can ask, "Who can tell me what we are supposed to
be doing now?" Someone will check the routine poster and remind the class about what they are supposed to be doing. This is
a simple way of allowing children to have control that invites cooperation instead of the teacher trying to be in control in ways
that invite resistance.

AVOIDING BEDTIME HASSLES

The following story demonstrates how avoiding morning hassles
is also dependent on some routines that take place the night

before as part of the routines that help avoid bedtime hassles. It also demonstrates the need to use concepts such as taking time for training and following through with dignity and respect.

Mrs. Felix took time to train Matthew to dress himself when he was two years old. She purchased the kinds of clothes that are easy to put on and take off. She then went through the procedure with Matthew several times. Once she was sure he knew how, she never allowed him to retrain her into doing it for him.

Since Matthew went to a morning preschool, Mrs. Felix got him up early enough to have plenty of time for dressing and eating so that Mr. Felix could take him to school on his way to work. She explained to Matthew that if he didn't get dressed on time, she would put his clothes in a paper bag so that he could get dressed in the car before going in to school—an excellent logical consequence.

They established the following routines beginning the night before school. At seven o'clock Matthew would get into his pajamas before his bedtime snack. Next came the bathroom routine. Matthew's family enjoyed the routine (tradition) of taking turns getting out everyone's toothbrush and putting toothpaste on them. Matthew loved climbing up on his stool and squeezing the toothpaste on everyone's brush—even though lots of toothpaste also spilled over onto the counter. As each family member went to the bathroom and discovered the toothpaste already on their brush, they would sing out, "Thank you." Then his mom or dad would take Matthew into his room and have him pick out the clothes he wanted to wear the next day so that he could have them all ready for morning. (This routine avoids the hassle of trying to decide what to wear in the morning when time pressures make it so inviting for a child to demand something he can't find or that is in the dirty-clothes hamper. As he grows older, he will also learn to lay out his books, coat, and everything else he will need in the morning.) His mom or dad would then talk to him about his day, read him a story, and tuck him into bed with a goodnight kiss.

Matthew had his own clock radio that woke him up in the morning. He liked to come snuggle with his parents in their bed for a few minutes—a nice way for them to wake up. When they all got up, Matthew would go to his room, get dressed, and come to the kitchen to help with breakfast. (In the Felix family, everyone has a job to do at breakfast time. Their jobs changed each week at their family meeting.) Matthew's favorite job was scrambling the eggs—a job two-year-old children do very well after a "time for training." If Matthew finished his routines before it was time to leave, he could then play with his toys.

One cold, rainy day, Matthew dawdled and was not ready when it was time to leave. His father took naked Matthew under one arm, his clothes in a bag under the other arm, and walked out into the pouring rain just as a neighbor came out to get his newspaper. (Sometimes you can't worry about what others think when you are teaching your children about responsibility.)

Matthew cried all the way to school. His dad kindly said, "I'll pull over and you can get dressed if you want to." However, Matthew was testing, so getting dressed would not have been any fun. When Matthew got to school, his teacher (who also believes in these principles) kindly said to him, "Oh hi, Matthew. I see you didn't get dressed yet. Take your clothes into my office and come out as soon as you are dressed." And he did.

About a month later Matthew tested again. This time he had his pajamas on, and this time he got dressed in the car before going in to school. He had already learned that crying didn't work. From then on Matthew was usually dressed on time. A few times his mother would notice him dawdling and say, "It looks as if you have decided to get dressed in the car." Matthew didn't like that idea, so he would hurry and finish getting dressed. Mother could have eliminated taking responsibility for even these reminders by allowing Matthew to experience the logical consequences again.

Some people have questioned this example because they thought it was humiliating to take Matthew to school naked. I can assure you that Matthew didn't care. Of course you wouldn't do this with a four-year-old.

His dad could have made this experience humiliating to Matthew by "piggybacking" (as explained in chapter five) by adding blame and shame to what would otherwise be a logical consequence. His dad did not say, "It serves you right! Maybe next time you'll hurry up. You are making me late. All the kids will probably laugh at you for not getting dressed." That would have made the experience humiliating.

One mother who heard this story tried a slight variation. Her four-year-old daughter, Selena, did not get dressed in time to leave for preschool, so her mom put her clothes in a paper bag and had Selena get into the car in her pajamas. She did not take Selena into her preschool in her pajamas. Instead she parked the car in the driveway next to a window in the preschool. She told her daughter, "Honey, I'll be sitting in the office where I can see you. Come in to the school as soon as you are dressed." Selena sat in the car, pouting, for about five minutes. Then she got dressed (maybe she was bored) and came into the preschool.

QUALITY BEDTIME SHARING

One reason children give their parents such a hard time at bedtime is because they can feel that their parents are trying to get rid of them. It is understandable that at the end of a long day, parents look forward to peace and quiet. Instead, they usually experience the frustration of bedtime hassles. Spending a few minutes of quality bedtime sharing is important for helping to eliminate frustrations.

When children sense that you are in a hurry to get away from them, they feel discouraged about belonging. They then engage in discouraged behavior by demanding drinks, bathroom privileges, or crying about fears. When they sense you really enjoy being with them for a few minutes of quality sharing, they feel a sense of belonging and don't need to misbehave.

Sharing the saddest and the happiest events of the day works well to help children feel content. A fringe benefit is that parents enjoy it too. Sharing means you also talk about your saddest and happiest times of the day. Listen first while your child shares; then you can share. This type of sharing is most effective when it is the last part of a bedtime routine. When children experience quality bedtime sharing, they feel the kind of belonging that occurs when someone takes the time to listen and to share of himself or herself. This is usually enough to motivate children to fall asleep contentedly.

AVOIDING MEALTIME HASSLES

Mealtimes have become such a battleground that you would think children would rather be hungry than eat. It is not that they would rather be hungry, but they would rather feel powerful than eat. It is almost impossible to make children eat, but that doesn't keep parents from trying. Many times parents think they have succeeded, only to have their children vomit their food up again.

Mrs. Williams served four-year-old Sara oatmeal for breakfast. Sara wouldn't eat it, in spite of her mother's scolding. Mrs. Williams put it in the refrigerator and served it to Sara for lunch. She still wouldn't eat it, so she got it for dinner. Mrs. Williams was an authoritarian mother who dominated Sara in many areas. Sara did not know how to "win," except during mealtime. This one area where she could feel independent and powerful was so important that she was sacrificing her body. Sara got rickets.

Mrs. Williams took Sara to the doctor, who guessed what was happening. He was a wise man and advised, "Put nutritious food on the table, eat your own food, and leave her alone! Talk about pleasant things or else keep silent."

Mrs. Williams felt very bad about what had happened. The only reason she had harassed Sara about eating was that she loved her and mistakenly thought that nagging was the best way to get her to eat and be healthy. As with many controlling methods used with today's children, it had backfired and she had achieved the opposite of what she wanted. She took the doctor's advice and stopped the war over eating. Sara never became a hearty eater (she is a very small-boned child), but she ate enough to overcome the rickets and stay healthy.

It is interesting to talk to people who were raised during the Depression of the 1930s. They say that the only mealtime problem they had was "Will there be enough food?" No one cared if one person chose not to eat. That would just mean there would be more for someone else. Children did not develop eating problems in that kind of atmosphere.

GET CHILDREN INVOLVED

Getting children involved in planning and solutions is the best way to avoid mealtime problems. Take time during a family meeting to plan the meals for the following week.

The Ainge family invented the family meal-planning activity described in chapter nine. Together they filled in the columns for each day of the week for who would cook and what they would have for dinner. This created an atmosphere of cooperation. When they had all been in on the planning, the children were more willing to eat what someone else had chosen, because they had also had some choices.

The Ainge family also did the shopping together. They divided the shopping list into different sections of the grocery store.

Each member of the family took a different section. The children learned a lot about shopping while having fun together to get a chore done. It is easy to see why this family does not have "war games" at the dinner table. They have been encouraged to use their "power" to contribute, cooperate, and enjoy one another.

STAYING OUT OF CHILDREN'S FIGHTS

The best way to train your children to fight is to keep getting involved in their fights. Parents have a difficult time believing that the main reason children fight is to get parents involved. Parents who stay out of the arguments experience a drastic reduction in fighting.

Most parents recognize the typical pattern of sibling fights based on birth order. The oldest child is usually the most "bugable," and the youngest child usually gets the greatest payoff for getting the mother involved. Thus, the youngest does something to provoke the oldest. This provocation could be anything, from making a face at the oldest to disturbing something in the oldest's room.

When the oldest bites the bait and goes after the youngest, there is a loud scream of protest to the mother from the youngest. The mother becomes involved by scolding the oldest. When the oldest is able to convince her that the youngest started it, the mother replies with, "I don't care what he has done. You are the oldest, and you should know better."

If the mother would notice the look of triumph on the youngest child's face, she would gain much insight into the purpose (mistaken goal) of the behavior. The mother is collaborating in their training to fight as a way of seeking attention, power, or revenge. She reinforces the children's mistaken beliefs about how to find belonging and significance.

Mrs. Reeder decided to stay out of her children's fights. She chose a conflict-free time and explained to them that she really didn't like getting involved in their fights and that from now on she was sure they could figure out ways to solve their own problems. During a family meeting they discussed the Four Problem-Solving Steps outlined in chapter twelve.

The next day, Mrs. Reeder was walking down the hall and happened to see seven-year-old Troy hit five-year-old Shaun on the head with a cap gun. She felt she couldn't ignore that and went charging into the bedroom to stop the fight. As a flashback, she realized that when Shaun was hit, he fell back on the bed and mildly complained to Troy, "That hurt." Then Shaun saw his mother and he let out a loud cry of protest. Mrs. Reeder realized she had been hooked and quickly turned around and went to the bathroom and locked the door. Both children followed her and started banging on the door, each wanting to tell his side of the story.

As Mrs. Reeder sat in the bathroom listening to the boys banging on the door and arguing about who started it, she thought, Dreikurs is crazy! This isn't working! However, she stuck it out a little longer so that she could report back to her study group what happened. The children soon stopped pounding on the door and went away.

Mrs. Reeder continued to stay out of their fights by telling them, "I'm sure you can solve your own problems," whenever they came to her with a complaint. Meanwhile the family continued to discuss possible solutions to problems during family meetings so the children were learning problem-solving skills.

Mrs. Reeder knew this method had been effective when, about a month later, she overheard her four-year-old daughter, Colleen, say to Troy, "I'm going to tell Mom." Troy replied, "She will just tell you to solve your own problem." (Colleen must have known Troy was right, because she didn't tell her mom.)

Mrs. Reeder reported that fighting among her children diminished by about 75 percent. The remaining 25 percent of fights were much milder and more quickly solved.

There are circumstances when staying out of fights may be difficult or inadvisable:

- Some adults find it almost impossible to become unconcerned, even though they intellectually believe it to be the best thing to do.
- When children are very young, they may do serious damage to each other, such as a two-year-old hitting a six-month-old on the head with a toy fire truck. (Many adults use this excuse to get involved in the fights of older children.) If older children really want to hurt each other, they will do it when adults are not around. Adults should not assume the protective role with older children, unless they want it twenty-four hours a day.
- Teachers are responsible for student safety and cannot stay out of fights.

Some parents don't believe children fight mostly for the parents' benefit. They argue that their children fight even when they are not around. I always ask, "How do you know they fight when you are not around?"

They grin sheepishly as they admit, "Because they make sure I find out. They usually greet me at the door with all their complaints. Sometimes they even call me at work to get me involved. I can see now that they are still trying to make me judge, jury, and executioner—of the other guy."

If you can't stand to stay out of your children's fights, and decide to become involved, the most effective way is to "put your children in the same boat." Do not take sides or try to decide who is at fault. Chances are you wouldn't be right, because you never see everything that goes on. "Right" is always a matter of opinion. What seems right to you will surely seem unfair from at least one child's point of view. If you feel you must get involved to stop fights, don't become judge, jury, and executioner. Instead, put them in the same boat and treat them the same.

Mrs. Hamilton noticed two-year-old Marilyn hitting eight-month-old Sally. Mrs. Hamilton felt that Sally had not done anything to provoke Marilyn, but she still put them both "in the same boat." First she picked baby Sally up, put her in her crib, and said, "We'll come get you when you are ready to stop fighting." Then she took Marilyn to her room and said, "Come let me know when you are ready to stop fighting, and we'll go get the baby."

At first glance this may look ridiculous. Why put the baby in her crib for fighting when she was just sitting there, innocently, and doesn't understand her mom's admonition anyway? Many people guess that the purpose of treating them both the same is for the benefit of the older child to avoid feeling always at fault. Actually treating them the same benefits both children. When you take the side of the child you "think" is the victim, you are training that child to adopt a victim mentality. When you always "bully" the child you "think" started it, you are training that child to adopt a "bully" mentality.

We can't know for sure if Sally provoked Marilyn (innocently or purposefully). If she did, reprimanding Marilyn would not only be unfair, but it would teach Sally a good way to get her mother on her side. This is good victim training. If she did not provoke Marilyn, reprimanding Marilyn (because she is older) would teach Sally the possibility of getting special attention by provoking Marilyn. Marilyn might then adopt the mistaken belief that she is most significant as the "bad" child.

Still, people object that it doesn't make sense to put a baby, who did nothing wrong, in her crib. The point is not who did what. The point is that you treat both children the same so one doesn't learn "victim" mentality and the other doesn't learn "bully" mentality. Surely, the baby doesn't mind being put into her crib for few seconds. It is the gesture that counts.

Another way to put children in the same boat is to give them both the same choice. "You can either stop fighting or go outside to settle your fight." Or, "Would you like to go to separate rooms until you are ready to stop fighting, or to the same room to work on a solution?" "Would you both like to sit on my lap until you are ready to stop fighting?" Do or say whatever is comfortable for you—so long as they are treated the same.

I can still hear objections. But what if the older child really did hit the younger child for no reason? Shouldn't the older child be punished? Shouldn't the younger child be comforted?

Since you have read this far, you know that punishment is not an alternative. It is such a ridiculous example to give to children: "I'll hurt you to teach you not to hurt others."

I suggest you comfort the older child first, and then invite him or her to help you comfort the younger one. Again this is not rewarding the older child for "starting" it. It is recognizing that, for some reason, the older child is feeling discouraged. Maybe the older child is feeling dethroned by the younger child. Maybe the older child believes you love the younger one more. The reason isn't important right now. (But dealing with the belief behind the behavior is.) It is important to know when children feel discouraged and need encouragement.

Encouragement might look like this: "Honey, I can see that you are upset." (Validating feelings is very encouraging.) "Would a hug help?" Can you imagine her surprise to receive love and understanding instead of punishment and disdain? After she feels better you might say, "Would you be willing to help your little sister feel better? Do you want to give her a hug first, or do you want me to?" Can you see that these gestures encourage loving, peaceful actions?

Suppose the older child is too upset to give you a hug, or to want to hug the baby. Still, make the gesture. Then say, "I can see you aren't ready yet. I'm going to comfort your sister. When you are ready, you can come help me." The baby is not going to suffer that much more while you take a few seconds to comfort the older child—and you will avoid victim training that could invite the baby to decide, "The way to be special around here is to provoke my older sister."

If you are hearing these methods with your heart, you will get the idea. Put yourself in the shoes of your children. What would help you the most and teach you the most? And, don't forget to use your sense of humor.

One father would stick his thumb in front of his fighting children and say, "I'm a reporter for CBC. Who would like to be the first to speak into my microphone and give me your version of what is happening here?" Sometimes his children would just laugh, and sometimes they would each take a turn telling their version. When they told their versions of the fight, the father would turn to an imaginary audience and say, "Well, folks. You heard it here first. Tune in tomorrow to see how these brilliant children solve this problem." If the problem wasn't defused by then, the father would say, "Are you going to put the problem on the family meeting agenda so the whole family can help with suggestions, or can I meet you here tomorrow—same time, same station—for a report to our audience?"

When adults refuse to get involved in children's fights or put the children in the same boat by treating them the same for fighting, the biggest motive for fighting is eliminated.

NONVERBAL SIGNALS

Most of the methods discussed so far in this chapter are forms of nonverbal signals. They all incorporate other important concepts and attitudes, such as allowing for a cooling-off period and being kind and firm at the same time. They stress action rather than words. When words are necessary, the fewer the better. It is effective to involve children in a problem-solving session, where you decide on a plan that includes a nonverbal signal in order to give adults additional help in learning to keep their mouths shut.

Mr. Perry, a principal, decided to attend a parent study group at his school. He made it clear to the group that he was attending as a parent who would like to learn some skills to use with his own children.

One night he asked the group to help him solve the problem of getting his son, Mike, to take out the garbage. Mike always agreed to do it, but never did without constant reminders. The group gave Mr. Perry several suggestions, such as turning the television off until it was done or giving Mike a choice as to when he would do it. One parent suggested they try the nonverbal signal of turning Mike's empty plate over at the dinner table if he forgot to take the garbage out before dinner. Mr. Perry decided to try this.

First, the family discussed the garbage problem at a family meeting. Mike again reaffirmed that he would do it. Mrs. Perry said, "We appreciate your willingness to help, but we also realize how easy it is to forget. Would it be okay with you if we use a nonverbal signal so that we can stop nagging?"

Mike wanted to know what kind of signal.

Mr. Perry explained the idea of turning his empty plate over at the dinner table. If he came to the table and saw his plate turned over, that would remind him. He could then empty the garbage before coming to the table. Mike said, "That's okay with me."

It was eight days before Mike forgot to empty the garbage. (When children are involved in a problem-solving discussion, they usually cooperate for a while before testing the plan.) When he came to the table and saw his plate turned over, Mike started having a temper tantrum. He whined, "I'm hungry! I'll take the garbage out later! This is really dumb!"

I'm sure you can imagine how difficult it was for Mike's mom and dad to ignore this obnoxious behavior. Most parents would want to say, "Come on, Mike, you agreed, now stop acting like a baby!" If Mike continued his misbehavior, they would want to forget the plan and use punishment (which would stop the present obnoxious behavior, but would not solve the problem of getting the garbage emptied and allow Mike to learn responsibility).

Mr. and Mrs. Perry continued to ignore Mike's temper tantrum, even when he stomped into the kitchen, got the garbage, slammed the garage door on his way out, and then sulked and banged his fork on his plate all during dinner.

The next day Mike remembered to empty the garbage and was very pleasant during dinner. As a result of their consistency in following the agreed-upon plan, Mike did not forget to empty the garbage for two more weeks. When he saw his empty plate turned over again, he said, "Oh, yeah." He then took the garbage out, came to the table, turned his plate over, and was pleasant as he ate with the rest of the family.

Another reason it is difficult for parents to ignore obnoxious misbehavior is the feeling that they are letting children get away with something. They feel they are actually neglecting their duty to do something about it. This could be true, if there weren't some plan or purpose behind the ignoring. Mr. and Mrs. Perry let Mike "get away with" his temporary outburst (remember, things often get worse before they get better), but since it was part of an agreed-upon plan, they solved the problem of continuous nagging over neglected chores.

Mrs. Beal was frustrated because it irritated her so much when the children would come home from school and dump their books on the couch. Constant nagging was not producing any change. During a family meeting she told her children she didn't want to yell and nag anymore about this problem. She suggested the nonverbal signal of putting a pillow slip over the television as a reminder that there were books on the couch.

The children agreed to this plan, and it worked very well. Their mother no longer got involved beyond the signal. When the children saw the pillow slip, they either picked up their own books or reminded someone else to.

Several weeks later, Mrs. Beal wanted to watch her favorite soap opera after the children had gone to school. She was surprised to find a pillow slip on the television. She looked at the couch and saw the packages she had left there the night before, when she was in a hurry to fix dinner.

The whole family had a good laugh over this turn of events. They enjoyed this method, and from then on the children thought of many nonverbal signals as solutions to problems.

Mrs. Reed likes to use nonverbal signals in her fifth-grade classroom. She teaches them to her students almost as a second language on the first day of school. One is to have them give her the nonverbal signal of sitting quietly with their hands clasped on top of their desks when they were ready to listen. When she wants them to turn around and sit down during class or an assembly, she raises her right index finger and makes two small circles and then two up-and-down motions in the air to the rhythm of the words "Turn around and sit down." She also taught them a signal for quiet during extreme noise. She would clap her hands once. Everyone who heard the single clap would clap once. Then she would clap twice. By now, several students had heard the echo clap of their classmates and were ready to join the response of two claps. Two claps were usually enough to get everyone quiet. Once in a while it would take three claps before everyone would hear and echo with three claps.

Mrs. Norwood and her daughter Mary always felt bad after their fights and were quick to apologize. One day they discussed this and decided to see which one would be the first to remember to put her hand over her heart as a nonverbal signal for "I love you" in the middle of a fight. Mrs. Norwood shared that it was a bit embarrassing that Mary was usually the first to re-member.

CHOICES

One of the biggest mistakes for adults is to make demands in-stead of offering choices. Children often respond to choices when they will not respond to demands, especially when you fol-low the choice with, "You decide." Choices should be respect-ful and should focus attention on the needs of the situation. Choices are directly related to responsibility. Younger children are less capable of wide responsibility, so their choices are more limited. Older children are capable of broader choices, because they can assume responsibility for the consequences of their choice.

For instance, younger children might be given the choice of going to bed now or in five minutes. Older children might be given full responsibility for choosing their bedtime, because they also take full responsibility for getting themselves up in the morning and off to school without any hassles.

Choices are also directly related to the respect for, and conve-nience of, others. Younger children might be given the choice of coming to dinner on time or waiting until the next meal to eat, rather than expecting someone to cook and clean up more than once. Older children might be given the choice of being on time or fixing their own dinner and cleaning up any mess they make.

Whenever a choice is given, either alternative should be ac-ceptable to the adult. My first try at choices was to ask my three-year-old: "Do you want to get ready for bed?" She didn't. Obviously, the choice I offered was beyond the need (mine and hers) for her to go to bed, and the choice I offered did not in-clude an alternative I was willing to accept. I waited five minutes and started again by asking, "Would you like to wear your pink pajamas or your blue pajamas? You decide." She chose her blue pajamas and started putting them on. Adding, "You decide," after a choice is empowering. It adds emphasis to the fact that the child does have a choice.

What if they don't want either choice and want to do something else? If the something else is acceptable to you, fine. If it is not, say, "That isn't one of the choices." And then repeat the choices and, "You decide."

Children may not have a choice about many things, such as whether or not to do their homework. Homework needs to be done, but children can be offered a choice as to when they would like to do it, such as right after school, just before dinner, or after dinner.

"AS SOON AS, THEN . . ."

"As soon as you pick up your toys, then we will go to the park." This statement usually is more effective than "If you pick up your toys, we will go to the park." The first is heard by children as a kind but firm statement indicating what you are willing to do under a prescribed set of circumstances. The latter statement is heard by children (and usually meant by adults) as a challenge to a power contest. "As soon as, then" is effective when it doesn't have any energy attached to it. In other words, it doesn't matter to you if you go to the park or not. You know the kids want to, so it is up to them to meet the requirements. What you need to accept is that you may not go to the park because the children choose to avoid picking up their toys. If you are invested in going to the park try curiosity questions: "Who wants to go to the park? What needs to be done before we can go?"

Many teachers have found it effective to say, "As soon as you are ready, we will begin our lesson." They had an attitude of respect for themselves, their students, and the needs of the situation—the key to success in this method. "As soon as" should be said in a tone of voice that indicates you will withdraw from the situation until the requirements are met. You should then become unconcerned and let the child experience the consequences of his or her choice. If you do not become unconcerned, it will become a power contest no matter what words you use.

ALLOWANCE MONEY

Allowances can be a great teaching tool. When children have a regular allowance they can learn the value of money—if parents handle allowances effectively.

Allowance money should not be used for punishment or reward. Many parents use allowance money as leverage to try to make children responsible for their chores. They give out allowances as a reward when chores are done and withhold allowances as a punishment when chores are not done. Children will learn much more about money and responsibility when the threat is taken away. Use family meetings to teach responsibility regarding chores and keep allowance a separate issue.

When children have their own allowance, you can eliminate getting hooked when they see something they want at the store. Whenever Mary says, "I want that!" her mother replies, "Do you have enough money?" Mary usually doesn't, so her mother says, "Well, maybe you would like to save your allowance so you can buy it."

Mary usually thinks she wants it so bad that she will save her money faithfully until she can buy it. However, it is usually forgotten within hours. She usually doesn't really want it badly enough to save her own money, even though she would be glad to have her mom spend her money.

As children get older and want an expensive item like a bike, you might have them save ten dollars or more toward the bike. When children have some of their own money invested in things, they are much more responsible about taking care of them. Children can also use their allowance money to make up for damage they might do to property belonging to someone else.

REVIEW

All of the methods explained in this chapter can be effective when used and taught in a friendly manner. Your attitude, intent, and manner are the keys to success. Some adults use these methods in the same manner and for the same purposes as they use punishment. The punitive approach invites rebellion or blind submission. The positive approach invites cooperation, mutual respect, responsibility, and social responsibility.

Positive Discipline Tools

1. Take some cooling-off time because you do better when you feel better—the bathroom technique (for parents), the novel technique (for teachers), Positive Time-out (for children and adults).
2. Decide what you will do instead of what you will try to make children do.
3. Let your children know in advance what you plan to do.
4. Use kind and firm action—not words. (Keep your mouth shut and act.)
5. When words are necessary, make them few and stated kindly and firmly.
6. Use emotional withdrawal to stay out of power struggles and wait for a calm time to focus on solutions.
7. Use routine charts to avoid power struggles.
8. Avoid bedtime hassles by sharing happiest and saddest moments while tucking children in.
9. Avoid power struggles by getting children involved in solutions.

10. Stay out of children's fights—or treat children the same.
11. First comfort the one who did the hurting. Then invite that child to help you comfort the one who was hurt.
12. Validate feelings.
13. Give hugs.
14. Use your sense of humor.
15. Get children involved in mealtime planning, cooking, and cleaning.
16. Establish nonverbal reminders with children for what needs to be done.
17. Offer choices instead of making demands.
18. Use "As soon as _____, then _____."
19. Use allowance money to teach money management—not for punishment or reward.

Questions

1. What are several methods that can be used as a cooling-off period?
2. What is the rationale for the method "Decide what you will do, not what you will make the children do"? Why is it effective?
3. What are the six points to remember to increase the effectiveness of the foregoing methods?
4. What does it mean to become unconcerned when using this method? What should you do if you cannot become unconcerned?
5. What does it mean to emotionally withdraw?
6. What should always take place after a cooling-off period or any other form of withdrawal?
7. What are the key concepts necessary to avoid morning and bedtime hassles?
8. Why does quality bedtime sharing help avoid bedtime hassles?

9. What are the negative results of getting involved in children's fights?

10. What is the procedure you should follow when you decide to stay out of children's fights?

11. What are the three circumstances when it may not be advisable to stay out of fights?

12. When the decision has been made to get involved in children's fights, what is the most effective method to use?

13. What does it mean to "put them in the same boat"? What negative results does this help avoid?

14. What are nonverbal signals? What can be accomplished by using them?

15. What are the benefits of giving choices?

16. What are some guidelines for assuring the effectiveness of choices?

17. What are the advantages of following the suggestions for allowance money?

18. What are the keys to success in using any of the methods suggested in this book?

Chapter Twelve

LOVE AND JOY IN
HOMES AND CLASSROOMS

The primary goal of Positive Discipline is to enable both adults and children to experience more joy, harmony, cooperation, shared responsibility, mutual respect, and love in their life and relationships. We often act as though we have forgotten that love and joy are the whole point of living and working with children, and find ourselves acting out of fear, judgment, expectations, blame, disappointment, and anger. Then we wonder why we feel so miserable.

THREE REMINDERS

Following are three reminders that show us how to avoid detours that keep us from experiencing love, joy, and satisfaction in our relationships with children.

1. What We Do Is Never as Important as How We Do It

The feeling and attitude behind what we do will determine the "how." The feeling behind words is often most evident in our tone of voice.

The other day I came home from a trip and was welcomed by a sink full of dirty dishes. I felt discouraged and angry and started scolding and criticizing. "We have agreed that everyone will put their dishes in the dishwasher. How come no one keeps their agreements when I'm not around?"

I looked for someone to blame, but everyone claimed, "I didn't do it."

From a negative feeling I said, "Okay, we have to have a family meeting and decide what to do about this."

Can you imagine the outcome if we had tried to have a family meeting based on my feelings of blame and criticism? We would not have found the kind of effective solution that comes from an atmosphere of love and respect. My attacking attitude would have inspired defensiveness and counterattacks instead of harmony.

I realized what I was doing and immediately changed directions. I could see that my negative attitude would not produce the results I wanted—to say nothing of how miserable it made me feel at the time. As soon as I changed my attitude, my feelings changed and I had an immediate inspiration about how to get positive results.

I said to my family, "Let's go out for pizza. Then we will have a family meeting to look for solutions instead of blame."

Based on those feelings, we had a very successful family meeting. We laughingly agreed that it must have been a phantom who had left the dishes in the sink. When we stopped looking for blame and concentrated on solutions, Mark and Mary came up with a great plan. They proposed that we would all be assigned two days a week for KP duty to take care of the phantom's dirty dishes. As you might guess, fewer dishes were left in the sink after this friendly discussion where everyone took responsibility to solve the problem.

Acting from negative thoughts and feelings is a guaranteed

detour away from love, joy, and positive results. By dismissing our negative attitudes, we allow our natural good feelings and common sense to rise to the surface.

2. See Mistakes as Opportunities to Learn

Throughout this book, I have discussed the importance of helping children experience mistakes as opportunities to learn. When adults do not apply this principle to themselves, it is an immediate detour away from love, joy, and positive results, as illustrated in the following example:

Mickey, a second grader, kicked a classmate. The teacher, Mrs. Heaton, was very upset with Mickey. She wanted to teach him not to hurt other people. She took him outside the classroom door to reprimand him. She said, "How would you like it if other people kicked you?"

In her attempt to teach him how it felt, she kicked him—a little harder than she meant to. An aide was walking by and witnessed this incident. The aide reported it to the principal.

Mrs. Heaton felt very bad about what she had done. She believes in the principles of Positive Discipline and has been trying to implement them for years. She called to ask, "What went wrong? How could I have done such a thing? What else could I do?"

First Mrs. Heaton was assured that she is very normal. Is there a parent or teacher on this planet who has not "lost it" and reacted in anger instead of acting in ways that would be more beneficial for long-range results?

Second, Mrs. Heaton was acknowledged for being aware that she had made a mistake. She was encouraged to pat herself on the back instead of beating up on herself. Too many parents and teachers would not realize they had made a mistake.

Third, Mrs. Heaton was acknowledged for wanting to improve and do better. She was encouraged to see this as a gift (or a wake-up call) that motivated her to seek answers for future improved behavior on her part.

The Positive Discipline books are full of what else to do instead of reacting. That is not the point here. The point is that we need to realize that all human beings get hooked into reacting instead of acting. Most adults truly mean well—they simply want to teach children to be more respectful. The problem is that, when reacting, we use disrespectful behavior (we misbehave) in our attempts to teach respect. While reacting, we become more interested (without thinking about it) in making a child "pay" through blame, shame, and pain for what he or she has done. We are not thinking about the long-term effects on the child. If we were, we would not be reacting.

Fortunately, this can be the beginning, not the end. We have found that no matter how many times we react, and forget to use the principles of Positive Discipline, we can always go back to the principles and clean up the messes we made while reacting. It is true, over and over again, that mistakes are wonderful opportunities for learning.

After learning from a mistake, adults will find that children are very forgiving when they use the Three R's of Recovery. It took Mrs. Heaton more than a week to recover from her humiliation and self-flagellation. Then she took Mickey aside and apologized. She said, "Mickey, I'm so sorry I kicked you. I was so mad at you for kicking Joey but did the same thing I was mad at you for. That wasn't very smart of me, was it?"

Mickey just looked at her sheepishly, but she had his attention. She continued, "It wasn't very nice of me either, was it?"

Mickey stuck out his lower lip and shook his head.

Mrs. Heaton asked, "Does it make you feel any better to hear me say 'I'm sorry'?"

Mickey nodded.

Mrs. Heaton continued. "How do you think it would make Joey feel if you told him you were sorry?"

Mickey muttered, "Better."

Mrs. Heaton asked, "How would you feel about apologizing to Joey, and then the three of us could get together and work on ways to handle the problem you were having with Joey. Or we could put it on the class-meeting agenda and get the whole class to help. Which would you prefer?"

Mickey said, "Just us."

Mrs. Heaton asked, "How much time do you need to apologize to Joey and ask him if he would join us for a problem-solving session?"

Mickey brightened and said, "I can do it today."

Mrs. Heaton said, "Great. You let me know when you and Joey are ready, and we'll set a time."

Mrs. Heaton, Mickey, and Joey got together the next day and discussed each boy's perception of what had happened, what caused it to happen, how they felt about it, what they had learned from the experience, and their ideas about how to solve the problem. They also discussed the concept of mistakes as opportunities for learning. The boys walked away feeling very pleased about an agreement they had made to avoid fighting in the future.

This is an excellent example of how a mistake provides many opportunities for learning. Mrs. Heaton was able to model taking responsibility for a mistake and apologizing. She then helped Mickey feel good about apologizing for his mistake. She was able to help the boys practice listening to each other's perceptions of the experience. Finally, they practiced the wonderful life skill of brainstorming for solutions and agreeing on one that they would both like to try.

Can we ever say it enough? Mistakes are wonderful opportunities for learning—for adults and children.

Adults could learn more about the principle of mistakes as opportunities for learning by observing toddlers when they're learning to walk. Toddlers don't waste time feeling inadequate every time they fall. They simply get up and go again. If they are hurt by the fall, they may cry for a few minutes before they get on their way again, but they don't add blame, criticism, or other self-defeating messages to their experience. We can help our children maintain this simple way of experiencing life by rediscovering the value of mistakes for ourselves.

Thinking we have to be perfect is a well-traveled detour away from love and joy in life. The Four R's of Recovery (as discussed in chapter two) can put us back on course.

3. Sometimes We Have to Learn the Same Thing Over and Over Again

How many parents have said, "How many times do I have to tell you?"

These parents set themselves up for disappointment and frustration if they don't understand that the answer may be, "Over and over and over." (I often believe that children don't really understand what we try to teach them until they have their own children and try to teach them the same things.)

Mrs. Bordeau expressed such relief in hearing this principle. She said, "I thought that it would take only one family meeting to get my children to cooperate in doing their chores. Since their enthusiasm didn't last longer than a week, I just assumed it wasn't working and went back to daily nagging."

Mrs. Bordeau didn't realize how much progress she had made to get enthusiasm for even a week. I told her about the three-week syndrome (explained in chapter nine) and how I have accepted with gratitude that dealing with chores once every three weeks is much nicer than daily nagging and frustration.

Children are not the only ones who need opportunities to

learn over and over again. Otherwise, why would we need to use the Four R's of Recovery so often? A detour to misery is feeling inadequate or frustrated every time we or our children do not learn something once and for all. The road to love and joy includes not only acceptance that we will make mistakes but that we will have opportunities to learn over and over again. It is an important part of the learning process.

Many methods have been presented in this book. If they are seen only as techniques, they will fail. Many positive attitudes have also been presented. When the methods are put together with the positive attitudes, they become concepts that create an atmosphere of love, mutual respect, cooperation, and enjoyment between children.

This chapter includes many concepts that require adult participation and guidance in order to help children develop a strong foundation. An attitude of love and joy is essential. And it helps to look for the positive aspects of a situation.

FINDING THE POSITIVE IN A SITUATION

Lori was suspended from school for having cigarettes in her locker. She told her dad, "I don't know how they got there! I was just putting them in my pocket to take them to the principal when a teacher came by and sent me to the office." Dad had a hard time believing that Lori didn't know how the cigarettes got into her locker, since it has a combination lock. He also found it hard to believe that she was putting them in her pocket to take them to the principal. He felt disappointed that Lori would lie to him because they had always been such a close and loving family. He was also worried that she was beginning to ruin her life by getting involved in smoking, drinking, and drugs.

Dad felt like scolding and punishing and letting her know how disappointed he was. Instead he decided to look for the positive. It is never difficult to find, if you are willing to look for it. As he got into Lori's world he could understand that she was probably having a tough time deciding how to stick with family values and still be part of the crowd. He also realized that the only reason Lori would lie to him would be because she loved him so much that she wouldn't want to disappoint him.

With this understanding, Dad approached Lori. Instead of scolding and punishing, he kindly said, "Lori, I'll bet it is really difficult trying to figure out how to stick up for what you believe and yet not be called a 'party pooper' by your friends."

Lori felt such relief as she said, "Yes, it is."

Dad went on, "And I'll bet that if you would ever lie to us, it would be because you love us so much you wouldn't want to disappoint us." Lori got tears in her eyes and could only nod in agreement. Dad added, "Lori, we would be disappointed if you did something that would hurt you, but if you don't know that you can always tell us anything, then we aren't doing a good enough job in letting you know how much we love you—unconditionally." Lori gave her dad a big hug, and they just held each other for a while.

They never did directly discuss the problem of smoking and lying. Over a year has gone by, and Lori seems to delight in letting her mom and dad know every time she resists the temptation to do something contrary to her values. She also feels proud that she is influencing her friends to stick up for their values.

GIVING CHILDREN THE BENEFIT OF THE DOUBT

Every child wants to succeed. Every child wants to have good relationships with others. Every child wants to have a sense of belonging and significance. When we remember this, we will give misbehaving children the benefit of the doubt. Instead of assuming they want to be difficult, we will assume they want positive results and are simply confused about how to achieve them. They don't have the knowledge, the skills, or the maturity to find belonging and significance in useful ways. It is our job to help them develop what they need. To be effective, our approach must be based on an attitude, "I know you want to succeed. How can I help?" When we have this attitude, children are more likely to feel loved unconditionally.

EXPRESSING UNCONDITIONAL LOVE

Children need to know that they are more important than anything they do. They need to know that they are more important than the material possessions in our lives. Fred's mom made some mistakes before she remembered this important point.

Fred broke one of his mother's prize antique vases. She was so heartbroken over it that she sat down and cried. Fred felt very bad about what he had done, but finally asked, "Mommy, would you feel that bad if something happened to me?"

Children often don't know how important and loved they are. Sometimes parents and teachers focus so much on misbehavior that they lose sight of the child—and the child loses sight of himself or herself.

I was counseling one family whose daughter had stolen some clothing (as a joke, she claimed) from a friend she was mad at. The mother and sister were so upset about this that they were calling her a thief and wondering if there wasn't something basically wrong with her. I asked them why they were so upset. What was their real concern? The mother answered that she was afraid her daughter might end up in juvenile hall. I asked why that was a problem. The mother shared that she was concerned about how much that would hurt her daughter. I then asked the mother how she thought her daughter felt about being called a thief and being accused of having something wrong with her. She admitted that she could see how much she was already hurting her daughter while claiming to be concerned that she would be hurt.

I asked the daughter which she felt would hurt her more, going to juvenile hall or what she was now experiencing with her mother. She said, "This hurts much worse."

Since the daughter is a teenager, there is no way her mother can control her. This girl needs to experience the consequences of her behavior, and love and support from her mother.

It is so easy to get things backward so that our intended message is lost. This mother was humiliating her daughter because she loved her and meant to save her from being hurt. All her daughter heard was the humiliation, which she interpreted to mean, "Mother doesn't even like me."

I know you love your children, and you know you love your children, but do they know you love them? You might be surprised if you ask.

One mother asked her three-year-old, "Do you know I really love you?"

The reply was, "Yes, I know you love me if I be good."

A teenager replied to the same question, "I know you love me if I get good grades."

We often nag our children to do better. We want them to be better because we love them and think they will be happier if they do what we think is good for them. They usually do not hear that we want them to do better for them. What they hear is, "I can never do anything good enough. I can't live up to your expectations. You want me to be better for you, not for me."

Remember that children do better when they feel better. Nothing feels better than unconditional love. Most parents are not aware that they are being unloving when they use punishment. In fact, most parents use punishment in the name of love. In our book *Parents Who Love Too Much*,[1] we use the following example to show how parents use punishment when other methods would be more effective, and how many adults think, "I was punished, and I turned out just fine."

Yes, most of us turned out just "fine," even though we were punished. We can laugh at some of the punishments we received as a child—and even say we deserved them. However, if we had been allowed to learn from our mistakes instead of being made to pay for them, is it possible we might be even better than "fine"?

In the following story, Stan was led through a process that helped him understand the difference between punishment (that helped him turn out just fine) and nonpunitive discipline that could have helped him so much more.

Stan told his parenting group about a time he cheated on a fifth-grade test. He said, "I was stupid enough to write some answers on the palm of my hand. The teacher saw me open my fist to find an answer." This teacher grabbed Stan's paper and, in front of everyone in the class, tore it up. He received an F on the test and was publicly called a cheater. The teacher told his parents. His father gave him a whipping and grounded him for a month. Stan said, "I never cheated again, and I certainly deserved the F."

The group leader helped him explore this experience to help everyone in the class see if there might have been a more productive way to handle this situation.

Leader: Does everyone agree with Stan that he deserved the F?

Group: Yes.

Leader: Would that have been enough to teach him the consequences of his choices, or did he need the punishment also?

Group: Hmmmmm.

Leader: What do you think, Stan? How did you feel about getting the F for cheating?

Stan: I felt very guilty and very embarrassed.

Leader: What did you decide from that?

Stan: That I wouldn't do it again.

Leader: What did you decide after receiving the whipping? (punishment)

Stan: That I was a disappointment to my parents. I still worry about disappointing them.

Leader: So how did the punishment help you?

Stan: Well, I had already decided I wouldn't cheat again. The guilt and embarrassment of getting caught in front of others was enough to teach me that lesson. Actually, the worry about disappointing my parents is a real burden.

Leader: If you had a magic wand and could change the script of that event, how would you change it? How would you change what anyone said or did?

Stan: Well, I wouldn't cheat.

Leader: And after that?

Stan: I don't know.

Leader: Who has any ideas you could give Stan? It is usually easier to see possibilities when you aren't emotionally involved. What could Stan's teacher or parents have done or said that would have demonstrated kind and firm discipline?

Group member: I'm a teacher, and I'm learning a lot from this. The teacher could have taken Stan aside and asked him why he was cheating.

Leader: Stan, what would you have answered to that?

Stan: That I wanted to pass the test.

Group member: Then I could appreciate his desire to pass and ask him how he felt about cheating as a way to accomplish that.

Stan: I would promise never to do it again.

Group member: I would then tell him he would have to

receive an F for this test but that I was glad he had learned to avoid cheating. I would then ask him to prepare a plan for me about what he would do to pass the next test.

Stan: I would still feel guilty and embarrassed about cheating, but I would also appreciate the kindness along with the firmness. Now I see what that means.

Leader: Now do you have any ideas how you could use your magic wand to change what your parents did?

Stan: It would have been nice if they had acknowledged how guilty and embarrassed I felt. They could have empathized about what a tough lesson that was for me to learn. Then they could express their faith in me to learn from my experience and to do the right thing in the future. They could reassure me that they would love me no matter what, but that they hoped I wouldn't disappoint myself in the future. Wow, what a concept— to worry more about disappointing myself than my parents. I find that very encouraging.

Several points are made by this discussion about nonpunitive parenting:

1. Nonpunitive parenting does not mean letting children "get away" with their behavior.
2. Nonpunitive parenting does mean helping children explore the consequences of their choices in a supportive and encouraging environment so that lasting growth and learning can take place.
3. Most people turned out "fine" even if they were punished—and they might have learned even more had they received both kindness and firmness to learn from mistakes.

Stan's father did not have the benefit of understanding the long-term results of his parenting methods. He did not have the benefit of understanding the importance of getting into the child's world. He did not know that children do better when they feel better. He did not know the power of unconditional love combined with kindness and firmness at the same time. If he had, Stan might have felt more empowered through the Four Steps for Winning Cooperation.

THE FOUR STEPS FOR WINNING COOPERATION

The Four Steps for Winning Cooperation (which were presented in chapter two) are excellent for helping you get into the child's world. Use these steps whenever you feel a gap in your communication that is creating hostility and resentment. Both of you will feel understood after using this process.

Most parents want their children to get better grades. Children often interpret this to mean that grades are more important than they are. The Four Steps for Winning Cooperation might be helpful when our children doubt the benefits of your suggestions.

1. Express understanding for the child's feelings: "Does it seem to you that I want you to get better grades for me or for you?"
2. Show empathy without condoning: "I can understand how it might seem like you can't do things good enough for me. When my parents wanted me to do better, I felt like I was supposed to live for them and their expectations."
3. Share your real feelings: "I honestly want you to get better grades because I think you would benefit. I know it can seem like a drag now, but a good education opens many doors to you in the future and offers you more choices."

4. Invite the child to focus on a solution: "How can we work this out so that you can work on improvement that you see as beneficial to you rather than criticism from me?"

Creating an atmosphere of cooperation is essential for teaching communication and problem-solving skills that incorporate the essence of social responsibility. When children have good communication and problem-solving skills, they will greatly improve the quality of their interpersonal relationships and life circumstances. The best way to teach these skills is to model them with your own behavior when working with children. Example is the best teacher.

TEACH AND MODEL COMMUNICATION AND PROBLEM-SOLVING SKILLS

Family meetings and class meetings give children and adults the opportunity to practice many communication and problem-solving skills together. If you have been using this process, you have probably noticed your children using skills they learned during the meetings in other areas of their lives.

Positive Discipline includes many options for communication and problem solving besides family and class meetings. The same skills used in meetings can also be used for problem solving between two people. Curiosity questions provide a great platform for communication and problem solving, as do the Four Steps for Winning Cooperation—to name just a few. Another possibility is to teach children the following four problem-solving steps when they're trying to resolve a conflict on a one-to-one basis.

Four Problem-Solving Steps

1. Ignore it. (It takes more courage to walk away than to stay and fight.)
    a. Do something else. (Find another game or activity.)
    b. Leave long enough for a cooling-off period, then follow up with the following steps.
2. Talk it over respectfully.
    a. Tell the other person how you feel. Let him or her know you don't like what is happening.
    b. Listen to what the other person says about how he or she feels and what he or she doesn't like.
    c. Share what you think you did to contribute to the problem.
    d. Tell the other person what you are willing to do differently.
3. Agree together on a solution. For example:
    a. Work out a plan for sharing or taking turns.
    b. Apologize.
4. Ask for help if you can't work it out together.
    a. Put it on the agenda. (This can also be a first choice and is not meant to indicate a last resort.)
    b. Talk it over with a parent, teacher, or friend.

After discussing these skills, have the children role-play the following hypothetical situations. Have them solve each of the situations four different ways (one for each of the steps).

- Fighting over whose turn it is to use the tetherball.
- Shoving in line.
- Calling people bad names.
- Fighting over whose turn it is to sit by the window in the car.

Teachers can put the Four Problem-Solving Steps on a poster for children to refer to. Some teachers require that children use these steps before they put a problem on the class meeting agenda. Other teachers prefer the class meeting process because it teaches so many other skills. Instead of making one better than the other (class meetings or one-on-one), let children choose which option they would prefer at the moment.

Mrs. Underwood explained how she uses the Four Problem-Solving Steps. The children in her third-grade class have permission to leave the room at any time to use the problem-solving steps with another person. Quite often she will watch two children leave the room and then see them sitting by the fence talking. A few minutes later they come back to the classroom and go about their business. She has explained to the children that they do not need to share their discussion with anyone else if they don't want to. During class meetings she will ask if anyone would like to share how they have solved a problem.

Parents can teach these skills when their children come to them with a problem. Have them wait for a cooling-off period or use the Four Steps for Winning Cooperation so that they will be ready for problem solving. We sometimes use these steps during bedtime sharing.

HELP CHILDREN DEVELOP A SENSE OF RESPONSIBILITY

All the concepts taught in this book help children develop a sense of responsibility. Children will not learn responsibility if adults keep doing for children what they can and should do for themselves.

Parents are not the only ones who do things for children that they could do for themselves. There are many ways teachers could allow children to help. Students would learn more responsibility if teachers would pretend they could not use their arms or legs. Imagine the jobs children would then be allowed to do. They would then feel needed, which would lead to feelings of belonging and significance.

TAKE FULL RESPONSIBILITY YOURSELF

What about adult responsibility? It is not helpful to blame ourselves and feel guilty. It is helpful to be aware of mistakes we might be making so that we can know what to do to correct them and produce the results we want.

What would happen if adults assumed full responsibility for creating whatever they complain about? How would things be different if parents and teachers were aware of their own misbehavior (lack of knowledge or lack of skills) as well as the misbehavior (lack of knowledge, skills, and maturity) of children? It would be so much easier to focus on solutions after everyone takes responsibility without blame or shame.

Whenever adults get into power struggles or revenge mode, do not get into the child's world, do not take time for training, forget to be kind and firm at the same time, use a disrespectful tone of voice, or use any other kind of punishment, they will probably inspire "discouraged" behavior in their children.

HAVE COMPASSION FOR YOURSELF

Remember, mistakes are wonderful opportunities for learning. Have compassion for yourself when you make mistakes—and learn from them. I have been learning from parenting mistakes for twenty-five years. Even though I make many mistakes, I love these principles because they are wonderful guidelines to help me get back on track every time I get lost.

Before I learned to have compassion for myself, I was very hard on myself every time I didn't practice what I preach. I would cry on my husband's shoulder, "How can I travel around telling other parents and teachers how to be more effective with children when I don't always do it myself?" He would remind me of other concepts I preach:

- Mistakes are wonderful opportunities for learning.
- Focus on the positive. (I do use these principles more often than I don't.)
- Have the courage to be imperfect, since it is part of being human.
- Cool off—and then fix it.

Having compassion for yourself means remembering these concepts and continuing to love yourself and love life. With a loving attitude, things will always get better.

REINFORCE YOUR LEARNING

If you like the concepts presented in *Positive Discipline*, I strongly urge you to read the book again. I guarantee that you will get at least ten times more out of it during a second reading. Repetition is always important for increasing learning, but you will also find that you will see things you totally missed the first time. Many of the concepts presented in the beginning will make more sense because you are now familiar with the rest of the concepts and will be able to put it all together.

I know from personal experience, and from reports from hundreds of parents and teachers, that these concepts really work when they are used correctly. Positive Discipline is an effective and positive way of solving current problems. Even more important, it gives children the foundation they need to continue building their lives independently in effective and positive directions.

Adults have a leadership responsibility to help children develop characteristics that will enable them to live happy, productive lives. It is our job to provide them with a good foundation that they can build upon. Teaching them self-discipline, responsibility, cooperation, and problem-solving skills helps them establish an excellent foundation. When children exhibit these characteristics and skills, they will feel a greater sense of belonging and significance that will manifest itself through positive behavior.

Positive Discipline is not about perfection. It is so gratifying to hear parents say, "My children are still not perfect, and neither am I, but we sure do enjoy one another more." It is wonderful to hear teachers say, "It is true that kids aren't the same as they used to be, so I'm glad I have learned other ways, besides control, to work effectively with children today." These principles do not guarantee perfection—just a whole lot more love and joy along the way.

REVIEW

Positive Discipline Tools

1. The feeling behind what you do is more important than what you do.
2. See mistakes as opportunities for learning.
3. Be patient with yourself as you have to learn the same things over and over. This is an important part of the learning process.
4. Express unconditional love.
5. Give children the benefit of the doubt.
6. Use the Four Steps for Winning Cooperation.
7. Teach and model communication and problem-solving skills.
8. Help children develop a sense of responsibility.
9. Take full responsibility for your part in any conflict.

10. Have compassion for yourself.

11. Reinforce your learning by reading and practicing over and over.

Questions

1. What is the primary goal of Positive Discipline?

2. What are the reasons why *how* we do something is more important than *what* we do? Share personal examples of how the impact of something you do would be different if you changed *how* you did it.

3. How many times can we learn from the same mistake? Discuss whether this applies to all mistakes or if there are some we are justified in feeling bad about.

4. What happens if a method is used without the proper feelings and attitudes behind it?

5. How is the concept of "turning out just fine," even though you were punished, misleading?

6. What are the Four Problem-Solving Steps? How might children benefit from learning them?

7. What can adults learn from taking full responsibility?

8. What happens if you don't have compassion for yourself? What happens if you do have compassion for yourself?

9. What are the benefits of seeing the positive in everything?

10. What is the importance of conveying unconditional love? Discuss the differences between what adults mean and what children hear.

11. Why would anyone want to read a book more than once?

Appendix I

STARTING A POSITIVE DISCIPLINE
STUDY GROUP

In 1965 I was struggling. I wanted to be a good mother, but it did not come naturally for me. I was so grateful to learn the concepts taught in this book, but found I often reverted to old habits. Leading parent study groups kept me on track and significantly deepened my understanding and improved my practical application of skills.

Since the first edition of *Positive Discipline* Lynn Lott and I expanded an experiential model for teaching parenting classes. The manual for this model is called *Teaching Parenting the Positive Discipline Way*. It is full of experiential activities that are much more effective than lectures in teaching principles and skills. We offer two-day training sessions for facilitators of parent education classes.[1]

Because I now prefer the experiential model for parent classes, I hesitated to include this section in the present edition. However, I have had feedback from many parents who have shared that they benefited significantly by using the following schedule and information.

GETTING STARTED

You could start with just a few friends and neighbors, or you may want to jump right in and practice with a larger group. School principals are often willing to cooperate and would be happy to send the flyer on page 313 to parents. Remember, you don't have to be an expert. Let your group members know that you are all in this together and that you have as much to learn as they do, even though you are the facilitator. Find a cofacilitator if you can. Then simply follow the schedule beginning on page 314.

THE PROBLEM-SOLVING FORM

It is very effective to involve parent study group participants in helping one another brainstorm for solutions to problems. We find out how much we know when we can be objective with someone else's concern.

There is a problem-solving form on page 319 to use as a guide for discussing specific situations. Group facilitators might like to copy several of these forms to distribute to each member during the first session. When someone thinks of a specific problem, it can be written down and saved to share with the group at the appropriate time. Knowing that they will be able to work on specific situations later will encourage group members to stay on task when other material is being covered.

The most wonderful thing about leading a parent study group is that you will learn more than anyone. The exciting thing is that learning is a lifelong process. Don't get discouraged. Just keep leading study groups and keep learning.

SAMPLE FLYER

How To Achieve Positive Discipline at Home and at School

Attend a Parent Study Group

Learn how to help children develop:

- Self-discipline
- Problem-solving skills
- Responsibility
- Self-esteem

If you have hassles with children over such problems as:

Fighting	Responsibility
Chores	Mealtime
Homework	Getting up and off to
Bedtime	school without nagging
Sharing	Back talk

you will learn to understand why children misbehave. You will also learn specific, nonpunitive methods to help solve these problems.

When: Thursday evenings from 7:00 to 9:00 for six weeks beginning on _____

Where: School library

Cut and return to school:

☐ Yes, I would like to attend.

☐ I am unable to attend on Thursdays, but contact me for another day.

Name _____ Phone _____

STUDY GROUP SCHEDULE

Week One

Introduction: Discuss the principles regarding groups explained in the Introduction, and in the Group Participation challenges on pages 316–318.

Birth-order exercise: This exercise, found at the end of chapter three, is a good get-acquainted activity.

Problem-solving form (see page 319): Pass out several of these to all the group members so that they can remember situations they want to work on in the fourth week. (Read "Using the Problem-Solving Form" on page 320 so you will be familiar with its use.)

Reading assignment: Assign the chapters and questions to be discussed next week. (There should be a reading assignment each week corresponding to whatever is on the agenda for the following week.)

Homework assignment: Chapters one, two, and three.

Week Two

Exercise: Have group members choose a partner and describe a time when they experienced one of the Four R's of Punishment described in chapter one. Then invite sharing with the large group.

Exercise: Take a few minutes to reflect on a situation with a child that might have been different if you had started with a message of love. Share with a partner. Invite sharing with the large group.

Discuss the tools and questions at the end of chapters one, two, and three. Ask participants to share a time when they could have used one of the tools.

Homework Assignment: Chapters four, five, and six.

Problem-solving form (see page 319): Pass out copies to each participant. Let them know that you will ask for a volunteer each week to use the form to find solutions to a specific concern. (Even if their problem isn't chosen, they will learn a lot from the one that is chosen.)

Week Three

Discussion questions and tools for chapters four, five, and six.

Problem-solving form (see page 319): Ask for volunteers who would like to work on specific challenges they have listed on their form. You may have time for more than one.

Homework assignment: Chapters seven, eight, and nine.

Week Four

Discussion questions and tools for chapters seven, eight, and nine.

Problem-solving form: Ask for volunteers who would like to work on specific challenges they have listed on their form. You may have time for more than one.

Homework assignment: Ask everyone to try a family meeting and report next week.

Homework assignment: Chapter ten.

Week Five

Discussion questions and tools for chapter ten.

Ask everyone to make a guess about their lifestyle priority and how it may affect their parenting—both assets and liabilities.

Problem-solving form: Ask for volunteers who would like to work on specific challenges they have listed on their form. You may have time for more than one.

Homework assignment: Chapters eleven and twelve.

Week Six

Discussion questions and tools for chapters eleven and twelve.

Problem-solving form: Ask for volunteers who would like to work on specific challenges they have listed on their form. You may have time for more than one.

Closing activity: Ask participants to close their eyes and think of the three most important concepts they have learned and how they have used or will use these concepts with their children. Ask them to take a few minutes to record their thoughts on a piece of paper. Then invite each participant to share the most important thing they are taking with them as they leave the group. Let the group decide if they would like to keep meeting to work on specific challenges using the problem-solving form.

GROUP PARTICIPATION CHALLENGES

The value of study groups and some suggestions for group procedure were presented in the Introduction. It is further suggested that you present the following ideas at the first meeting.

There are several personalities that may cause problems in groups. Problems can be avoided when each member is aware of these situations and takes responsibility to cooperate as a group. It is most effective to discuss typical problems before they occur, so people don't feel personally criticized.

The Monopolizer

I am sure you have had the experience of being in a group with a monopolizer. This can be deadly for everyone else in the group. If you know that this is one of your problems, try the following:

• Count to five before speaking. This gives others a chance for a turn.

- Limit your comments to those you think will be interesting to others, as well as to yourself.
- Make your comments short and to the point. Most monopolizers repeat themselves and summarize several times.
- Make sure you are staying on the subject being discussed.
- Be aware of other group members who may not be as assertive as you are. Help them get into the conversation. (See signs to watch for in the quiet one.)

The Quiet One

After reading about the monopolizer, don't get the idea that you shouldn't talk in a study group. A study group will not be successful without group participation.

There are many reasons why an individual may be a quiet member of the group. The two we should be most aware of are (a) the person who can't get a word in edgewise because of monopolizers and (b) the person who prefers to remain silent because that is his or her learning style.

You can tell the difference by watching body language. The person who would like to say something usually leans forward and starts to speak before being drowned out by someone else. He or she may raise her hand first, whereas others just speak up. More assertive group members can help this person by saying, "Mary, did you have something you wanted to say?"

On the other hand, don't embarrass those who prefer to remain quiet by calling on them when they would prefer not to speak.

The Debater

Remember that the purpose of a Positive Discipline parent or teacher study group is to learn to understand and practice these concepts. This does not mean it is the only way. However, it is one very effective way to work with children. If time is spent discussing other theories, there will not be time to cover the present theory for full understanding and practical application.

The Self-righteous One

Some people become so enthusiastic about these principles that they want to convert others immediately. For example, a wife might go home from a study group and say to her husband, "This is the way we are going to do it from now on." A spouse may be inspired to try some of these techniques, after having the opportunity to observe the effectiveness of your example, but is sure to resist pressure to change.

Of course, it is nice if both adults are working together on the same approach, but it is not necessary. Children are so clever that they can switch their behavior according to the approach of the adult with whom they are interacting. It will not hurt them to experience different approaches from different adults.

The only person you can change is yourself. Use the approach that suits you.

The Doubter ("Yes, But . . .")

All the techniques suggested in this book have been used successfully by many parents and teachers. Anticipating that something won't work is often a good excuse to avoid trying it out.

While learning, choose only the suggestions you are willing to try. You don't have to buy the whole package to achieve many of the benefits.

PROBLEM-SOLVING FORM

Describe the problem interaction in detail. (When was the last time it happened?)

_____

_____

How did it make you feel? (Irritated, threatened, hurt, or inadequate?)

_____

_____

What did you do in response to the child's behavior?

_____

_____

What was the child's response to what you did?

_____

_____

What is your guess about the child's mistaken goal?

_____

_____

What are some alternative suggestions you could try next time the problem occurs? (Record suggestions from the group here.)

_____

_____

USING THE PROBLEM-SOLVING FORM

It is a good idea to make several copies of the problem-solving form for each member of the group. During the first few weeks, this will help group members remember the situations they would like to discuss after learning the basic concepts in the first six chapters of this book.

When it is time to discuss these situations, have the group guess the mistaken goal. Group members should attempt to get at the primary feelings of the adult. Listen for tone of voice and discrepancies. Does the adult claim slight annoyance or inadequacy when his or her tone of voice and description of the problem indicate power—a desire to make the child do it his or her way? Is anger or frustration a cover-up for feeling threatened or hurt?

Once the mistaken goal has been determined, the group should give several suggestions for the parent or teacher to try. These suggestions should include as many concepts and tools as possible, including some specific ideas for encouragement. The person with the problem can then choose one or more of these ideas.

The next group meeting should begin with a report on the effectiveness of the suggestions. If the suggestions were not effective, the group will usually be able to help the person understand why. For example, he or she may have forgotten to use a respectful tone of voice or may not have waited for a cooling-off period.

Following are some examples of situations that were presented to a group and the solutions that were suggested.

Six-year-old Matt always thinks things are unfair. One morning while his mom was talking to Matt, she reached down to smooth out the bedspread on his younger brother's bed. Matt said, "That's not fair. You always help him and not me." Mom shared with the group that she felt annoyed. Further questioning from the group revealed that she felt hurt. She tries so hard to be fair, but Matt accuses her of being unfair. The group then guessed that Matt was also feeling hurt because of his perception that his mom favored his younger brother. They came up with two suggestions:

1. Use the Four Steps for Winning Cooperation. Verbalize what you think he is feeling. Share a time you yourself felt things were unfair. Let him know you understand. Explain your desire to be fair because of equal love for both. Seek a solution, with Matt's help, as to what can be done.
2. Spend special time with Matt. This could be part of the solution.

Mrs. James shared her concern because her first-grade student, Scott, had developed a pattern of not completing his work. She initially thought his goal must be either attention or power, because she knew he was very capable, as shown by past performance. One suggestion from the group was to do goal disclosure with Scott, which would at least give Mrs. James more feedback as to what his goal was. Mrs. James wanted some practice with this technique, so she role-played Scott while another member of the group did goal disclosure. As she got into Scott's world, she was amazed to discover that his goal was probably revenge. She was also a close friend of Scott's family and realized the problem had started after she had taken some time off for a vacation. Scott had shared real concern with his parents that she might not come back. Since this really hurt him, he was afraid to get too close when she did come back. Instead, his behavior indicated passive revenge. Mrs. James was eager to try goal disclosure with Scott so that they could then talk about this and do some problem solving—after the steps of winning cooperation.

Mrs. Roberts, a preschool teacher, shared her problem with Steven, who always played in the block area but wouldn't help pick them up. At first Mrs. Roberts felt she was just frustrated but she came to realize she was upset because she couldn't make him do what he should do. After identifying the goal as power, the group came up with the following suggestions:

1. Take time for training. Make sure he knows exactly what is expected.
2. Ask questions: "Do you like to play in the blocks? What are you supposed to do when finished? How many blocks do you think you can pick up during cleanup time?"
3. Give a choice, including a logical consequence. "Would you like to pick up the blocks now or during story time? Would you like to pick up the blocks or give up the privilege of playing with the blocks?"
4. Redirect power behavior. Let him be in charge of cleanup.

Mrs. Roberts chose the fourth alternative as the one she thought would appeal to Steven and solve the problem.

Mrs. Sedgewick complained about six-year-old Scott not respecting his toys and picking them up. It was clear to the group that her voice indicated power that was escalating to revenge. The following possibilities were suggested by the group:

1. "Own" the problem. Share how much it bothers you to see the toys cluttering the house. Admit that you may have purchased more toys than he wants or needs.
2. Ask for help and solutions to your problem.
3. Take time for training and organization. Make drawstring bags or get ice-cream cartons for different sets of toys. Get agreement from Scott that only one bag or carton can be down at a time, that one must be picked up before another one is used.

4. Give a choice. Either he can pick the toys up or you
   will. If you pick them up, they stay up until he shows
   enough interest and responsibility. If this doesn't
   happen, then he definitely has too many toys to care.

DEVELOPING SOCIAL RESPONSIBILITY THROUGH PEER COUNSELING

Social responsibility was a key factor in the implementation of a peer counseling program with fifth- and sixth-grade students who were using their leadership skills in disruptive ways. I took Adler literally and determined that the best way to help these students redirect their leadership skills to constructive uses was to teach them to help other students.

Fifth- and sixth-grade teachers were sent a memo asking them to recommend students who were natural leaders for participation in a peer counseling training program. The memo read: "We would like to train some peer counselors. Please write down the names of three students you feel are capable leaders, even though their leadership may not now be in a positive direction."

The recommended students were then interviewed to see if they were interested in making a commitment to go through training and to do peer counseling. It was explained that they would need to volunteer one or two lunch periods per week to do counseling with other students. Those who were interested then completed four training sessions, where they learned the five steps of William Glasser's Reality Therapy.[1]

REALITY THERAPY

Step One: Making Friends

The entire first training session was devoted to this first step. The students were asked to brainstorm about the most important aspect of friendship and ways to create an atmosphere of trust. The most important aspect of friendship they came up with was an attitude of:

- Caring
- Concern
- Desire to help
- Respect.

To create an atmosphere of friendship, they decided one needs to:

- Greet the person by name.
- Tell your name.
- Show understanding.
- Tell about yourself. For example, explain your duties as a peer counselor or share an experience you have had in a situation similar to the referral problem.
- Help the person relax.
- Use your sense of humor.
- Express a willingness to work together on solutions that will help solve the problem.

Each student was given a copy of the results of the brainstorming, along with the caution that it was not necessary to use these steps in order, or even to use every one of them every time. They were also invited to be creative and add new ideas.

In the second training session the students were taught steps two through five of Reality Therapy.

Step Two: What Are You Doing?

1. Learn specifically what is going on to cause the problem by asking curiosity questions regarding the problem. These questions usually help the student see his or her part in the problem.
2. Students don't usually start at the beginning, so ask, "What happened before that?" Keep asking this question after each explanation until you feel you have found the beginning.

Step Three: Is It Helping?

Ask the following questions:

1. What are the consequences of what you are doing?
2. What is the payoff? What do you gain?
3. What is the price you pay? What problems does it cause you?

Step Four: Make a Plan to Do Better

What could be done differently to solve the problem?

1. Ask the counselee for suggestions.
2. Offer possible alternatives yourself.

Step Five: Get a Commitment

Ask the counselee:

1. Will you do it?
2. When will you do it?

ROLE-PLAYING

The final two training sessions were spent role-playing situations such as:

- A student who has been referred for fighting on the playground.
- A student who has been disrespectful to a teacher.
- A student who refuses to do classwork.

At first, peer counseling was done by two students working together with an adult supervisor (myself or volunteer teachers). As soon as they demonstrated confidence and competency, they worked in pairs as co-counselors without direct supervision. A supervisor was always nearby in case help was requested.

Counselees were referred by teachers, who filled out a referral slip with the name of the student and the problem. After seeing the student, the peer counselors were asked to write the solution arrived at on the referral slip. One copy of the slip was returned to the teacher and the other was kept for follow-up and record-keeping purposes.

Most counselees seemed very willing to talk to a peer counselor. The peer counselors showed great insight and skill in zeroing in on the problems and possible solutions, as in the following example.

One of the counselees was having difficulty getting along with a teacher. The peer counselor stated that he understood, because he had once had that problem. The peer counselor then went on to point out that maybe the teacher was having problems and needed some encouragement. He also pointed out that since the student couldn't do anything about the teacher's behavior, he should work on his own. The student and peer counselor worked out a plan for the counselee to be encouraging and to do his work so that the teacher wouldn't have a reason to be upset at him.

The idea of encouragement and personal accountability caught on and spread among the students when it was promoted by the peer counselors.

Teachers demonstrated enthusiasm and support for the program by referring many students. They also gave credit to the peer counseling program for changing from negative to positive the leadership skills of the students involved.

LETTER TO PARENTS

Edit this letter to meet your needs.

Dear Parents,

The purpose of this letter is to give you information about an exciting program being implemented at _____ school that is designed to help your child develop the Significant Seven Perceptions and Skills that are essential for success in today's society. A detailed description of the Significant Seven Perceptions and Skills is attached. Another benefit of the program we are implementing is that it teaches self-discipline, responsibility, cooperation, and problem-solving skills. It is a program that focuses on nonpunitive solutions to problems. All punishment (blame, shame, and pain) is eliminated and is replaced by focusing on solutions based on kindness, firmness, dignity, and respect. Too many people mistakenly think discipline and punishment are the same. They are not. Discipline comes from the root word *discipulis,* which means "a follower of truth, principle, or a revered teacher"—or "to teach." True discipline comes from an internal locus of control (self-discipline), not an external locus of control (punishments and rewards inflicted by someone else). Punishment comes from an external locus of control and is designed to inflict blame, shame, and pain. Of course, adults who inflict punishment on children mistakenly believe it will help them do better. Even though punishment may stop behavior for the moment, the long-term results are usually negative—rebellion, resentment, revenge, or retreat into sneakiness or low self-esteem. An easy way to test this theory is to remember how you felt and what you wanted to do after someone inflicted blame, shame, or pain on you.

Where did we ever get the crazy idea that in order to get children to *do* better, first we have to make them *feel* worse? Children *do* better when they *feel* better. Don't we all?

The program we have been referring to is called Positive Discipline in the Classroom. A pivotal process in this program is class meetings. During class meetings students and teachers work together to solve problems that are detrimental to individuals, fellow students, teachers, or the learning environment. Students are taught to help one another learn from mistakes and to find nonpunitive solutions. During the class meetings students learn to give and receive compliments, listen respectfully, understand and respect differences, brainstorm to come up with solutions, and choose solutions that will be the most helpful for individuals or the group as a whole. They soon learn that it is okay to be accountable for the choices they make because they won't be punished for poor choices, but will be helped to learn from them.

Some parents are afraid class meetings will be like a kangaroo court or that their child will be humiliated in front of the group. Nothing could be further from the truth. It is true that, in the beginning, students are not used to helping one another, seeing mistakes as wonderful opportunities to learn, and looking for helpful solutions. Most students have learned too well (from adults) how to inflict blame, shame, and pain. They must be taught to find nonpunitive solutions.

Positive Discipline is based on the premise of maintaining dignity and respect for all at all times. One example of a class-meeting method that ensures helpfulness instead of punishment is that students involved in a problem are invited to choose the brainstormed solution that will be most helpful to them. When an issue involves everyone in the class, a vote may be taken. If a solution doesn't work, students are invited to put the problem on the agenda again for more discussion and brainstorming for solutions.

Research has demonstrated that children who have strength in the Significant Seven Perceptions and Skills are at low risk for all the problems faced by youth today: violence and vandalism, drug abuse, teenage pregnancy and suicide, low motivation and achievement, and dropping out of school. On the other hand, students who do not have strength in these perceptions and skills are at high risk for the problems of youth today.

We do not know of any other program that so effectively helps students learn and practice all of the Significant Seven Perceptions and Skills—and, as a fringe benefit, eliminates most discipline problems in classrooms. Think of the potential benefits these skills will bring to future work and family relationships. These skills are equally, if not more, important than academic skills.

We hope you will be as excited as we are about the implementation of class meetings as part of our regular curriculum to create Positive Discipline in the Classroom. We invite you to visit anytime.

Teacher _____ Principal _____

In the book *Raising Self-Reliant Children in a Self-Indulgent World,*[1] H. Stephen Glenn and Jane Nelsen identify the Significant Seven Perceptions and Skills necessary for developing capable people. They are:

1. Strong perceptions of personal capabilities—"I am capable."
2. Strong perceptions of significance in primary relationships—"I contribute in meaningful ways and I am genuinely needed."
3. Strong perceptions of personal power or influence over life—"I can influence what happens to me."
4. Strong intrapersonal skills: the ability to understand personal emotions and to use that understanding to develop self-discipline and self-control.
5. Strong interpersonal skills: the ability to work with others and develop friendships through communicating, cooperating, negotiating, sharing, empathizing, and listening.
6. Strong systemic skills: the ability to respond to the limits and consequences of everyday life with responsibility, adaptability, flexibility, and integrity.
7. Strong judgmental skills: the ability to use wisdom and to evaluate situations according to appropriate values.

NOTES

Chapter One

1. Rudolf Dreikurs and Vicki Soltz, *Children the Challenge* (New York: Plume, 1991).
2. H. Stephen Glenn and Jane Nelsen, *Raising Self-Reliant Children in a Self-Indulgent World* (New York: Three Rivers Press, 2000).
3. John Platt, *Life in the Family Zoo* (Sacramento, Calif.: Dynamic Training Seminars, 1991).

Chapter Two

1. Jane Nelsen, Lynn Lott, and H. Stephen Glenn, *Positive Discipline in the Classroom,* 3rd ed. (New York: Three Rivers Press, 2000).

Chapter Three

1. Stella Chess and Alexander Thomas, *Know Your Child* (New York: Basic Books, 1987).
2. Jane Nelsen, Cheryl Erwin, and Roslyn Duffy, *Positive Discipline for Preschoolers,* 3rd ed. (New York: Three Rivers Press, 2006).
3. Wayne S. Frieden and Marie Hartwell-Walker, *Family Songs.* Available as downloadable MP3 files at www.focusingonsolutions.com.

Chapter Four

1. Jane Nelsen, Cheryl Erwin, and Roslyn Duffy's *Positive Discipline The First Three Years,* 2nd ed., and *Positive Discipline for Preschoolers,* 3rd ed. (New York: Three Rivers Press, 2006) are filled with information about age-appropriate and developmentally appropriate behavior and how they relate to parenting.
2. John Taylor, *Person to Person* (Saratoga, Calif.: R & E Publishers, 1984).
3. David Walsh and Nat Bennett, *WHY Do They Act That Way?: A Survival Guide to the Adolescent Brain for You and Your Teen* (New York: Free Press, 2004).
4. Jane Nelsen and Lynn Lott, *Positive Discipline for Teenagers* (New York: Three Rivers Press, 2000).

Chapter Five

1. Rudolf Dreikurs and Vicki Soltz, *Children the Challenge* (New York: Plume, 1991), p. 80.
2. Op cit., p. 84.

Chapter Six

1. Jane Nelsen, Lynn Lott, and H. Stephen Glenn, *Positive Discipline in the Classroom,* 3rd ed. (New York: Three Rivers Press, 2000).

Chapter Seven

1. From *Positive Discipline in the Classroom Teacher's Guide,* www.empoweringpeople.com.
2. This example was taken from Jane Nelsen, Lynn Lott, and H. Stephen Glenn, *Positive Discipline A–Z* (New York: Three Rivers Press, 1999).

Chapter Eight

1. Jane Nelsen, Lynn Lott, and H. Stephen Glenn, *Positive Discipline in the Classroom,* 3rd ed. (New York: Three Rivers Press, 2000).
2. Jane Nelsen and Lynn Lott, *Positive Discipline in the Classroom Teacher's Guide.* Available from Empowering Books, Tapes, and Videos, 1-800-456-7770, www.empoweringpeople.com.
3. Op cit.
4. Jane Nelsen, Cheryl Erwin, and Roslyn Duffy, *Positive Discipline for Preschoolers* (New York: Three Rivers Press, 1994), p. 261.

Chapter Nine

1. *A Positive Discipline Family Meeting Album* e-book is available at www.focusingonsolutions.com.
2. Jane Nelsen and Lynn Lott, *Positive Discipline for Teenagers* (New York: Three Rivers Press, 2000).
3. Jane Nelsen and Cheryl Erwin, *Positive Discipline for Single Parents* (New York: Three Rivers Press, 1999).
4. Excerpts from *The Positive Discipline Family Meeting Album,* an e-book by Jane Nelsen. Available at www.focusingonsolutions.com.

Chapter Ten

1. Jane Nelsen, an e-book and book on tape. Available at www.focusingonsolutions.com. Empowering People, 2005.

Chapter Eleven

1. Jane Nelsen, *Positive Time-Out and Over 50 Ways to Avoid Power Struggles in Homes and Classrooms* (New York: Three Rivers Press, 1999).
2. Jane Nelsen, Lynn Lott, and H. Stephen Glenn, *Positive Discipline A–Z* (New York: Three Rivers Press, 2005).

3. Jane Nelsen et al., *Positive Discipline in the Classroom: A Teacher's A–Z Guide* (New York: Three Rivers Press, 2001).

Chapter Twelve

1. Jane Nelsen and Cheryl Erwin, *Parents Who Love Too Much* (New York: Three Rivers Press, 2000).

Appendix I

1. Information on the manual and training is available at www.posdis.org. A nonprofit organization has been created (Positive Discipline Association) for the training of Certified Positive Discipline Associates, research, and two-day workshops (Positive Discipline in the Classroom and Teaching Parenting the Positive Discipline Way).

Appendix II

1. William Glasser, *Reality Therapy: A New Approach to Psychiatry* (New York: Harper and Row, 1975).

Appendix III

1. H. Stephen Glenn and Jane Nelsen, *Raising Self-Reliant Children in a Self-Indulgent World* (New York: Three Rivers Press, 1987).

SUGGESTED READINGS

Adler, Alfred. *What Life Could Mean to You.* London: One World, 1992.

_____. *Social Interest.* London: One World, 1998.

Allred, G. Hugh. *How to Strengthen Your Marriage and Family.* Provo, Utah: Brigham Young University Press, 1976.

_____. *Mission for Mother: Guiding the Child.* Salt Lake City, Utah: Book Crafts, 1968.

Ansbacher, Heinz, and Rowena Ansbacher. *Individual Psychology of Alfred Adler.* New York: Harper Perennial, 1964.

Chess, Stella, and Alexander Thomas. *Know Your Child.* New York: Basic Books, 1987.

Dinkmeyer, Don, and Rudolf Dreikurs. *Encouraging Children to Learn: The Encouragement Process.* Philadelphia: Brunner-Routledge, 2000.

Dinkmeyer, Don, and Gary McKay. *Raising a Responsible Child.* New York: Simon & Schuster, 1973.

Dreikurs, Rudolf. *Social Equality: The Challenge of Today.* Chicago: Contemporary Books, 1971.

Dreikurs, Rudolf, and Loren Grey. *A New Approach to Discipline: Logical Consequences.* New York: Plume, 1989.

Dreikurs, Rudolf, Bronia Grunwald, and Floy Pepper. *Maintaining Sanity in the Classroom*. New York: Taylor and Francis, 1998.

Dreikurs, Rudolf, and Vicki Soltz. *Children: The Challenge*. New York: Plume, 1991.

Frieden, Wayne S., and Marie Hartwell-Walker. *Family Songs* Available as downloadable MP3 files at www.focusingonsolutions.com.

Glasser, William. *Reality Therapy: A New Approach to Psychiatry*. New York: Harper and Row, 1975.

Glenn, H. Stephen, and Michael L. Brock. *7 Strategies for Developing Capable Students*. New York: Three Rivers Press, 1998.

Glenn, H. Stephen, and Jane Nelsen. *Raising Self-Reliant Children in a Self-Indulgent World*. New York: Three Rivers Press, 2000.

Hoffman, Edward. *The Drive for Self: Alfred Adler and the Founding of Individual Psychology*. New York: Addison-Wesley, 1994.

Kohn, Alfie. *Punished by Rewards*. New York: Houghton Mifflin, 1999.

Kvols, Kathy. *Redirecting Children's Misbehavior*. Seattle: Parenting Press, 1997.

Lott, Lynn, and Jane Nelsen. *Parenting Your Pup*. New York: Rodale, 2005.

————. *Teaching Parenting the Positive Discipline Way: A Manual for Parent Education Groups*. Lehi, Utah: Empowering People, 1990. www.empoweringpeople.com.

Nelsen, Jane. *Positive Time-Out and Over 50 Ways to Avoid Power Struggles in Homes and Classrooms*. New York: Three Rivers Press, 1999.

————. *Serenity: Eliminating Stress and Finding Joy and Peace in Life and Relationships.* Lehi, Utah: Empowering People, 2005; an e-book available at www.positivediscipline.com.

Nelsen, Jane, and Cheryl Erwin. *Parents Who Love Too Much.* New York: Three Rivers Press, 2000.

————. *Positive Discipline for Childcare Providers.* New York: Three Rivers Press, 2002.

————. *Positive Discipline for Step Families.* Lehi, Utah: Empowering People, 2005; an e-book available at www.positive discipline.com.

Nelsen, Jane, Cheryl Erwin, and Carol Delzer. *Positive Discipline for Single Parents,* 2nd ed. New York: Three Rivers Press, 1999.

Nelsen, Jane, Cheryl Erwin, and Roslyn Duffy. *Positive Discipline for Preschoolers,* 3rd ed. New York: Three Rivers Press, 2006.

————. *Positive Discipline the First Three Years,* 2nd ed. New York: Three Rivers Press, 2006.

Nelsen, Jane, Cheryl Erwin, Mary Hughes, and M. Michael Brock. *Positive Discipline for Christian Families.* Lehi, Utah: Empowering People, 2005; an e-book available at www.positive discipline.com.

Nelsen, Jane, Linda Escobar, Kate Ortolano, Roslyn Duffy, and Deborah Owens-Sohocki. *Positive Discipline: A Teacher's A–Z Guide.* New York: Three Rivers Press, 2001.

Nelsen, Jane, Riki Intner, and Lynn Lott. *Positive Discipline for Parents in Recovery.* Lehi, Utah: Empowering People, 2005; an e-book available at www.positivediscipline.com.

Nelsen, Jane, and Lisa Larson. *Positive Discipline for Working Parents.* New York: Three Rivers Press, 2003.

Nelsen, Jane, and Lynn Lott. *Positive Discipline in the Classroom: A Teacher's Guide,* Lehi, Utah: Empowering People 1992, www.empoweringpeople.com.

———. *Positive Discipline for Teenagers.* New York: Three Rivers Press, 1997.

Nelsen, Jane, Lynn Lott, and H. Stephen Glenn. *Positive Discipline A–Z,* 3rd ed. New York: Three Rivers Press, 2006.

———. *Positive Discipline in the Classroom,* 3rd ed. New York: Three Rivers Press, 2000.

Platt, John. *Life in the Family Zoo.* Sacramento, Calif.: Dynamic Training Seminars, 1991.

Taylor, John. *Person to Person.* Saratoga, Calif.: R & E Publishers, 1984.

Walsh, David, and Nat Bennett. *WHY Do They Act That Way?: A Survival Guide to the Adolescent Brain for You and Your Teen.* New York: Free Press, 2005.

Walton, F. X. *Winning Teenagers Over.* Columbia, S.C.: Adlerian Child Care Books, 1980.

INDEX

Jane Nelsen is a popular keynote speaker and workshop presenter for conferences and teacher-in-service. Her topics include:

Twenty-one Tools for Avoiding Power Struggles while Teaching Children Valuable Social and Life Skills

Positive Discipline for Raising Self-Reliant Children

Positive Discipline: Birth to Five

Empowering Teenagers and Yourself in the Process

Positive Discipline in the Classroom

Don't Believe Everything You Think: Four Principles for Eliminating Stress and Finding Serenity in Life and Relationships

She also coordinates a referral service for parent education coaching by phone.

For more information go to www.positivediscipline.com.